STUDENT ATLAS OF
WORLD
POLITICS
5th EDITION

About the Author

J ohn L. Allen is professor and chair of the Department of Geography at the University of Wyoming and professor emeritus of geography at the University of Connecticut, where he taught from 1967 to 2000. He is a native of Wyoming and received his bachelor's degree in 1963 and his M.A. in 1964 from the University of Wyoming, and his Ph.D. in 1969 from Clark University. His areas of special interest are perceptions of the environment and the impact of human societies on environmental systems. Dr. Allen is the author and editor of many books and articles as well as several other student atlases, including the best-selling *Student Atlas of World Geography*.

STUDENT ATLAS OF
WORLD POLITICS
5th EDITION

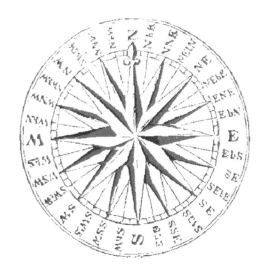

John L. Allen
University of Wyoming

McGraw-Hill/Dushkin
A Division of The McGraw-Hill Companies

Book Team

Vice President & Publisher   *Jeffrey L. Hahn*
Production Manager   *Brenda S. Filley*
Manager   *Theodore Knight*
Project Editor   *Ava Suntoke*
Developmental Editor   *Michael J. Butler*
Designers   *Charles Vitelli, Eldis N. Lima*
Typesetting Supervisor   *Juliana Arbo*
Typesetter   *Cynthia L. Vets*
Proofreader   *Robin N. Charney*
Cover design   *Tom Goddard*
Cartography   *Midwest Educational Graphics, Madison, WI*
Copier Coordinator   *Larry Killian*

We would like to thank Digital Wisdom Incorporated for allowing us
to use their Mountain High Maps cartography software. This software was
used to create maps 63, 64, 65, 66, 67, 68, 69, 70, 71, 72, 73, 74

McGraw-Hill/Dushkin

A Division of The **McGraw·Hill** Companies

The credit section for this book begins on page 193 and is considered an
extension of the copyright page.

ISBN 0-07-251191-5   ISSN: 1526-4556

Printed in the United States of America

1 0 9 8 7 6 5 4 3

A Note to the Student

International politics is a drama played out on the world stage. If the events of and subsequent to September 11, 2001, have taught us anything, it is that the drama is very real and the stage is indeed a worldwide one. The maps in this atlas serve as the stage settings for the various scenes in this drama; the data tables are the building materials from which the settings are created. Just as the stage setting helps bring to life and give meaning to the actions and words of a play, so can these maps and tables enhance your understanding of the vast and complex drama of global politics, including the emergence of global terrorism as a political instrument. Use this atlas in conjunction with your text on international politics or international affairs. It will help you become more knowledgeable about the international stage as well as the actors.

The maps and data sets in the *Student Atlas of World Politics*, Fifth Edition, are designed to introduce you to the importance of the connections between geography and world politics. The maps are not perfect representations of reality—no maps ever are—but they do represent models, or approximations of the real world, that should aid in your understanding of the world drama.

You will find your study of this atlas more productive in relation to your study of international politics if you examine the maps on the following pages in the context of five distinct analytical themes:

1. *Location: Where Is It?* This involves a focus on the precise location of places in both absolute terms (the latitude and longitude of a place) and in relative terms (the location of a place in relation to the location of other places). When you think of location, you should automatically think of both forms. Knowing something about absolute location will help you to understand a variety of features of physical geography, since these key elements are often closely related to their position on the earth. But it is equally important to think of location in relative terms. The location of places in relation to other places is often more important in influencing social, economic, and cultural characteristics than are the factors of physical geography. Certainly the relative location of the World Trade Center was crucial to its identification as both a symbolic and actual center of economic activity, and this identification played an important role in its selection as a target for terrorist action.

2. *Place: What Is It Like?* This encompasses the political, economic, cultural, environmental, and other characteristics that give a place its identity. You should seek to understand the similarities and differences of places by exploring their basic characteristics. Why are some places with similar environmental characteristics so very different in economic, cultural, social, and political ways? Why are other places with such different environmental characteristics so seemingly alike in terms of their institutions, their economies, and their cultures? The place characteristics of parts of the world American students have known little about (like Afghanistan) have now emerged as vital components of our necessary understanding of the implementation of military and political strategies.

3. *Human/Environment Interactions: How Is the Landscape Shaped?* This theme focuses on the ways in which people respond to and modify their environments. On the world stage, humans are not the only part of the action. The environment also plays a role in the drama of international politics. But the characteristics of the environment do not exert a controlling influence over human activities; they only provide a set of alternatives from which different cultures, in different times, make their choices. Observe the relationship between the basic elements of physical geography such as climate and terrain and the host of ways in which humans have used the land surfaces of the world. To know something of the relationship between people and the environment in the arid parts of the Old World is to begin to understand the nature of

political, economic, and even religious conflicts between the inhabitants of those regions and others.

4. *Movement: How Do People Stay in Touch?* This examines the transportation and communication systems that link people and places. Movement or "spatial interaction" is the chief mechanism for the spread of ideas and innovations from one place to another. It is spatial interaction that validates the old cliché, "the world is getting smaller." We find McDonald's restaurants in Tokyo and Honda automobiles in New York City because of spatial interaction. The spread of global terrorism is, first and foremost, a process of spatial interaction; advanced transportation and communication systems have made possible such events as transpired in New York City in September 2001, and these systems have transformed the world in which your parents were born. And the world that greets your children will be very different from your world. None of this would happen without the force of movement or spatial interaction.

5. *Regions: Worlds Within a World.* This theme, perhaps the most important for this atlas, helps to organize knowledge about the land and its people. The world consists of a mosaic of "regions" or areas that are somehow different and distinctive from other areas. The region of Anglo-America (the United States and Canada) is, for example, different enough from the region of Western Europe that geographers clearly identify them as two unique and separate areas. Yet, despite their differences, Anglo-Americans and Europeans share a number of similarities: common cultural backgrounds, comparable economic patterns, shared religious traditions, and even some shared physical environmental characteristics. Conversely, although the regions of Anglo-America and Central Asia are also easily distinguished as distinctive units of the Earth's surface with some shared physical environmental characteristics, the inhabitants of these two regions have fewer similarities and more differences than is the case with Anglo-America and Western Europe: different cultural traditions, different institutions, different linguistic and religious patterns. An understanding of both the differences and similarities between regions like Anglo-America and Europe on the one hand, or Anglo-America and Central Asia on the other, will help you to understand much that has happened in the past or that is currently transpiring in the world around you. At the very least, an understanding of regional similarities and differences will help you to interpret what you read on the front page of your daily newspaper or view on the evening news report on your television set.

Not all of these themes will be immediately apparent on each of the 74 maps and 14 tables in this atlas. But if you study the contents of the *Student Atlas of World Politics*, Fifth Edition, along with the reading of your text and think about the five themes, maps, tables, and text will complement one another and improve your understanding of global politics. As Shakespeare said, "All the world's a stage"; your challenge is to understand both the stage and the drama being played on it.

A Word About Data Sources

At the very outset of your study of this atlas, you should be aware of some limitations of the maps and data tables. In some instances, a map or a table may have missing data. This may be the result of the failure of a country to report information to a central international body (like the United Nations or the World Bank). Alternatively, it may reflect shifts in political boundaries, internal or external conflicts, or changes in responsibility for reporting data have caused certain countries to delay their reports. It is always our wish to be as up-to-date as is possible; earlier editions of this atlas were lacking more data than this one and subsequent versions will have still more data, particularly on the southeastern European countries, the independent countries part of the former Soviet Union, or on African and Asian nations that are just beginning to reach a point in their economic and political development where they can consistently report reliable information. In the meantime, as events continue to restructure our world, it's an exciting time to be a student of international events!

John L. Allen

Acknowledgments

The author wishes to recognize with gratitude the advice, suggestions, and general assistance of the following reviewers:

Robert Bednarz
Texas A & M University

Gerald E. Beller
West Virginia State College

Kenneth L. Conca
University of Maryland

Femi Ferreira
Hutchinson Community College

Paul B. Frederic
University of Maine at Farmington

James F. Fryman
University of Northern Iowa

Michael Gold-Biss
St. Cloud State University

Herbert E. Gooch III
California Lutheran University

Lloyd E. Hudman
Brigham Young University

Edward L. Jackiewicz
Miami University of Ohio

Artimus Keiffer
*Indiana University–Purdue University
    at Indianapolis*

Richard L. Krol
Kean College of New Jersey

Jeffrey S. Lantis
The College of Wooster

Robert Larson
Indiana State University

Elizabeth J. Leppman
St. Cloud State University

Mark Lowry II
United States Military Academy at West Point

Max Lu
Kansas State University

Taylor E. Mack
Mississippi State University

Kenneth C. Martis
West Virginia University

Calvin O. Masilela
West Virginia University

Patrick McGreevy
Clarion University

Tyrel G. Moore
University of North Carolina at Charlotte

David J. Nemeth
The University of Toledo

Emmett Panzella
Point Park College

Daniel S. Papp
University System of Georgia

Lance Robinson
United States Air Force Academy

Jefferson S. Rogers
University of Tennessee at Martin

Barbara J. Rusnak
United States Air Force Academy

Mark Simpson
University of Tennessee at Martin

Jutta Weldes
Kent State University

Table of Contents

Part IV   Population and Human Development   59

Part V   Food, Energy, and Materials   71

Part VI   Environmental Conditions   81

Part VII   Regions of the World   87

Part VIII   World Countries: Data Tables   101

Part IX   Geographic Index   162

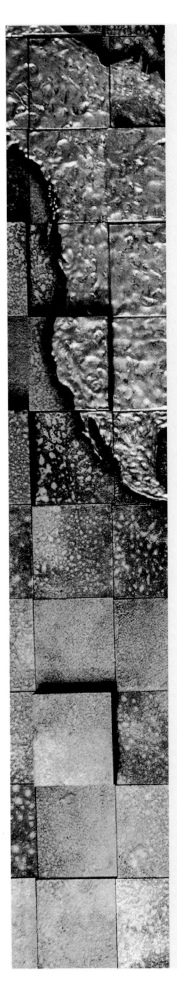

Part I

The Contemporary World

Map 1 Current World Political Boundaries

The international system includes states (countries) as the most important component. The boundaries of countries are the primary source of political division in the world, and for most people nationalism is the strongest source of political identification.

Scale: 1 to 125,000,000

Note: All world maps are Robinson projection.

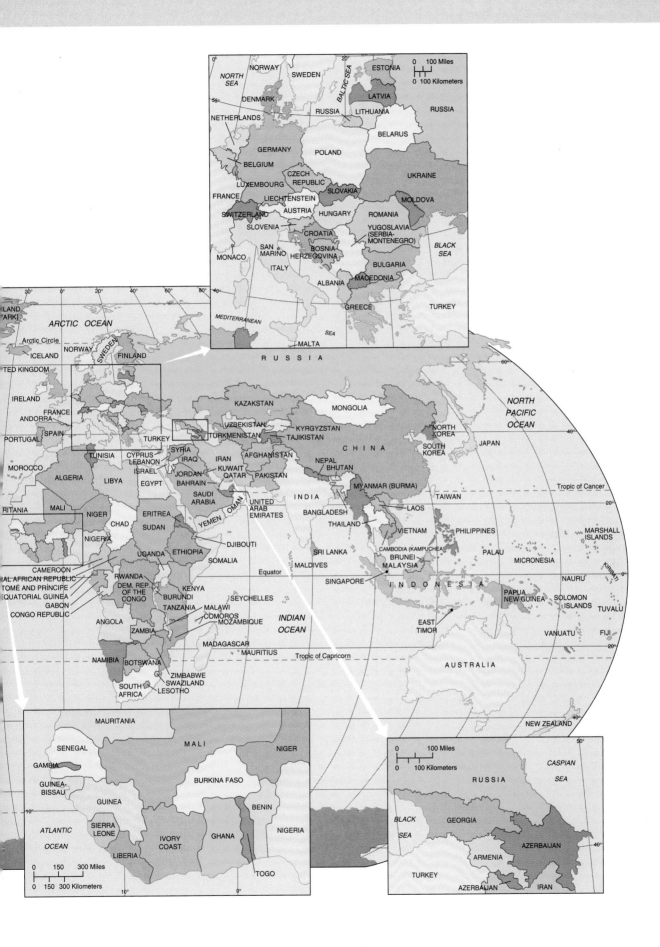

Map 2 World Climate Regions

Climates of the World

Tropical Moist Climates
- Rain Forest
- Monsoon
- Savanna

Dry Climates
- Warm Desert
- Warm Steppe
- Cool Desert
- Cool Steppe

Midlatitude Climates
- Summer Dry or Mediterranean
- Moist Subtropical
- Marine West Coast
- Cool Forest
- Subarctic

Polar Climates
- Tundra
- Ice Cap

Azonal Climates
- Undifferentiated Highlands

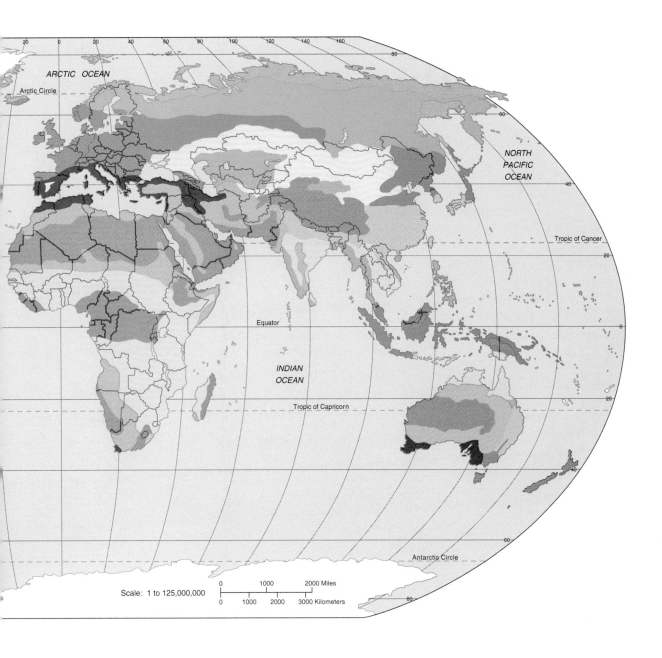

Of the world's many physical geographic features, climate (the long-term average of such weather conditions as temperature and precipitation) is the most important. It is climate that conditions the types of natural vegetation patterns and the types of soil that will exist in an area. It is also climate that determines the availability of our most precious resource: water. From an economic standpoint, the world's most important activity is agriculture; no other element of physical geography is more important for agriculture than climate.

Map 3 World Topography

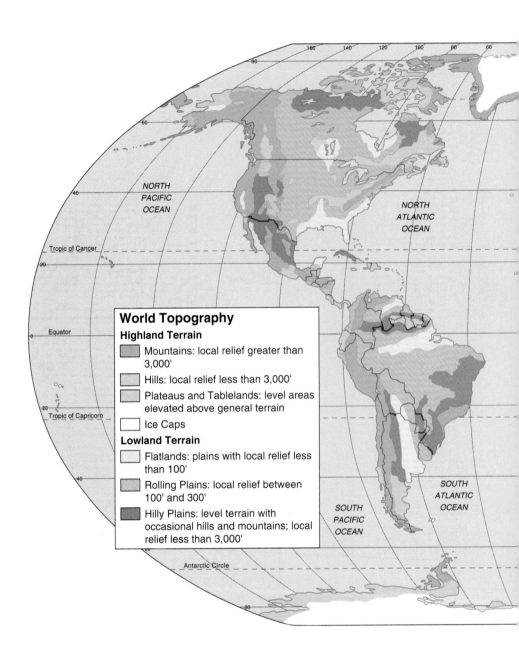

World Topography

Highland Terrain

Mountains: local relief greater than 3,000'

Hills: local relief less than 3,000'

Plateaus and Tablelands: level areas elevated above general terrain

Ice Caps

Lowland Terrain

Flatlands: plains with local relief less than 100'

Rolling Plains: local relief between 100' and 300'

Hilly Plains: level terrain with occasional hills and mountains; local relief less than 3,000'

Second only to climate as a conditioner of human activity—particularly in agriculture and in the location of cities and industry—is topography or terrain. It is what we often call "landforms." A comparison of this map with the map of land use (Map 6) will show that most of the world's productive agricultural zones are located in lowland regions. Where large regions of agricultural productivity are found, we tend to find urban concentrations and, with cities, industry. There is also a good spatial correlation between the map of landforms and the map showing the distribution and density of the human population (Map 7). Normally, the world's land-

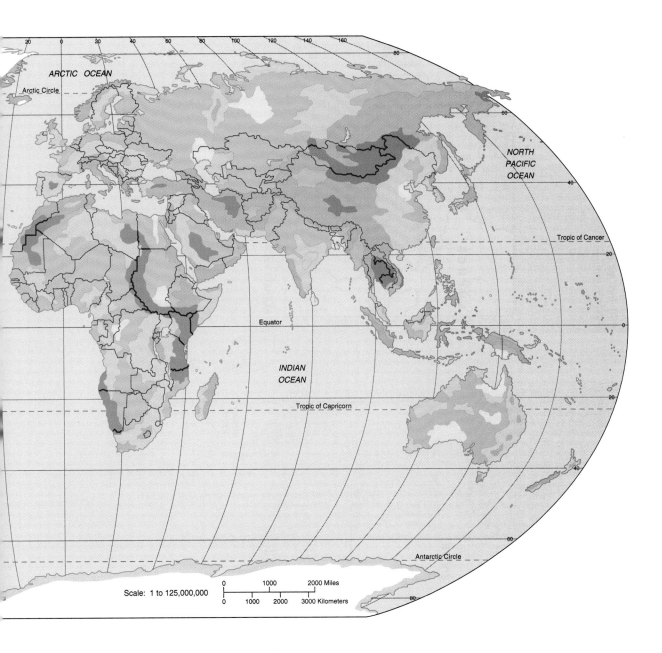

forms shown on this map are the result of extremely gradual primary geologic activity, such as the long-term movement of crustal plates (sometimes called continental drift). This activity occurs over hundreds of millions of years. Also important is the more rapid (but still slow by human standards) geomorphological or erosional activity of water, wind, and glacial ice; and waves, tides, and currents. Some landforms may be produced by abrupt or cataclysmic events, such as a major volcanic eruption or a meteor strike, but these are relatively rare and their effects are usually too minor to show up on a map of this scale.

Map 4 World Ecological Regions

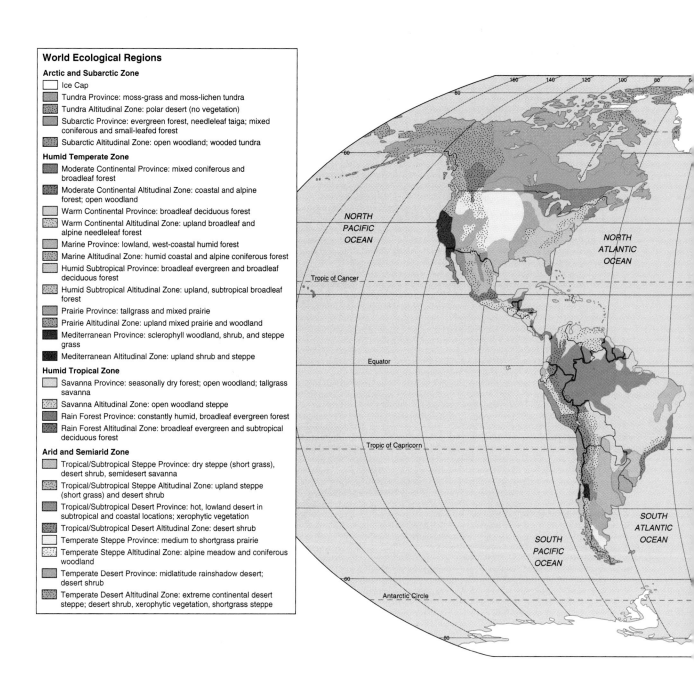

World Ecological Regions

Arctic and Subarctic Zone

- Ice Cap
- Tundra Province: moss-grass and moss-lichen tundra
- Tundra Altitudinal Zone: polar desert (no vegetation)
- Subarctic Province: evergreen forest, needleleaf taiga; mixed coniferous and small-leafed forest
- Subarctic Altitudinal Zone: open woodland; wooded tundra

Humid Temperate Zone

- Moderate Continental Province: mixed coniferous and broadleaf forest
- Moderate Continental Altitudinal Zone: coastal and alpine forest; open woodland
- Warm Continental Province: broadleaf deciduous forest
- Warm Continental Altitudinal Zone: upland broadleaf and alpine needleleaf forest
- Marine Province: lowland, west-coastal humid forest
- Marine Altitudinal Zone: humid coastal and alpine coniferous forest
- Humid Subtropical Province: broadleaf evergreen and broadleaf deciduous forest
- Humid Subtropical Altitudinal Zone: upland, subtropical broadleaf forest
- Prairie Province: tallgrass and mixed prairie
- Prairie Altitudinal Zone: upland mixed prairie and woodland
- Mediterranean Province: sclerophyll woodland, shrub, and steppe grass
- Mediterranean Altitudinal Zone: upland shrub and steppe

Humid Tropical Zone

- Savanna Province: seasonally dry forest; open woodland; tallgrass savanna
- Savanna Altitudinal Zone: open woodland steppe
- Rain Forest Province: constantly humid, broadleaf evergreen forest
- Rain Forest Altitudinal Zone: broadleaf evergreen and subtropical deciduous forest

Arid and Semiarid Zone

- Tropical/Subtropical Steppe Province: dry steppe (short grass), desert shrub, semidesert savanna
- Tropical/Subtropical Steppe Altitudinal Zone: upland steppe (short grass) and desert shrub
- Tropical/Subtropical Desert Province: hot, lowland desert in subtropical and coastal locations; xerophytic vegetation
- Tropical/Subtropical Desert Altitudinal Zone: desert shrub
- Temperate Steppe Province: medium to shortgrass prairie
- Temperate Steppe Altitudinal Zone: alpine meadow and coniferous woodland
- Temperate Desert Province: midlatitude rainshadow desert; desert shrub
- Temperate Desert Altitudinal Zone: extreme continental desert steppe; desert shrub, xerophytic vegetation, shortgrass steppe

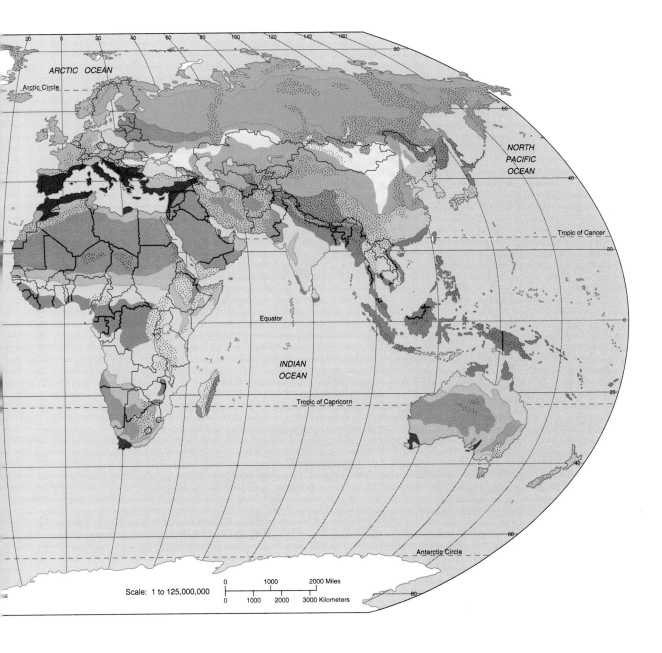

ARCTIC OCEAN

Arctic Circle

NORTH
PACIFIC
OCEAN

Tropic of Cancer

Equator

INDIAN
OCEAN

Tropic of Capricorn

Antarctic Circle

Scale: 1 to 125,000,000

| 0 | 1000 | 2000 Miles |

| 0 | 1000 | 2000 | 3000 Kilometers |

Ecology is the study of the relationships between living organisms and their environmental surroundings. Ecological regions are distinctive areas within which unique sets of organisms and environments are found. Within each ecological region, a particular combination of vegetation, wildlife, soil, water, climate, and terrain defines that region's habitability, or ability to support life, including human life. Like climate and landforms, ecological relationships are crucial to the existence of agriculture, the most basic of our economic activities, and important for many other kinds of economic activity as well.

Map **5** World Natural Hazards

Natural Hazards

Temporary (seasonal) pack ice: open water during summer months

Permanent pack ice: some open water leads during summer months

Permanent ice sheet

Severe sea fog: common enough to restrict navigation

Desert region: agriculture limited to irrigation

Area subject to desertification: soil and hydrology changes by humans

Tornado region: high risk of damaging storms

Tornado region: moderate risk of damaging storms

Tropical storm tracks (hurricanes, cyclones, typhoons); less than five per year

Tropical storm tracks (hurricanes, cyclones, typhoons); more than five per year

Selected rivers subject to severe flooding

• Major flood disasters in the 20th century

Southern limit of continuous permafrost (permantly frozen subsoil)

Equatorward limit of large iceberg drift

• Major earthquakes (in the 20th century)

• Major volcanic activity (in the 20th century)

Coastal areas subject to tsunamis: "tidal" waves produced by submarine volcanic/ earthquake activity

Unlike other elements of physical geography, natural hazards are unpredictable. There are certain regions, however, where the *probability* of the occurrence of a particular natural hazard is high. This map shows regions affected by major natural hazards at rates that are higher than the global norm. Persistent natural hazards may undermine the utility of an area for economic purposes. Some scholars suggest that regions of environmental instability may be regions of political instability as well.

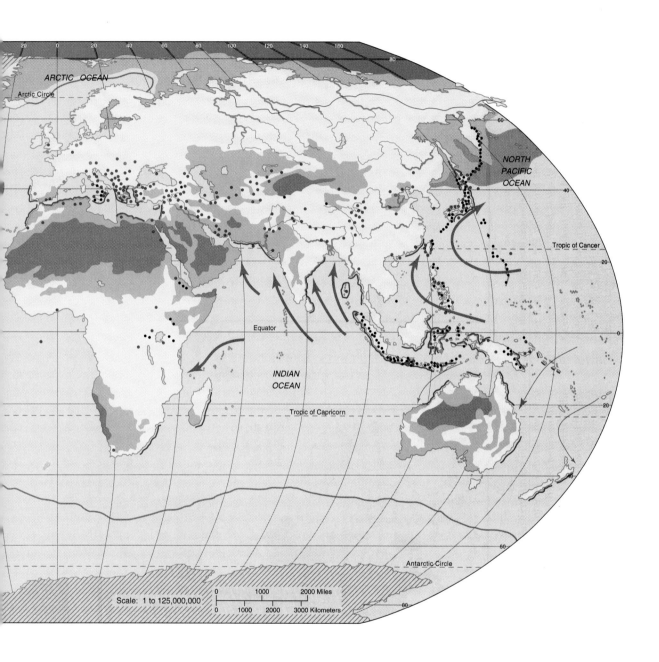

ARCTIC OCEAN

Arctic Circle

NORTH
PACIFIC
OCEAN

Tropic of Cancer

Equator

INDIAN
OCEAN

Tropic of Capricorn

Antarctic Circle

Scale: 1 to 125,000,000

| 0 | 1000 | 2000 Miles |
| 0 | 1000 | 2000 | 3000 Kilometers |

Map 6 Land Use Patterns of the World

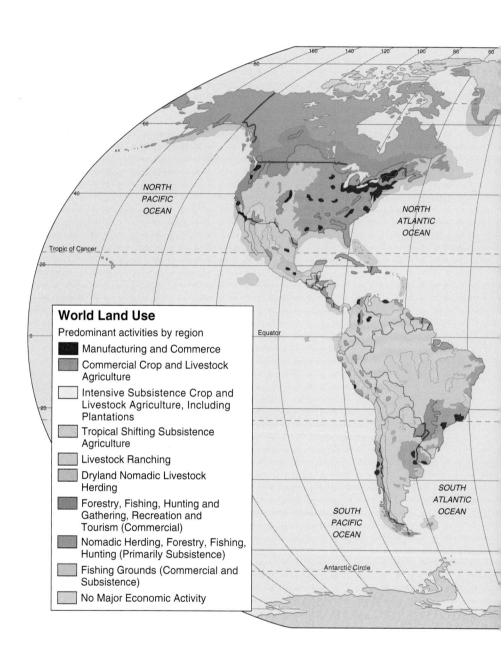

World Land Use

Predominant activities by region

- Manufacturing and Commerce
- Commercial Crop and Livestock Agriculture
- Intensive Subsistence Crop and Livestock Agriculture, Including Plantations
- Tropical Shifting Subsistence Agriculture
- Livestock Ranching
- Dryland Nomadic Livestock Herding
- Forestry, Fishing, Hunting and Gathering, Recreation and Tourism (Commercial)
- Nomadic Herding, Forestry, Fishing, Hunting (Primarily Subsistence)
- Fishing Grounds (Commercial and Subsistence)
- No Major Economic Activity

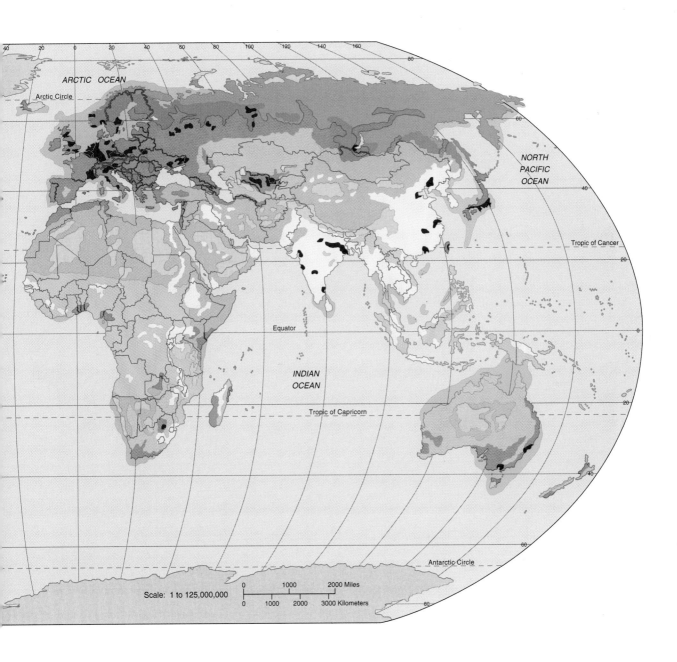

Many of the major land use patterns of the world (such as urbanization, industry, and transportation) are relatively small in area and are not easily seen on maps, but the most important uses people make of the earth's surface have more far-reaching effects. This map illustrates, in particular, the variations in primary land uses (such as agriculture) for the entire world. Note the differences between land use patterns in the more developed countries of the temperate zones and the less developed countries of the tropics.

Map 7 World Population Density

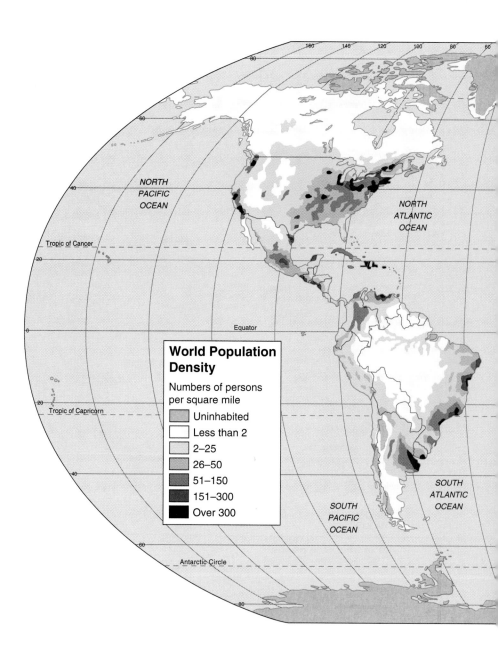

No feature of human activity is more reflective of environmental conditions than where people live. In the areas of densest populations, a mixture of natural and human factors has combined to allow maximum food production, maximum urbanization, and maximum centralization of economic activities. Three great concentrations of human population appear on the map—East Asia, South Asia, and Europe—with a fourth, lesser concentration in eastern North America (the "Megalopolis" region of the United States and Canada). One of these great population clusters—South Asia—is still growing rapidly and is expected to become even more densely populated during the twenty-first century. The other concentrations are likely to remain about

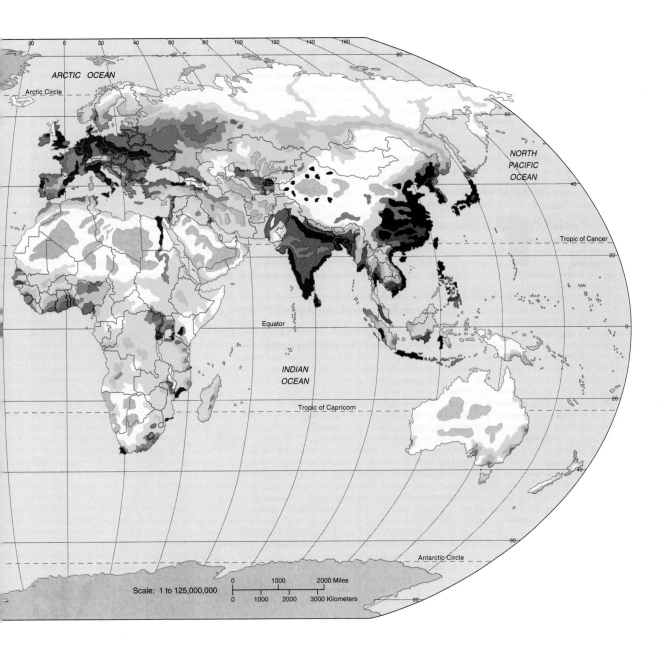

as they now appear. In Europe and North America, this is the result of economic development that has caused population growth to level off during the last century. In East Asia, population has also begun to grow more slowly. In the case of Japan and the Koreas, this is the consequence of economic development; in the case of China, it is the consequence of government intervention in the form of strict family planning. The areas of future high density (in addition to those already existing) are likely to be in Middle and South America and Africa, where population growth rates are well above the world average.

Map 8 World Religions

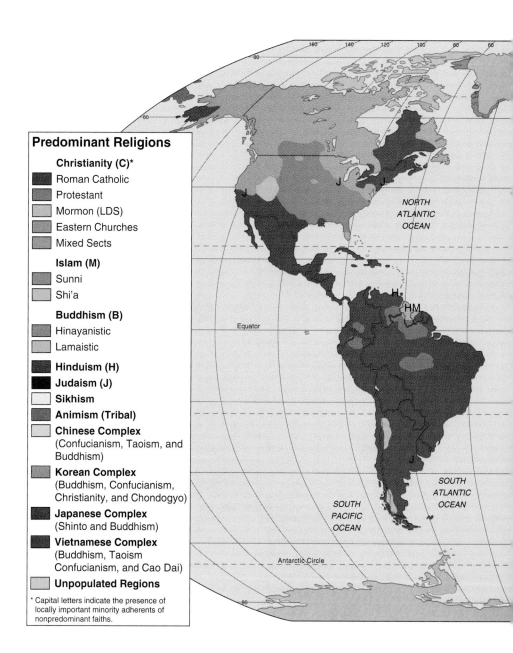

Predominant Religions

Christianity (C)*
- Roman Catholic
- Protestant
- Mormon (LDS)
- Eastern Churches
- Mixed Sects

Islam (M)
- Sunni
- Shi'a

Buddhism (B)
- Hinayanistic
- Lamaistic

Hinduism (H)

Judaism (J)

Sikhism

Animism (Tribal)

Chinese Complex
(Confucianism, Taoism, and Buddhism)

Korean Complex
(Buddhism, Confucianism, Christianity, and Chondogyo)

Japanese Complex
(Shinto and Buddhism)

Vietnamese Complex
(Buddhism, Taoism Confucianism, and Cao Dai)

Unpopulated Regions

* Capital letters indicate the presence of locally important minority adherents of nonpredominant faiths.

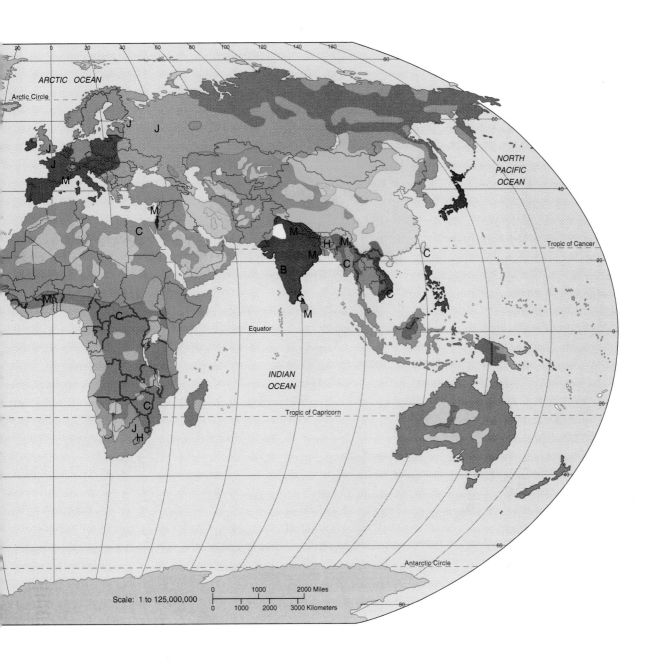

Religious adherence is one of the fundamental defining characteristics of culture. A depiction of the spatial distribution of religions is, therefore, as close as we can come to a map of cultural patterns. More than just a set of behavioral patterns having to do with worship and ceremony, religion is an important conditioner of how people treat one another and the environments that they occupy. In many areas of the world, the ways in which people make a living, the patterns of occupation that they create on the land, and the impacts that they make on ecosystems are the direct consequence of their adherence to a religious faith.

Map 9 World Languages

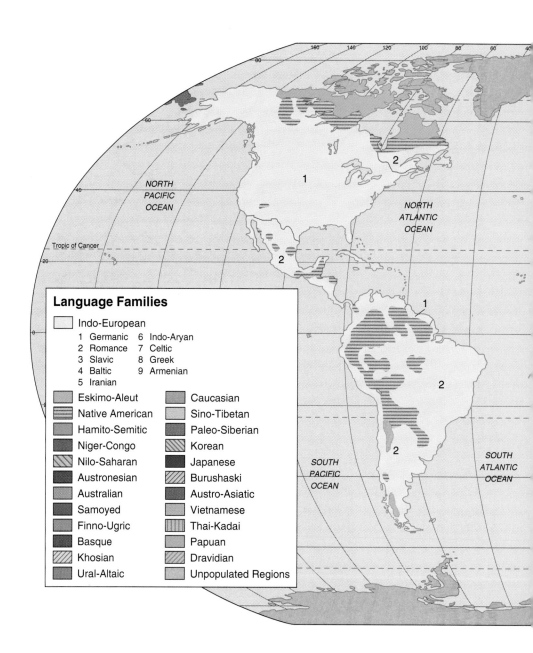

Language Families

☐ Indo-European
  1 Germanic 6 Indo-Aryan
  2 Romance   7 Celtic
  3 Slavic   8 Greek
  4 Baltic   9 Armenian
  5 Iranian

Eskimo-Aleut   Caucasian
Native American   Sino-Tibetan
Hamito-Semitic   Paleo-Siberian
Niger-Congo   Korean
Nilo-Saharan   Japanese
Austronesian   Burushaski
Australian   Austro-Asiatic
Samoyed   Vietnamese
Finno-Ugric   Thai-Kadai
Basque   Papuan
Khosian   Dravidian
Ural-Altaic   Unpopulated Regions

NORTH
PACIFIC
OCEAN

NORTH
ATLANTIC
OCEAN

Tropic of Cancer

SOUTH
PACIFIC
OCEAN

SOUTH
ATLANTIC
OCEAN

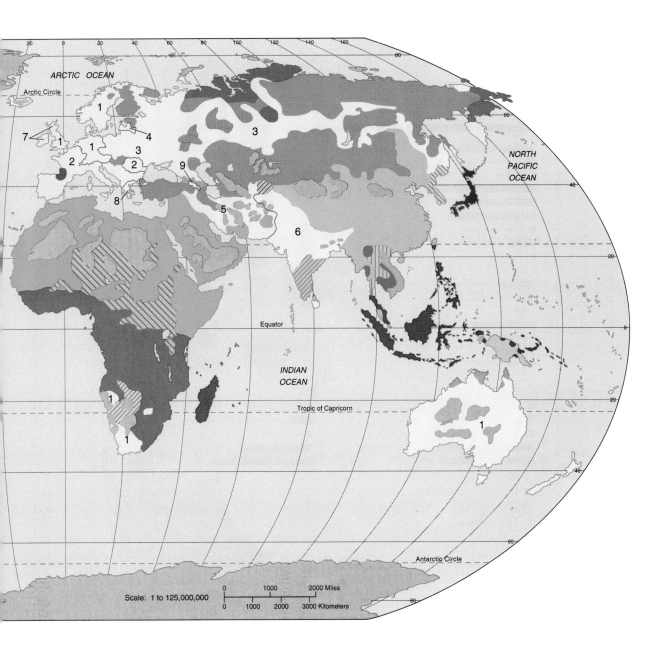

Like religion, language is an important defining characteristic of culture. It is perhaps the most durable of all cultural traits. Even after centuries of exposure to other languages or of conquest by speakers of other languages, the speakers of a specific tongue will often retain their own linguistic identity. As a geographic element, language helps us to locate areas of potential conflict, particularly in regions where two or more languages overlap. Many, if not most, of the world's conflict zones are areas of linguistic diversity. Language also provides clues that enable us to chart the course of human migrations, as shown in the distribution of Indo-European languages. And it helps us to understand some of the reasons behind important historical events; linguistic identity differences played an important part in the disintegration of the Soviet Union.

Map 10 World External Migrations in Modern Times

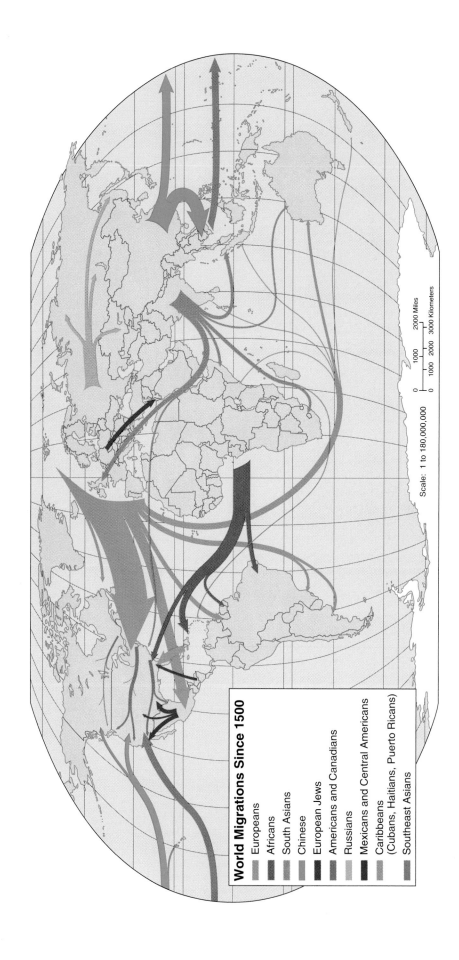

World Migrations Since 1500

- Europeans
- Africans
- South Asians
- Chinese
- European Jews
- Americans and Canadians
- Russians
- Mexicans and Central Americans
- Caribbeans (Cubans, Haitians, Puerto Ricans)
- Southeast Asians

Scale: 1 to 180,000,000

0   1000   2000 Miles

0   1000   2000   3000 Kilometers

Migration has had a significant effect on world geography, contributing to cultural change and development, to the diffusion of ideas and innovations, and to the complex mixture of people and cultures found in the world today. *Internal migration* occurs within the boundaries of a country; *external migration* is movement from one country or region to another. Over the last 50 years, the most important migrations in the world have been internal, largely the rural-to-urban migration that has been responsible for the recent rise of global urbanization. Prior to the mid-twentieth century, three types of external migrations were most important: *voluntary,* most often in search of better eco-

nomic conditions and opportunities; *involuntary or forced,* involving people who have been driven from their homelands by war, political unrest, or environmental disasters, or who have been transported as slaves or prisoners; and *imposed,* not entirely forced but which conditions make highly advisable. Human migrations in recorded history have been responsible for major changes in the patterns of languages, religions, ethnic composition, and economies. Particularly during the last 500 years, migrations of both the voluntary and involuntary or forced type have literally reshaped the human face of the earth.

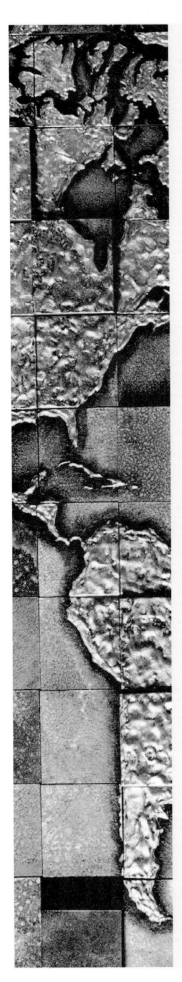

Part II

States: Alliances and Conflicts

Map 11 Political Boundary Types

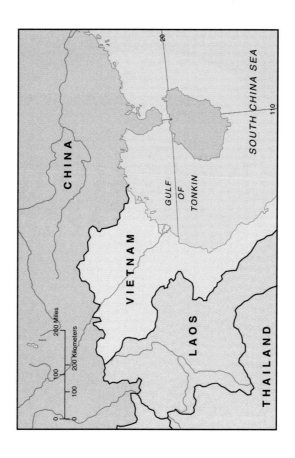

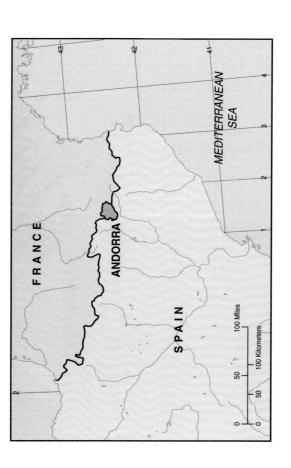

Antecedent: Antecedent boundaries are those that existed as part of the cultural landscape before the establishment of political territories. The boundary between Spain and France is the crest of the Pyrenees Mountains, long a cultural and linguistic barrier and a region of sparse population that is reflected on population density maps even at the world scale.

Subsequent: Subsequent boundaries are those that develop along with the cultural landscape of a region, part of a continuing evolution of political territory to match cultural region. The border region between Vietnam and China has developed over thousands of years of adjustment of territory between the two different cultural realms. Following the end of the Vietnam War, a lengthy border conflict between Vietnam and China suggests that the process is not yet completed.

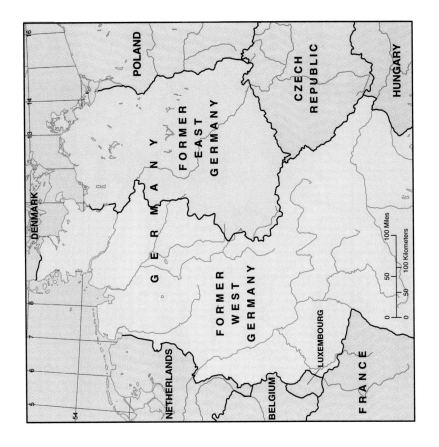

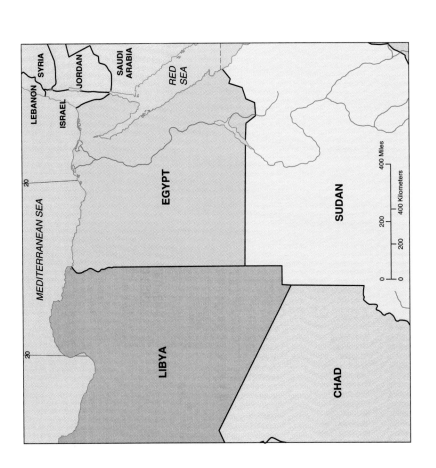

Relict: A relict boundary is like a relict landscape. The boundary between the former North and South Vietnam, along the Ben Hai River, is an example of a relict boundary. So too is the dividing line between the former Federal Republic of Germany (West Germany) and the German Democratic Republic (East Germany). Germany has been unified since 1990, with reintegration of the former Communist East into the West German economy happening progressively and more rapidly than expected. Nevertheless, there are still significant and visible differences between the urban German west and the rural east, between a progressive and modern economic landscape and a deteriorating one.

Superimposed: Superimposed boundaries are drawn arbitrarily across a uniform or homogenous cultural landscape. These boundaries often result from the occupation of territory by an expansive settlement process (see, for example, many of the boundaries of the western states in the United States) or from the process whereby colonial powers divided territory to suit their own needs rather than those of the indigenous population. The borders of Egypt, Libya, and Sudan meet in the center of a uniform cultural and physical region, artificially dividing what from a natural and human perspective is unified.

-23-

Map 12 Political Systems

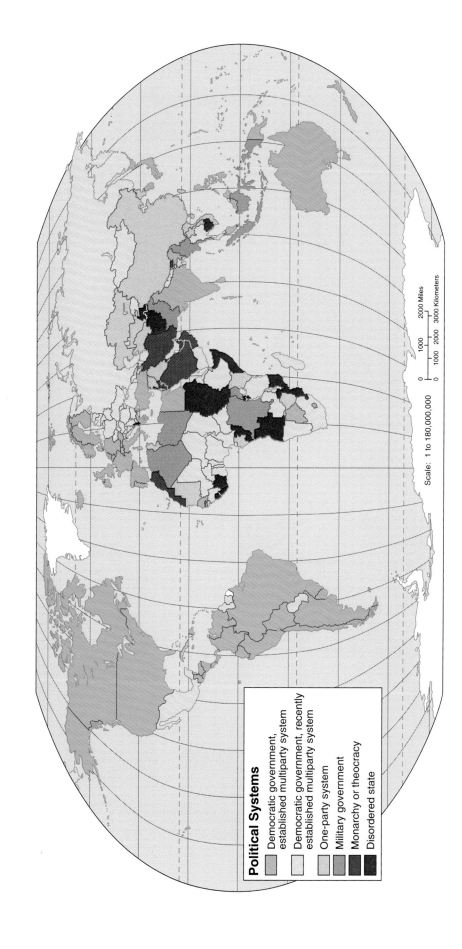

Political Systems

- Democratic government, established multiparty system
- Democratic government, recently established multiparty system
- One-party system
- Military government
- Monarchy or theocracy
- Disordered state

Scale: 1 to 180,000,000

0 1000 2000 Miles

0 1000 2000 3000 Kilometers

World political systems have changed dramatically during the last decade and may change even more in the future. The categories of political systems shown on the map are subject to some interpretation: established multiparty democracies are those in which elections by secret ballot with adult suffrage are and have been long-term features of the political landscape; recently established multiparty democracies are those in which the characteristic features of multiparty democracies have only recently emerged. The former Soviet satellites of eastern Europe and the republics that formerly constituted the USSR are in this category; so are states in emerging regions that are beginning to throw off the single-party rule that often followed the violent upheavals of the immediate postcolonial governmental transitions. The other categories are more or less obvious. One-party systems are states where single-party rule is constitutionally

guaranteed or where a one-party regime is a fact of political life. Monarchies are countries with heads of state who are members of a royal family; note that a number of countries that have monarchs, such as the U.K. and the Netherlands, do not fall into this category because the monarchs are titular heads of state only. Theocracies are countries in which rule is within the hands of a priestly or clerical class; today, this means primarily fundamentalist Islamic countries such as Iran. Military governments are frequently organized around a junta that has seized control of the government from civil authority; such states are often technically transitional, that is, the military claims that it will return the reins of government to civil authority when order is restored. Finally, disordered states are countries so beset by civil war or widespread ethnic conflict that no organized government can be said to exist within them.

Map 13 Sovereign States: Duration of Independence

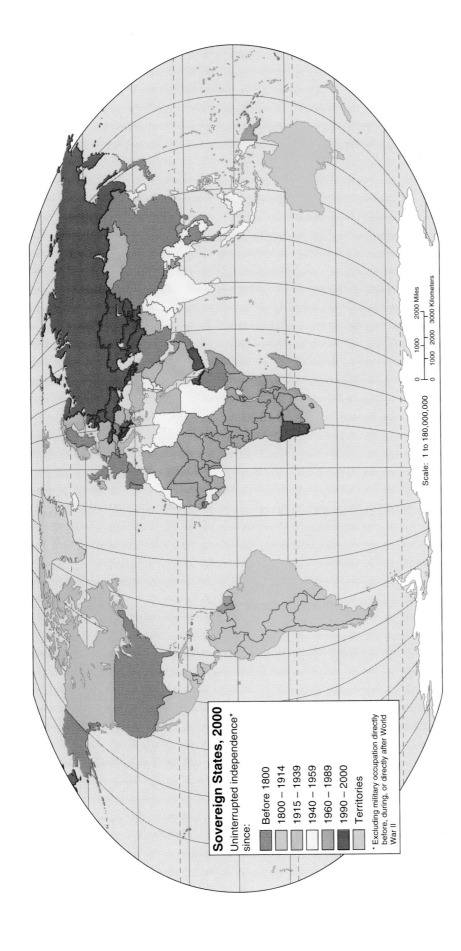

Sovereign States, 2000

Uninterrupted independence* since:

Before 1800
1800 – 1914
1915 – 1939
1940 – 1959
1960 – 1989
1990 – 2000
Territories

* Excluding military occupation directly before, during, or directly after World War II

Scale: 1 to 180,000,000

0   1000   2000 Miles

0   1000   2000   3000 Kilometers

Most countries of the modern world, including such major states as Germany and Italy, became independent after the beginning of the nineteenth century. Of the world's current countries, only 27 were independent in 1800. (Ten of the 27 were in Europe; the others were Afghanistan, China, Colombia, Ethiopia, Haiti, Iran, Japan, Mexico, Nepal, Oman, Paraguay, Russia, Taiwan, Thailand, Turkey, the United States, and Venezuela.) Following 1800, there have been four great periods of national independence. During the first of these (1800–1914), most of the mainland countries of the Americas achieved independence. During the second period (1915–1939), the countries of Eastern Europe emerged as independent entities. The third period (1940–1959) includes World War II and the years that followed, when independence for African and Asian nations that had been under control of colonial powers first began to occur. During the fourth period (1960–1989), independence came to the remainder of the colonial African and Asian nations, as well as to former colonies in the Caribbean and the South Pacific. More than half of the world's countries came into being as independent political entities during this period. Finally, in the last decade (1990–2000), the breakup of the existing states of the Soviet Union, Yugoslavia, and Czechoslovakia created 22 countries where only 3 had existed before.

Map 14 European Boundaries, 1914-1948

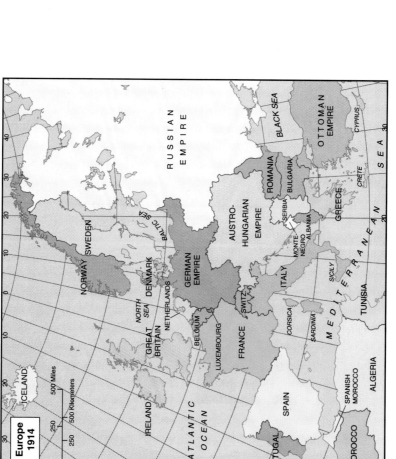

In 1914, on the eve of the First World War, Europe was dominated by the United Kingdom and France in the west, the German Empire and the Austro-Hungarian Empire in central Europe, and the Russian Empire in the east. Battle lines for the conflict that began in 1914 were drawn when the United Kingdom, France, and the Russian Empire joined together as the Triple Entente. In the view of the Germans, this coalition was designed to encircle Germany and its Austrian ally, which, along with Italy, made up the Triple Alliance. The German and Austrian fears were heightened in 1912–14 when a Russian-sponsored "Balkan League" pushed the Ottoman Turkish Empire from Europe, leaving behind the weak and mutually antagonistic Balkan states Serbia and

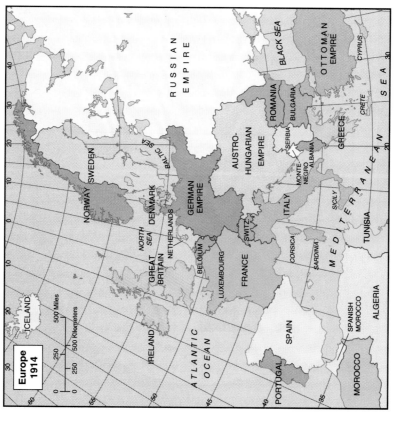

Montenegro. In August 1914, Germany and Austria-Hungary attacked in several directions and World War I began. Four years later, after massive loss of life and destruction, the central European empires were defeated. The victorious French, English, and Americans (who had entered the war in 1917) restructured the map of Europe in 1919, carving nine new states out of the remains of the German and Austro-Hungarian empires and the westernmost portions of the Russian Empire which, by the end of the war, was deep in the Revolution that deposed the czar and brought the Communists to power in a new Union of Soviet Socialist Republics.

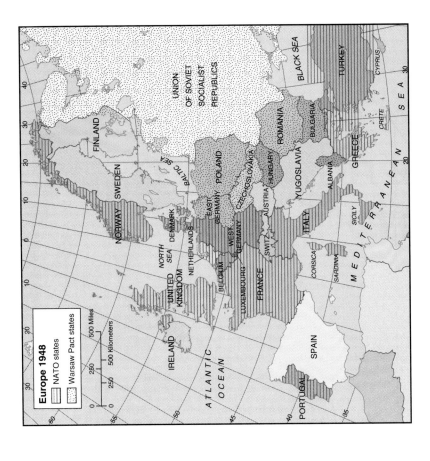

Europe 1948

NATO states

Warsaw Pact states

to the Atlantic and from the Black Sea to the Baltic. But the Axis powers of Germany and Italy could not withstand the greater resources and manpower of the combined United Kingdom–United States–USSR-led Allies and, in 1945, Allied armies occupied Germany. Once again, the lines of the central and eastern European map were redrawn. This time, a strengthened Soviet Union took back most of the territory the Russian Empire had lost at the end of the First World War. Germany was partitioned into four occupied sectors (English, French, American, and Russian) and later into two independent countries, the Federal Republic of Germany (West Germany) and the German Democratic Republic (East Germany). Although the Soviet Union's territory stopped at the Polish, Hungarian, Czechoslovakian, and Romanian borders, the eastern European countries (Poland, East Germany, Czechoslovakia, Hungary, Romania, Yugoslavia, Albania, and Bulgaria) became Communist between 1945 and 1948 and were separated by the Iron Curtain from the West.

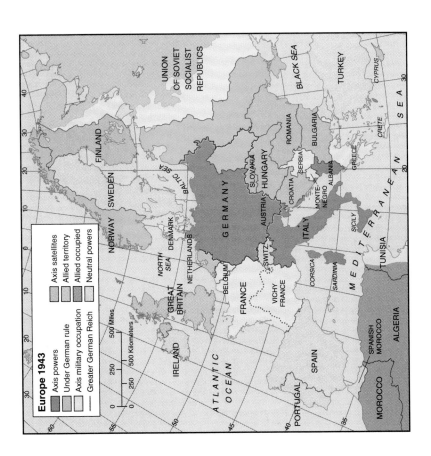

Europe 1943

Axis powers

Under German rule

Axis military occupation

Greater German Reich

Axis satellites

Allied territory

Allied occupied

Neutral powers

When the victorious Allies redrew the map of central and eastern Europe in 1919, they caused as many problems as they were trying to solve. The interval between the First and Second World Wars was really just a lull in a long war that halted temporarily in 1918 and erupted once again in 1939. Defeated Germany, resentful of the terms of the 1918 armistice and 1919 Treaty of Versailles and beset by massive inflation and unemployment at home, overthrew the Weimar republican government in 1933 and installed the National Socialist (Nazi) party led by Adolf Hitler in Berlin. Hitler quickly began making good on his promises to create a "thousand year realm" of German influence by annexing Austria and the Czech region of Czechoslovakia and allying Germany with a fellow fascist state in Mussolini's Italy. In September 1939 Germany launched the lightning-quick combined infantry, artillery, and armor attack known as *der Blitzkrieg* and took Poland to the east and, in quick succession, the Netherlands, Belgium, and France to the west. By 1943 the greater German Reich extended from the Russian Plain

Map 15 An Age of Bipolarity: The Cold War ca. 1970

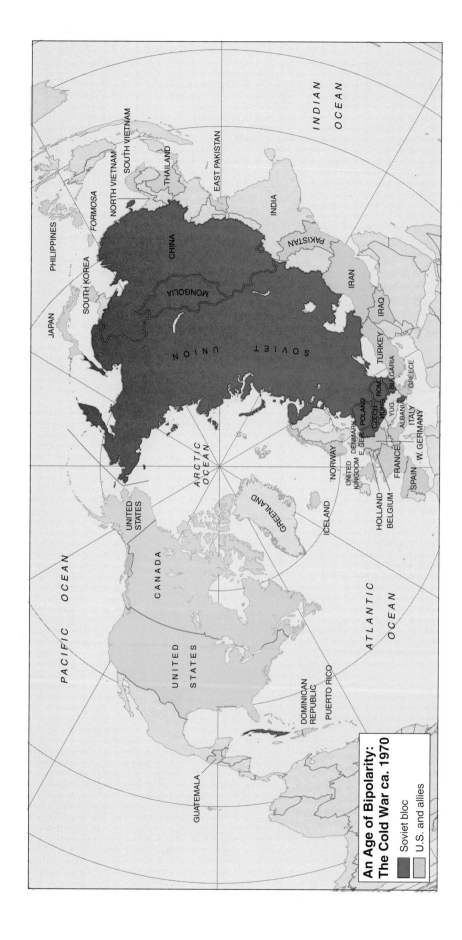

An Age of Bipolarity:
The Cold War 1970

Soviet bloc

U.S. and allies

Following the Second World War, the world was divided into two armed camps led by the United States and the Soviet Union. The Soviet Union and its allies, the Warsaw Pact countries, feared a U.S.-led takeover of the eastern European countries that became Soviet satellites after the war and the replacing of a socialist political and economic system with a liberal one. The United States and its allies, the NATO (North Atlantic Treaty Organization) countries, equally feared that the USSR would overrun western Europe. Both sides sought to defend themselves by building up massive military arsenals. The United States, adopting an international geopolitical strategy of con- tainment, sought to ring the Soviet Union with a string of allied countries and military bases that would prevent Soviet expansion in any direction. The levels of spending on military hardware contributed to the devolution of the Soviet Union, and the obsoles- cence of alliances and military bases in an age of advanced guidance and delivery sys- tems made the U.S. military containment less necessary. Following a peak in the early 1960s, the cold war gradually became less significant and the age of bipolar interna- tional power essentially ended with the dissolution of the USSR in 1991.

Map 16 Europe: Political Changes in the 1990s

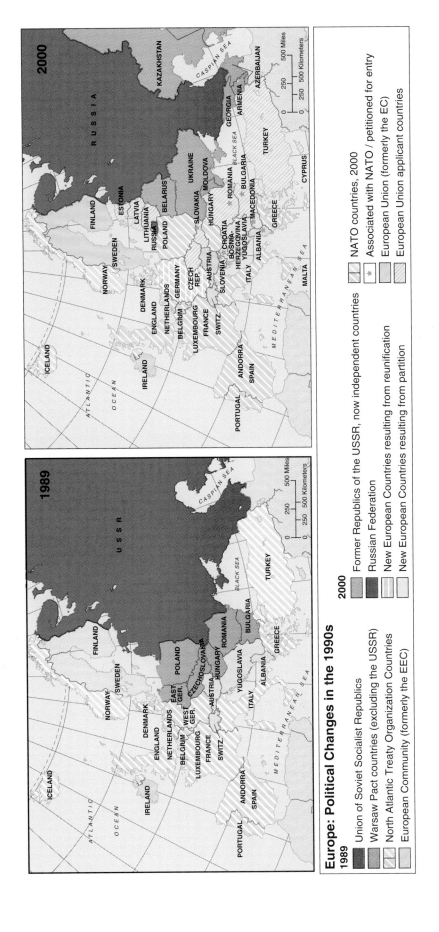

Europe: Political Changes in the 1990s

1989

- Union of Soviet Socialist Republics
- Warsaw Pact countries (excluding the USSR)
- North Atlantic Treaty Organization Countries
- European Community (formerly the EEC)

2000

- Former Republics of the USSR, now independent countries
- Russian Federation
- New European Countries resulting from reunification
- New European Countries resulting from partition
- NATO countries, 2000
- ★ Associated with NATO / petitioned for entry
- European Union (formerly the EC)
- European Union applicant countries

During the last decade of the twentieth century, one of the most remarkable series of political geographic changes of the last 500 years took place. The bipolar East-West structure that had characterized Europe's political geography since the end of the Second World War altered in the space of a very few years. In the mid-1980s, as Soviet influence over eastern and central Europe weakened, those countries began to turn to the capitalist West. Between 1989, when the country of Hungary was the first Soviet satellite to open its borders to travel, and 1991, when the Soviet Union dissolved into 15 independent countries, abrupt change in political systems occurred. The result is a new map of Europe that includes a number of countries not present on the map of 1989. These countries have emerged as the result of reunification, separation, or independence from the former Soviet Union. The new political structure has been accompanied by growing economic cooperation.

Map 17 The Middle East: Territorial Changes, 1918–Present

TERRITORIAL CHANGES IN THE MIDDLE EAST, WORLD WAR I TO PRESENT

- Ottoman Empire to World War I
- British control
- French control
- Kurdish homelands
- International boundaries in 1994

The Middle East, encompassing the northeastern part of Africa and southwestern Asia, has experienced a turbulent history. In the last century alone, many of the region's countries have gone from being ruled by the Turkish Ottoman Empire, to being dependencies of Great Britain or France, to being independent. Having experienced the Crusades and colonial domination by European powers, the region's predominantly Islamic countries are now resentful of interference in the region's affairs by countries with a European and/or Christian heritage. The tension between Israel (settled largely in the late nineteenth and twentieth centuries by Jews of predominantly European background) and its neighbors is a matter of European–Middle Eastern cultural stress as well as a religious conflict between Islamic Arab culture and Judaism.

Map 18 Africa: Colonialism to Independence, 1910–2000

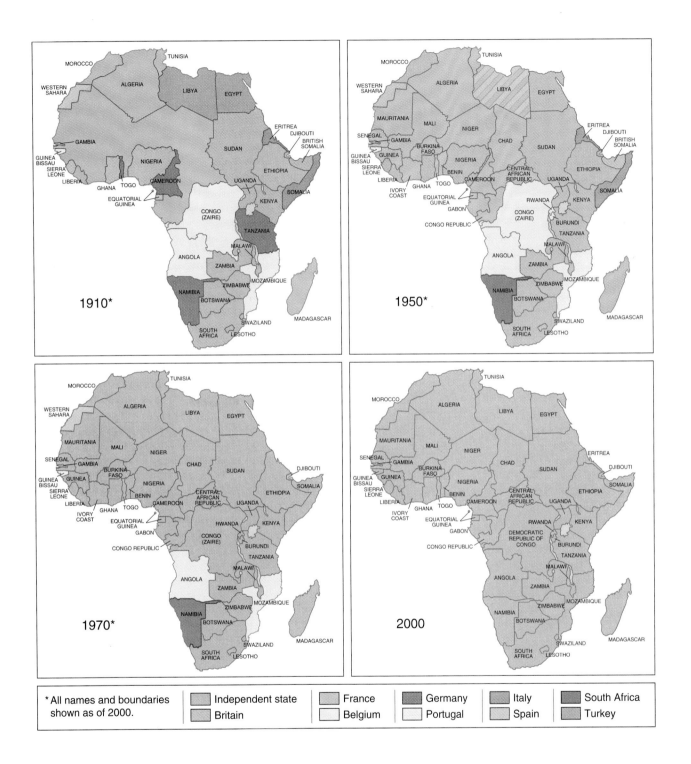

1910*

1950*

1970*

2000

* All names and boundaries shown as of 2000.	Independent state	France	Germany	Italy	South Africa
	Britain	Belgium	Portugal	Spain	Turkey

In few parts of the world has the transition from colonialism to independence been as abrupt as on the African continent. Unlike the states of Middle and South America, which generally achieved independence from their colonial masters in the early nineteenth century, most African states did not become independent until the twentieth century, often not until after World War II. In part because they retain borders that are legacies of their former colonial status, many of these recently created African states are beset by internal problems related to tribal and ethnic conflicts.

Map **19** Asia: Colonialism to Independence, 1930–2000

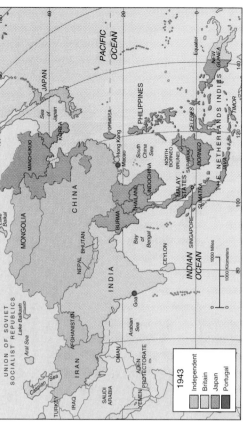

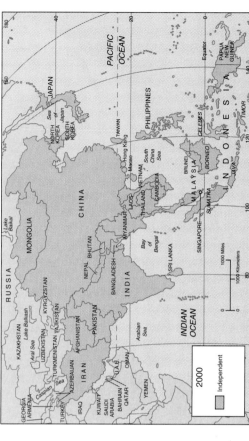

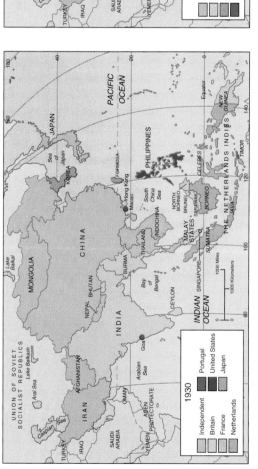

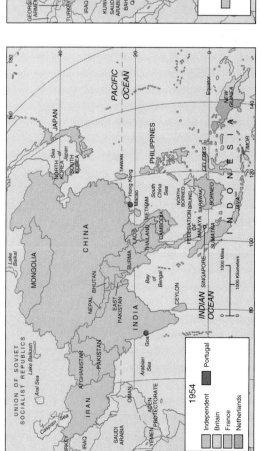

Asian countries, like those in Africa, have recently emerged from a colonial past. With the exception of China, Japan, and Thailand, virtually all Asian nations were until not long ago under the colonial control of Great Britain, France, Spain, the Netherlands, or the United States. For a short period of time between 1930 and 1945, Japan itself was a colonial power with considerable territories on the Asian mainland. The unraveling of colonial control in Asia, particularly in South and Southeast Asia, has precipitated internal conflicts in the newly independent states that make up a significant part of the political geography of the region. The last vestiges of European colonialism in Asia disappeared with the cession of Hong Kong (1997) and Macau (1999) to China.

Map 20 Global Distribution of Minority Groups

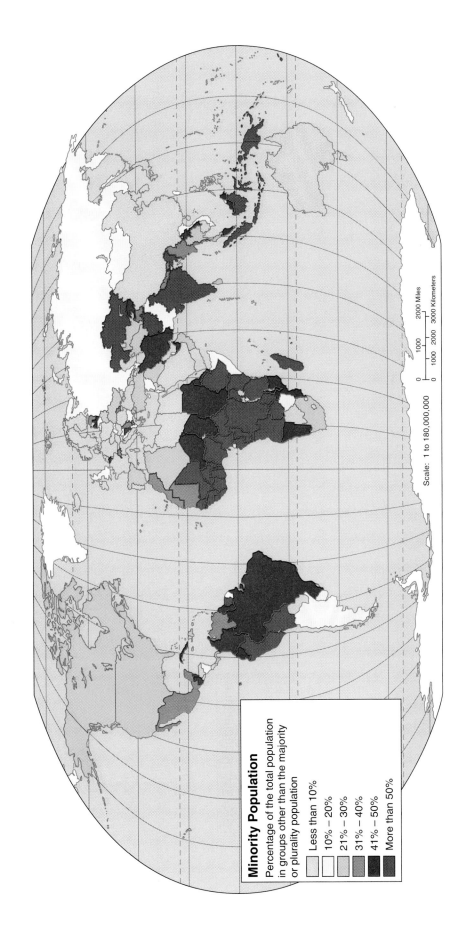

Minority Population

Percentage of the total population in groups other than the majority or plurality population

- Less than 10%
- 10% – 20%
- 21% – 30%
- 31% – 40%
- 41% – 50%
- More than 50%

Scale: 1 to 180,000,000

0   1000   2000 Miles

0   1000   2000   3000 Kilometers

The presence of minority ethnic, national, or racial groups within a country's population can add a vibrant and dynamic mix to the whole. Plural societies with a high degree of cultural and ethnic diversity should, according to some social theorists, be among the world's most healthy. Unfortunately, the reality of the situation is quite different from theory or expectation. The presence of significant minority populations played an important role in the disintegration of the Soviet Union; the continuing existence of minority populations within the new states formed from former Soviet republics threatens the viability and stability of those young political units. In Africa, national boundaries were drawn by colonial powers without regard for the geographical distribution of ethnic groups, and the continuing tribal conflicts that have resulted hamper both economic and political development. Even in the most highly developed regions of the world, the presence of minority ethnic populations poses significant problems: witness the separatist movement in Canada, driven by the desire of some French-Canadians to be independent of the English majority, and the continuing ethnic conflict between Flemish-speaking and Walloon-speaking Belgians. This map, by arraying states on a scale of homogeneity to heterogeneity, indicates areas of existing and potential social and political strife.

-33-

Map 21 Linguistic Diversity

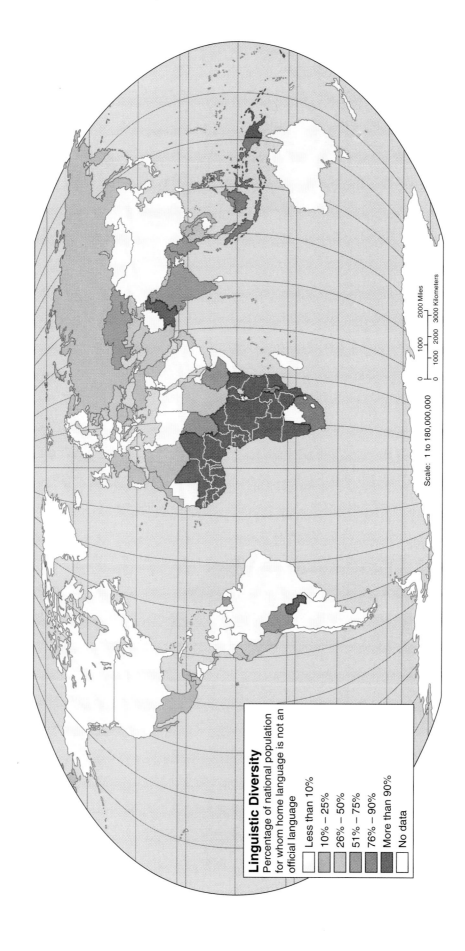

Linguistic Diversity

Percentage of national population
for whom home language is not an
official language

- Less than 10%
- 10% – 25%
- 26% – 50%
- 51% – 75%
- 76% – 90%
- More than 90%
- No data

Scale: 1 to 180,000,000

0   1000   2000 Miles

0   1000   2000   3000 Kilometers

Of the world's approximately 5,300 languages, fewer than 100 are official languages, those designated by a country as the language of government, commerce, education, and information. This means that for much of the world's population the language that is spoken in the home is different from the official language of the country of residence. The world's former colonial areas in Middle and South America, Africa, and South and

Southeast Asia stand out on the map as regions in which there is significant disparity between home languages and official languages. To complicate matters further, for most of the world's population, the primary international languages of trade and tourism (French and English) are neither home nor official languages.

Map 22 World Refugee Population

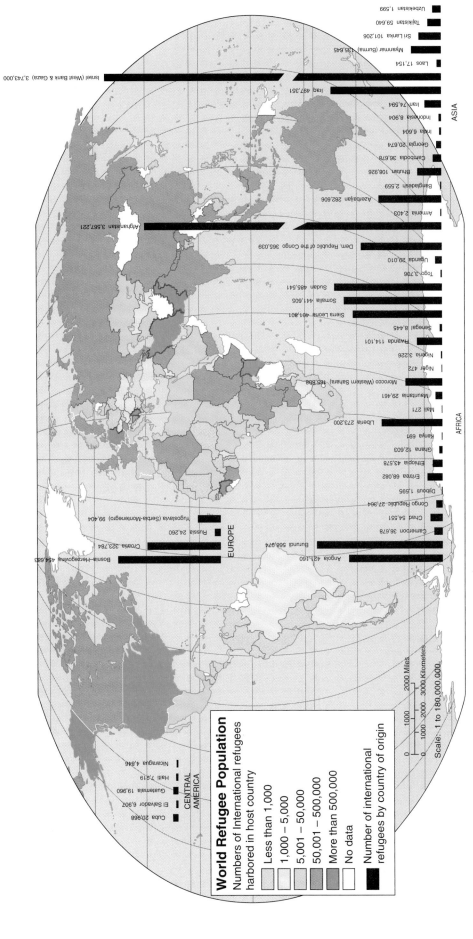

Refugees are persons who have been driven from their homes, normally by armed conflict, and have sought refuge by relocating. The most numerous refugees have traditionally been international refugees, who have crossed the political boundaries of their homelands into other countries. This refugee population is recognized by international agencies, and the countries of refuge are often rewarded financially by those agencies

for their willingness to take in externally displaced persons. In recent years, largely because of an increase in civil wars, there have been growing numbers of internally displaced persons—those who leave their homes but stay within their country of origin. There are no rewards for harboring such internal refugee populations.

Map 23   International Conflicts in the Post–World War II World

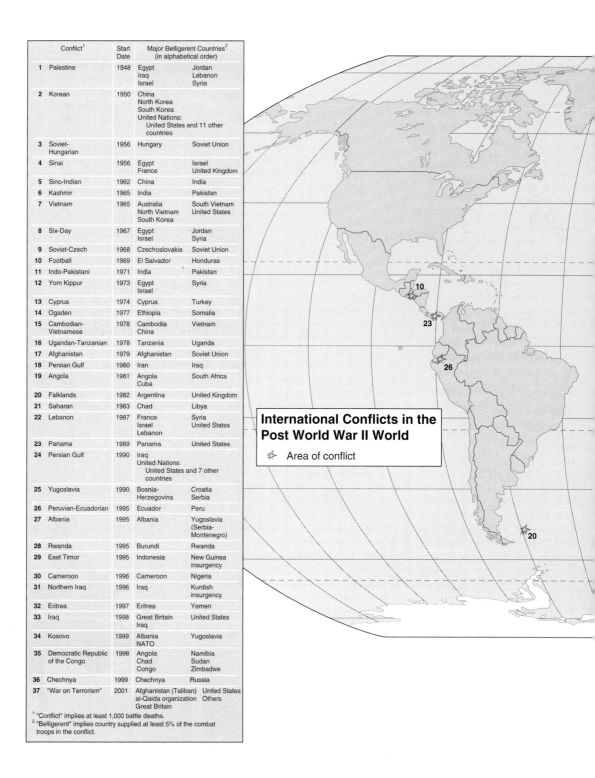

	Conflict[1]	Start Date	Major Belligerent Countries[2] (in alphabetical order)	
1	Palestine	1948	Egypt Iraq Israel	Jordan Lebanon Syria

2	Korean	1950	China
			North Korea
			South Korea
			United Nations:
			    United States and 11 other
			    countries	

3	Soviet-Hungarian	1956	Hungary	Soviet Union
4	Sinai	1956	Egypt France	Israel United Kingdom
5	Sino-Indian	1962	China	India
6	Kashmir	1965	India	Pakistan
7	Vietnam	1965	Australia North Vietnam South Korea	South Vietnam United States
8	Six-Day	1967	Egypt Israel	Jordan Syria
9	Soviet-Czech	1968	Czechoslovakia	Soviet Union
10	Football	1969	El Salvador	Honduras
11	Indo-Pakistani	1971	India	Pakistan
12	Yom Kippur	1973	Egypt Israel	Syria
13	Cyprus	1974	Cyprus	Turkey
14	Ogaden	1977	Ethiopia	Somalia
15	Cambodian-Vietnamese	1978	Cambodia China	Vietnam
16	Ugandan-Tanzanian	1978	Tanzania	Uganda
17	Afghanistan	1979	Afghanistan	Soviet Union
18	Persian Gulf	1980	Iran	Iraq
19	Angola	1981	Angola Cuba	South Africa
20	Falklands	1982	Argentina	United Kingdom
21	Saharan	1983	Chad	Libya
22	Lebanon	1987	France Israel Lebanon	Syria United States
23	Panama	1989	Panama	United States

24	Persian Gulf	1990	Iraq
			United Nations:
			    United States and 7 other
			    countries	

25	Yugoslavia	1990	Bosnia-Herzegovina	Croatia Serbia
26	Peruvian-Ecuadorian	1995	Ecuador	Peru
27	Albania	1995	Albania	Yugoslavia (Serbia-Montenegro)
28	Rwanda	1995	Burundi	Rwanda
29	East Timor	1995	Indonesia	New Guinea insurgency
30	Cameroon	1996	Cameroon	Nigeria
31	Northern Iraq	1996	Iraq	Kurdish insurgency
32	Eritrea	1997	Eritrea	Yemen
33	Iraq	1998	Great Britain Iraq	United States
34	Kosovo	1999	Albania NATO	Yugoslavia
35	Democratic Republic of the Congo	1998	Angola Chad Congo	Namibia Sudan Zimbadwe
36	Chechnya	1999	Chechnya	Russia
37	"War on Terrorism"	2001	Afghanistan (Taliban) al-Qaida organization Great Britain	United States Others

[1] "Conflict" implies at least 1,000 battle deaths.
[2] "Belligerent" implies country supplied at least 5% of the combat troops in the conflict.

International Conflicts in the Post World War II World

✦ Area of conflict

The Korean War and the Vietnam War dominated the post–World War II period in terms of international military conflict. But numerous smaller conflicts have taken place, with fewer numbers of belligerents and with fewer battle and related casualties. These smaller international conflicts have been mostly territorial conflicts, reflecting the continual readjustment of political boundaries and loyalties brought about by the end of colonial empires, and the dissolution of the Soviet Union. Many of these conflicts were not wars in the more traditional sense, in which two or more countries formally declare war on one another, severing diplomatic ties

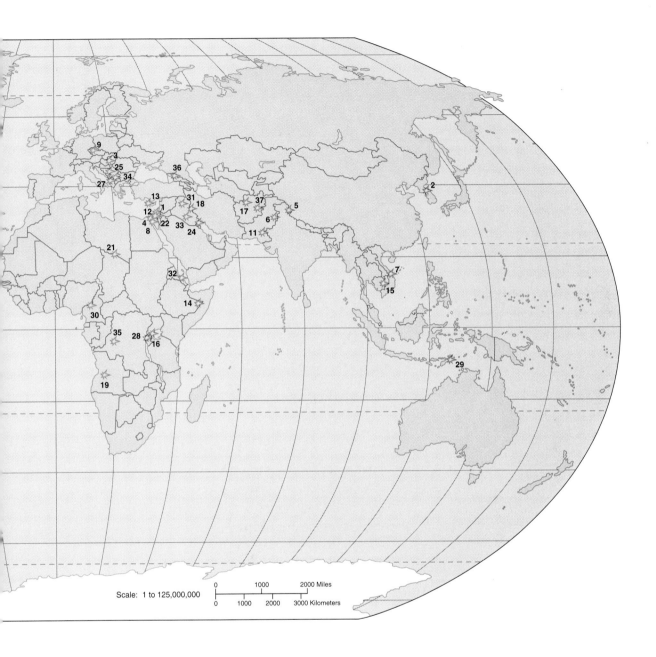

and devoting their entire national energies to the war effort. Rather, many of these conflicts were and are undeclared wars, sometimes fought between rival groups within the same country with outside support from other countries. The aftermath of the September 11, 2001, terrorist attacks on the United States indicate the dawn of yet another type of international conflict, namely a "war" fought between traditional nation-states and non-state actors.

Map 24 Post–Cold War International Alliances

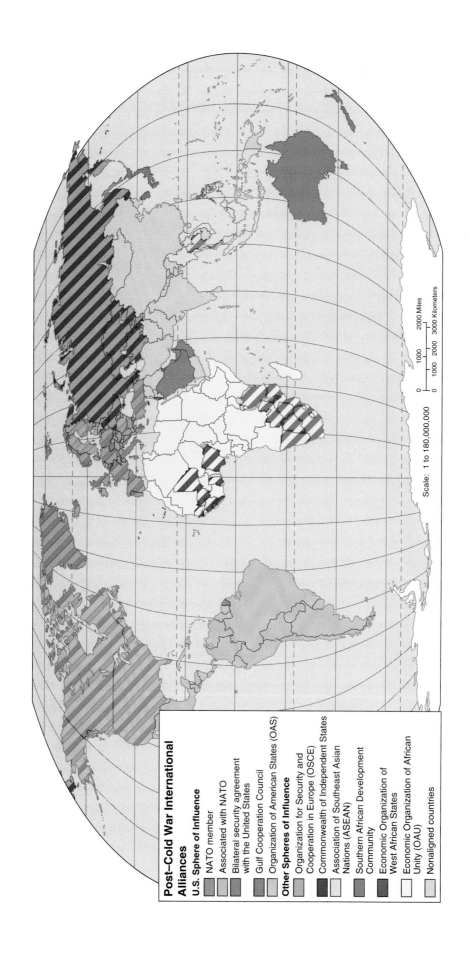

Scale: 1 to 180,000,000

0   1000   2000 Miles
0   1000   2000   3000 Kilometers

Post–Cold War International Alliances

U.S. Sphere of Influence
- NATO member
- Associated with NATO
- Bilateral security agreement with the United States
- Gulf Cooperation Council
- Organization of American States (OAS)

Other Spheres of Influence
- Organization for Security and Cooperation in Europe (OSCE)
- Commonwealth of Independent States
- Association of Southeast Asian Nations (ASEAN)
- Southern African Development Community
- Economic Organization of West African States
- Economic Organization of African Unity (OAU)
- Nonaligned countries

When the Warsaw Pact dissolved in 1992, the North Atlantic Treaty Organization (NATO) was left as the only major military alliance in the world. Some former Warsaw Pact members (Czech Republic, Hungary, and Poland) have joined NATO and others are petitioning for entry. The bipolar division of the world into two major military alliances of the twenty-first century economic alliances will begin to overshadow military ones in their relevance for the world's peoples.

nant political and military power. But other international alliances, such as the Commonwealth of Independent States (including most of the former republics of the Soviet Union), will continue to be important. It may well be that during the first few decades of the twenty-first century economic alliances will begin to overshadow military ones in their relevance for the world's peoples.

Map 25 Flashpoints, 2001

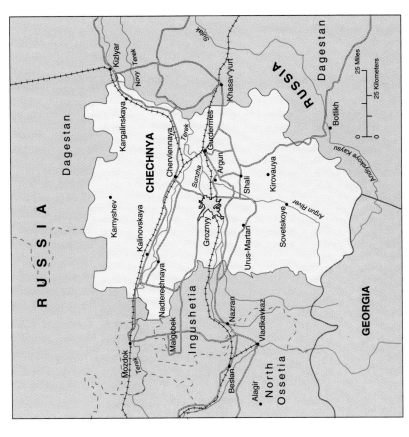

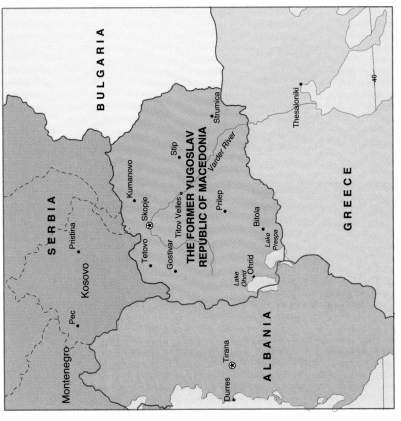

Chechnya: The area in southern Russia known as the Caucasus Region is home to a large variety of non-Russian ethnic groups; many are Muslim and resent centuries of Russian domination and Soviet-era totalitarianism. After the Soviet Union disintegrated in 1991, several of these ethnic groups began agitating for more autonomy from Moscow or for outright independence. One of the more vocal groups with a history of opposition to Moscow's rule were the Chechens. The Chechens declared themselves a sovereign nation in 1991 and by 1994 relations between the breakaway government in Chechnya and the Russian government had drastically deteriorated. In December of that year, Russian forces attacked Chechnya, beginning the first of two (1994–96 and 1999–present) full-scale military conflicts that have also crept into the neighboring Russian autonomous area of Dagestan, itself largely Muslim. In the mid- and late 1990s Russia experienced several terrorist attacks in cities throughout the nation which the Russian government attributed to Islamic extremists supporting Chechen independence. As a result, a second round of the conflict began in August 1999 with a full-scale Russian military assault on Dagestan and Chechnya. This assault is ongoing and continues to face intense resistance, with heavy casualties on both sides.

Macedonia: Since the fifteenth-century conquest of much of southeastern Europe by the Turkish Ottoman Empire, conflict in the Balkan region has been precipitated by ethnic and religious enmity between Orthodox Christians and Muslims. An area of particular concern has been the interface between predominantly Orthodox Macedonia and predominantly Muslim Albania, particularly in the border region the two share with the former Yugoslav republic of Kosovo. Tensions between the Macedonian government and its Albanian (Muslim) minority were heightened by the fallout from the conflict in Kosovo in the late 1990s between the Serbs and the Kosovar Albanians, backed by Albania. The resolution of this conflict by a NATO-led force in favor of the Kosovars led to emboldened feelings of Albanian patriotism in the region. Several sporadic incidents occurred along the Macedonian-Albanian border in late 2000, with more protracted and heavier combat between rebels and the Macedonian government forces occurring in the northern part of Macedonia (near the capital of Skopje) throughout 2001. The rebel forces assert they are only seeking to revise the Macedonian constitution and attain better rights for the Albanian minority in Macedonia. The Macedonian government is concerned that the Albanian minority centered in northern and western Macedonia wishes to secede and merge (along with Kosovo) into a Greater Albania, and suspects that Albania itself has encouraged this objective.

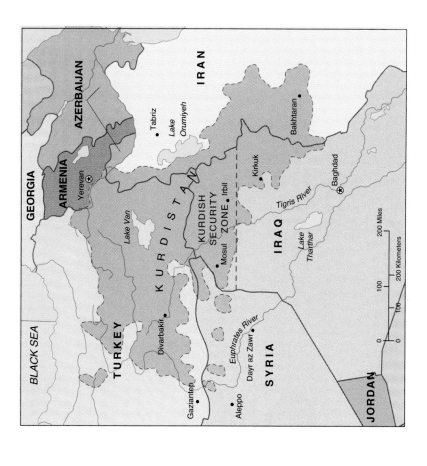

Iraq and Kurdistan: Where Turkey, Iran, and Iraq meet in the high mountain region of the Tauros and Zagros mountains, a nation of 25 million people exists. This nation is the Kurds, the occupants of this area for over 3,000 years but having no state, and receiving considerably less attention than other stateless nations like the Palestinians. Following the 1991 Gulf War between Iraq and a U.S.-led coalition of European and Arabic states, the United Nations demarcated a Kurdish "security zone" in northern Iraq. Continually under attack from Iraq to the south and beset internally by militant extremist groups like the Kurdish Workers party, the security zone is anything but. Unless three powerful states —Turkey, Iran, and Iraq—could be persuaded to give up major portions of their territory for the establishment of an independent Kurdistan, the security zone arrangement may be the closest the Kurds come to their ambition of territorial integrity and independence.

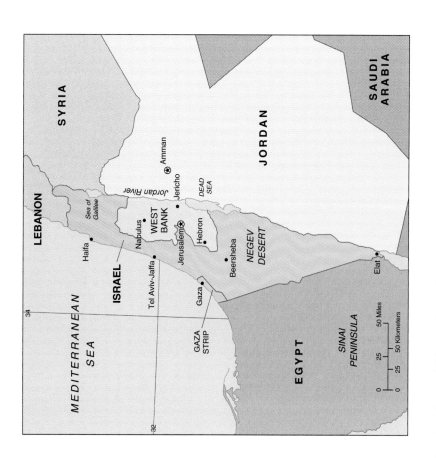

Israel and Its Neighbors: The modern state of Israel was created out of the former British Protectorate of Palestine, inhabited primarily by Muslim Arabs, after the Second World War. Conflict between Arabs and Israeli Jews has been a constant ever since. Much of the present tension revolves around the West Bank area, not part of the original Israeli state but taken from Jordan, an Arab country, in the Six-Day War of 1967. Many Palestinians had settled this part of Jordan after the creation of Israel and remain as a majority population in the West Bank region today. Israel has established many agricultural settlements within the region since 1967, angering Palestinian Arabs. For Israel, the West Bank is the region of ancient Judea and this region, won in battle, will not be ceded back to Palestinian Arabs without protracted or severe military action.

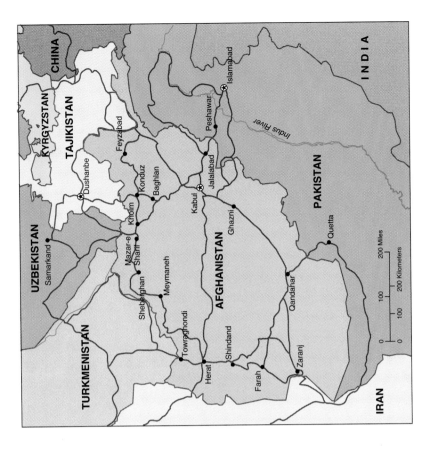

Afghanistan (Taliban and Al-Qaeda): In the aftermath of the tragic September 11, 2001, terrorist attacks on the World Trade Center and the Pentagon, the United States (backed by its allies) has declared a massive and global "war on terrorism" to varying degrees by its allies) has declared a massive and global "war on terrorism" and any states that may provide "safe harbor" to terrorists. To date, the most prominent target of this U.S. declaration of war has been the Taliban regime of Islamic extremists who controlled about 95 percent of the territory of the beleaguered nation of Afghanistan. International observers believe that the Taliban regime has welcomed and provided a base for the Al-Qaeda terrorist network dominated by Saudi expatriate and millionaire Osama bin Laden since the late 1990s. As a result of this intelligence, the U.S. and Britain have pursued a daily bombardment of key Al-Qaeda and Taliban installations inside Afghanistan and are poised to commit forces to a ground assault on that country (and possibly elsewhere) as this publication goes to press.

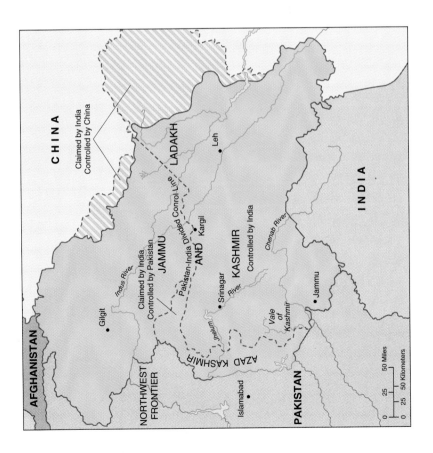

Jammu and Kashmir: When Britain withdrew from South Asia in 1947, the former states of British India were asked to decide whether they wanted to become part of a new Hindu India or a Muslim Pakistan. In the state of Jammu and Kashmir, the rulers were Hindu and the majority population was Muslim. The maharajah (prince) of Kashmir opted to join India, but an uprising of the Muslim majority precipitated a war between India and Pakistan over control of this high mountain region. In 1949 a cease-fire line was established by the UN, leaving most of the territory of Jammu and Kashmir in Indian hands. Since then Pakistan and India have waged intermittent skirmishes over the disputed territory that holds the headwaters of the Indus River, a life-giving stream to the desert Pakistan. In 1999 extremist Muslim groups demanding independence escalated the periodic battles into a full-fledged, if small, war between two of Asia's major powers—both possessing nuclear weapons.

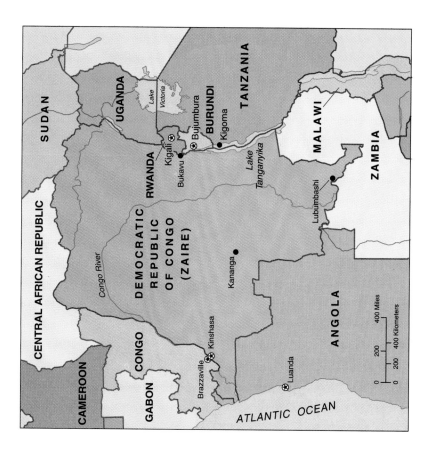

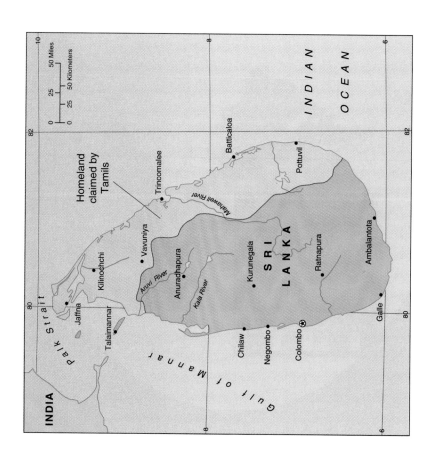

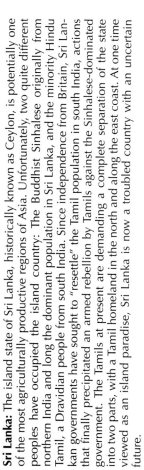

Congo: The war in the Democratic Republic of the Congo (formerly Zaire) has preoccupied the United Nations and African diplomats since 1999. Troops from Zimbabwe, Angola, Sudan, Chad and Namibia are now joined with the Congo's President Laurent Kabila against his former allies Rwanda, Burundi, and Uganda, who each back several separate Congolese rebel groups. The origins of the conflict lie in the overthrow of long-time dictator Mobutu Sese Seko by Kabila's army in May 1997 after a year of civil war. Kabila's failure to call elections or stabilize the country's economy led to further rounds of rebellion in the huge but fractious nation, rebellion supported by the economic and military assistance of neighboring Rwanda, Burundi, and Uganda. Diplomats have called the conflict "Africa's first world war", and fear that it may destabilize the southern half of the continent, leading to massive refugee flows and abject poverty.

Sri Lanka: The island state of Sri Lanka, historically known as Ceylon, is potentially one of the most agriculturally productive regions of Asia. Unfortunately, two quite different peoples have occupied the island country: The Buddhist Sinhalese originally from northern India and long the dominant population in Sri Lanka, and the minority Hindu Tamil, a Dravidian people from south India. Since independence from Britain, Sri Lankan governments have sought to "resettle" the Tamil population in south India, actions that finally precipitated an armed rebellion by Tamils against the Sinhalese-dominated government. The Tamils at present are demanding a complete separation of the state into two parts, with a Tamil homeland in the north and along the east coast. At one time viewed as an island paradise, Sri Lanka is now a troubled country with an uncertain future.

-42-

Map 26   Nations With Nuclear Weapons

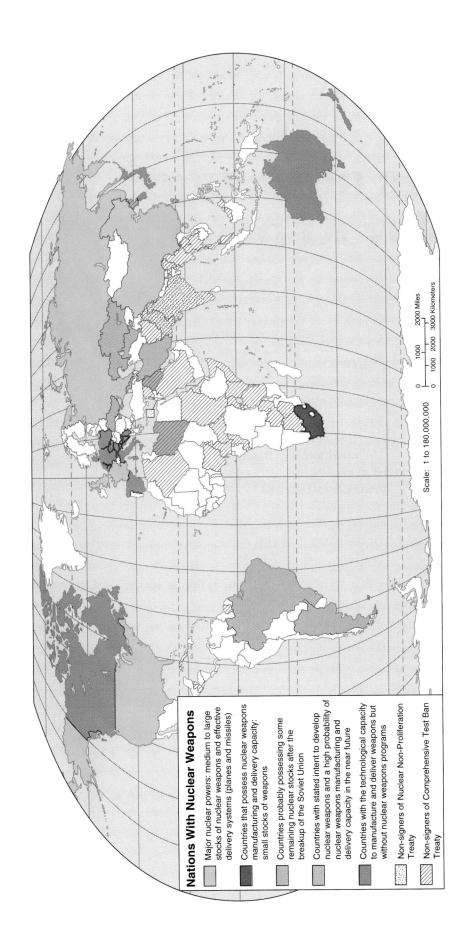

Nations With Nuclear Weapons

- Major nuclear powers: medium to large stocks of nuclear weapons and effective delivery systems (planes and missiles)
- Countries that possess nuclear weapons manufacturing and delivery capacity: small stocks of weapons
- Countries probably possessing some remaining nuclear stocks after the breakup of the Soviet Union
- Countries with stated intent to develop nuclear weapons and a high probability of nuclear weapons manufacturing and delivery capacity in the near future
- Countries with the technological capacity to manufacture and deliver weapons but without nuclear weapons programs
- Non-signers of Nuclear Non-Proliferation Treaty
- Non-signers of Comprehensive Test Ban Treaty

Scale: 1 to 180,000,000

0   1000   2000 Miles

0   1000   2000   3000 Kilometers

Since 1980, the number of countries possessing the capacity to manufacture and deliver nuclear weapons has grown dramatically, increasing the chances of accidental nuclear exchanges. In addition to the traditional nuclear powers of the United States, Russia, China, the United Kingdom, and France, some newly independent former Soviet republics (Ukraine, Kazakhstan, Uzbekistan, and Georgia) may retain some of the weapons systems from the old Soviet Union. Also, four other countries are now judged by many authorities to possess nuclear weapons capability: Israel, India, Pakistan, and South Africa. While the stockpile of weapons of these countries is small (ranging from a minimum of 510 weapons in Pakistan to a maximum of 50–200 weapons in Israel), the proliferation of countries capable of using nuclear warheads in wartime threatens global security. In addition to countries that already possess the capacity to make and deliver nuclear weapons, seven other countries—Argentina, Brazil, Iran, Iraq, Libya, North Korea, and Taiwan—have had active nuclear weapons programs and may possess nuclear weapons capacity. Finally, there are countries—virtually all of them in the developed economies of the world—that possess the technological capacity to manufacture nuclear weapons and delivery systems but have chosen not to develop nuclear weapons programs. These countries include, among others, Canada, most western and eastern European countries (other than Britain or France), South Korea, Japan, Australia, and New Zealand.

-43-

Map 27 Size of Armed Forces

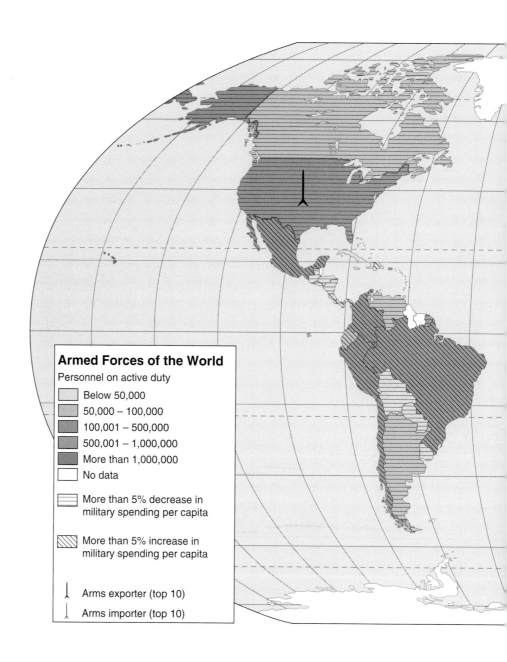

Armed Forces of the World

Personnel on active duty

- Below 50,000
- 50,000 – 100,000
- 100,001 – 500,000
- 500,001 – 1,000,000
- More than 1,000,000
- No data

More than 5% decrease in military spending per capita

More than 5% increase in military spending per capita

Arms exporter (top 10)

Arms importer (top 10)

While the size of a country's armed forces is still an indicator of national power on the international scene, it is no longer as important as it once was. The increasing high technology of military hardware allows smaller numbers of military personnel to be more effective. There are some countries, such as China, with massive numbers of military personnel but with relatively limited military power because of a lack of modern weaponry. Additionally, the use of rapid transportation allows personnel to be deployed about the globe or any region of it quickly; this also increases effectiveness of highly trained and well-armed smaller military units. Nevertheless, the world is still a long way from the predicted "push-button warfare" that many experts have

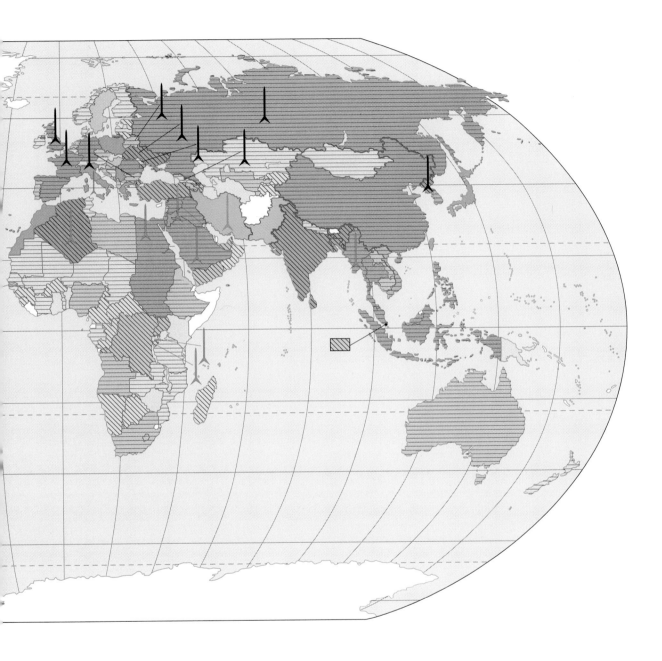

long anticipated. Indeed, the pattern of the last few years has been for most military conflicts to involve ground troops engaged in fairly traditional patterns of operation. Even in the Persian Gulf conflict, with its highly-publicized "smart bombs," the bulk of the military operation that ended the conflict was carried out by infantry and armor operating on the ground and supported by traditional air cover using conventional weaponry. Thus, while the size of a country's armed forces may not be as important as it once was, it is still a major factor in measuring the ability of nations to engage successfully in armed conflict.

Map 28 Military Expenditures as a Percentage of Gross National Product

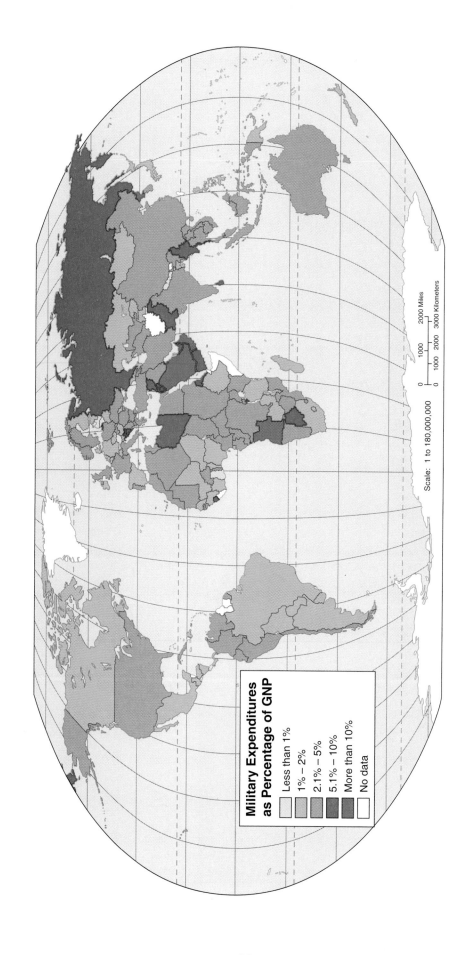

**Military Expenditures
as Percentage of GNP**

- Less than 1%
- 1% – 2%
- 2.1% – 5%
- 5.1% – 10%
- More than 10%
- No data

Scale: 1 to 180,000,000

0   1000   2000 Miles

0   1000   2000   3000 Kilometers

Many countries devote a significant proportion of their total central governmental expenditures to defense: weapons, personnel, and research and development of military hardware. A glance at the map reveals that there are a number of regions in which defense expenditures are particularly high, reflecting the degree of past and present political tension between countries. The clearest example is the Middle East. The steady increase in military expenditures by developing countries is one of the most alarming (and least well known) worldwide defense issues. Where the end of the cold war has meant a substantial reduction of military expenditures for the countries in North America and Europe and for Russia, in many of the world's developing countries military expenditures have risen between 15 percent and 20 percent per year for the past few years, averaging out to 7.5 percent per year for the past quarter century. Even though many developing countries still spend less than 5 percent of their gross national product on defense, these funds could be put to different uses in such human development areas as housing, land reform, health care, and education.

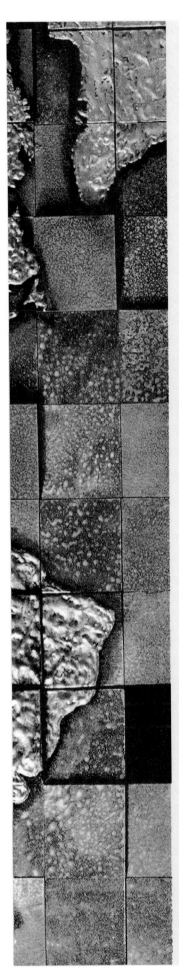

Part III

The Global Economy

Map 29 International Trade Organizations

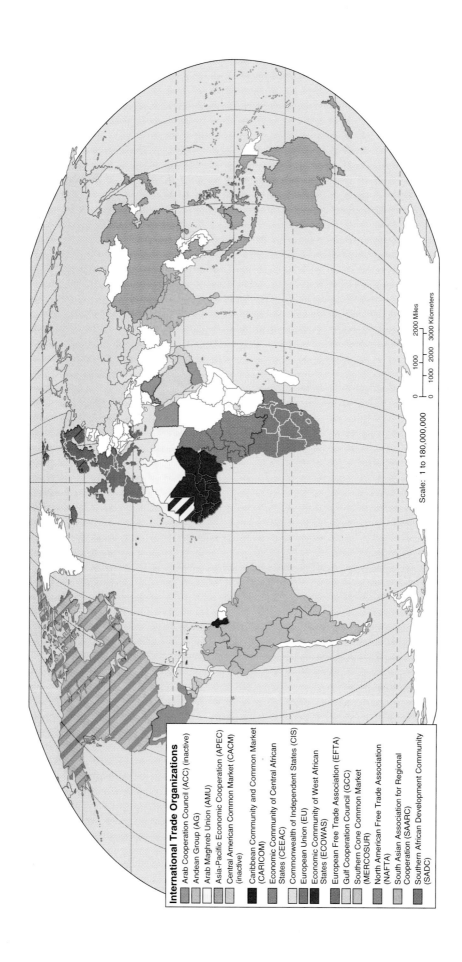

International Trade Organizations

Arab Cooperation Council (ACC) (inactive)
Andean Group (AG)
Arab Maghreb Union (AMU)
Asia-Pacific Economic Cooperation (APEC)
Central American Common Market (CACM) (inactive)
Caribbean Community and Common Market (CARICOM)
Economic Community of Central African States (CEEAC)
Commonwealth of Independent States (CIS)
European Union (EU)
Economic Community of West African States (ECOWAS)
European Free Trade Association (EFTA)
Gulf Cooperation Council (GCC)
Southern Cone Common Market (MERCOSUR)
North American Free Trade Association (NAFTA)
South Asian Association for Regional Cooperation (SAARC)
Southern African Development Community (SADC)

Scale: 1 to 180,000,000

0   1000   2000 Miles
0 1000 2000 3000 Kilometers

One of the most pervasive influences in the global economy over the last half century has been the rapid rise of international trade organizations. Pioneered by the European Economic Community, founded in part to assist in rebuilding the European economy after the World War II, these organizations have become major players in global movements of goods, services, and labor. Some have integrated to form financial and political unions, such as the European Community which has grown into the European Union. Others, like the Commonwealth of Independent States, are attempts to hold on to the remnants of better economic times. Still others, like the Asia-Pacific Economic Cooperation, are infant organizations that incorporate vastly different regions, states, and even economic systems, and are attempts to anticipate the direction of future economic growth. The role of the international trade organizations is likely to grow greater in the twenty-first century.

Map 30 Rich and Poor Countries: Gross National Income

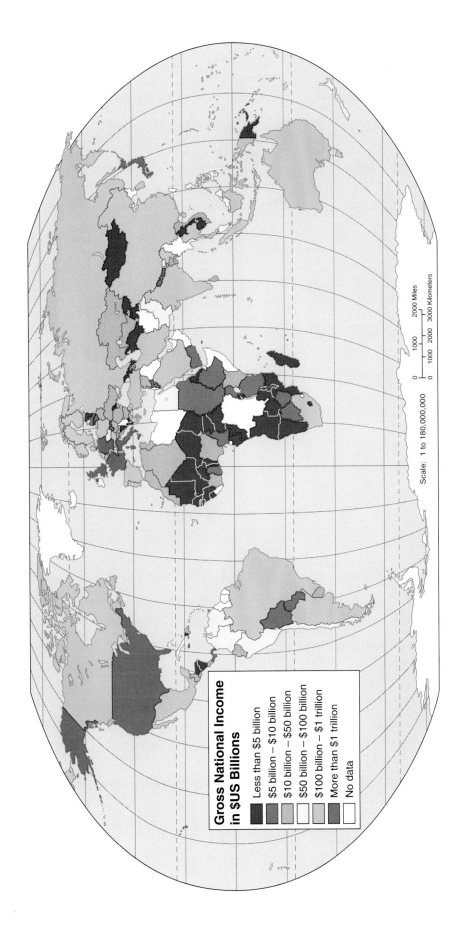

Gross National Income in $US Billions

- Less than $5 billion
- $5 billion – $10 billion
- $10 billion – $50 billion
- $50 billion – $100 billion
- $100 billion – $1 trillion
- More than $1 trillion
- No data

Scale: 1 to 180,000,000

0   1000   2000 Miles

0   1000   2000   3000 Kilometers

Gross National Income (GNI) is a new measure of the value of all the goods and services produced by a country, including its net income from abroad, during a year. Although GNI is used to measure relative levels of economic well-being, it is often misleading and incomplete: it does not, for example, take into account environmental deterioration, the accumulation or degradation of human and social capital, or the value of household work. In spite of its deficiencies, however, GNI is still a reasonable way to illustrate the vast differences in wealth that separate the poorest countries from the richest (as long as you keep in mind that it provides no measure of the distribution of wealth within a country). One of the more striking features of the map is the evidence that such a small number of countries possess so much of the world's wealth.

Map 31 Gross National Income Per Capita

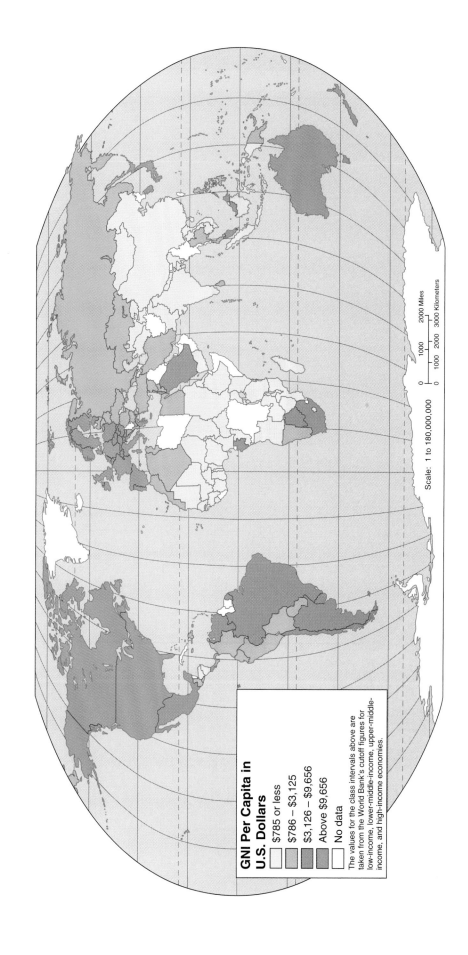

GNI Per Capita in U.S. Dollars

- $785 or less
- $786 – $3,125
- $3,126 – $9,656
- Above $9,656
- No data

The values for the class intervals above are taken from the World Bank's cutoff figures for low-income, lower-middle-income, upper-middle-income, and high-income economies.

Scale: 1 to 180,000,000

```
0          1000        2000 Miles
0     1000      2000      3000 Kilometers
```

Gross National Income in either absolute or per capita form should be used cautiously as a yardstick of economic strength because it does not measure the distribution of wealth among a population. There are countries (most notably, the oil-rich countries of the Middle East) where per capita GNI is high but where the bulk of the wealth is concentrated in the hands of a few individuals, leaving the remainder in poverty. Even within countries in which wealth is more evenly distributed (such as those in North America or Western Europe), there is a tendency for dollars or pounds sterling or francs or marks to concentrate in the bank accounts of a relatively small percentage of the population. Yet the maldistribution of wealth tends to be greatest in the less developed countries, where the per capita GNI is far lower than in North America and Western Europe, and poverty is widespread. In fact, a map of GNI per capita offers a reasonably good picture of comparative economic well-being. It should be noted that a low per capita GNI does not automatically condemn a country to low levels of basic human needs and services. There are a few countries, such as Costa Rica and Sri Lanka, that have relatively low per capita GNI figures but rank comparatively high in other measures of human well-being, such as average life expectancy, access to medical care, and literacy.

-50-

Map 32 Relative Wealth of Nations: Purchasing Parity

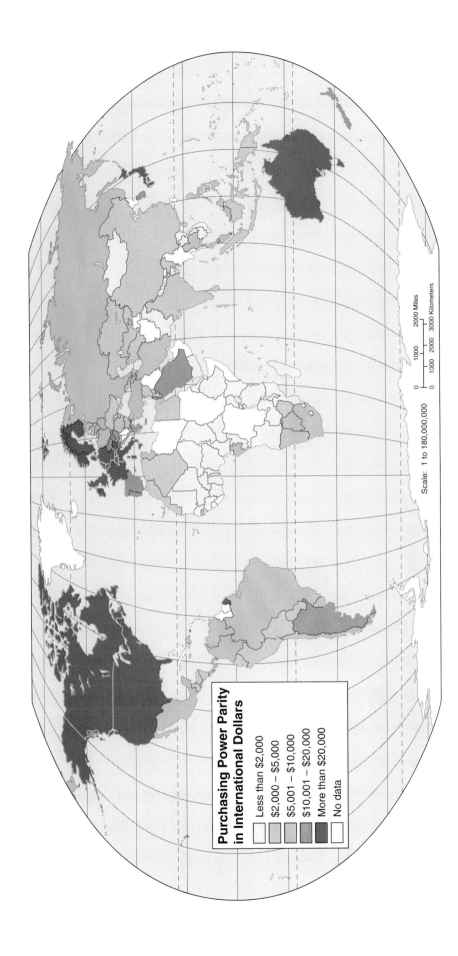

Purchasing Power Parity in International Dollars

- Less than $2,000
- $2,000 – $5,000
- $5,001 – $10,000
- $10,001 – $20,000
- More than $20,000
- No data

Scale: 1 to 180,000,000

0   1000   2000 Miles
0   1000   2000   3000 Kilometers

Of all the economic measures that separate the "haves" from the "have-nots," perhaps per capita Purchasing Power Parity (PPP) is the most meaningful. While per capita figures can mask significant uneven distributions within a country, they are generally useful for demonstrating important differences between countries. Per capita GNP and GDP (Gross Domestic Product) figures, and even per capita income, have the limitation of seldom reflecting the true purchasing power of a country's currency at home. In order to get around this limitation, international economists seeking to compare national currencies developed the PPP measure, which shows the level of goods and services that holders of a country's money can acquire locally. By converting all currencies to the "international dollar," the World Bank and other organizations using PPP can now show more truly comparative values, since the new currency value shows the number of units of a country's currency required to buy the same quantity of goods and services in the local market as one U.S. dollar would buy in an average country. The use of PPP currency values can alter the perceptions about a country's true comparative position in the world economy. More than per capita income figures, PPP provides a valid measurement of the ability of a country's population to provide for itself the things that people in the developed world take for granted: adequate food, shelter, clothing, education, and access to medical care. A glance at the map shows a clear-cut demarcation between temperate and tropical zones, with most of the countries with a PPP above $5,000 in the midlatitude zones and most of those with lower PPPs in the tropical and equatorial regions. Where exceptions to this pattern occur, they usually stem from a tremendous maldistribution of wealth among a country's population.

Map 33   International Flows of Capital

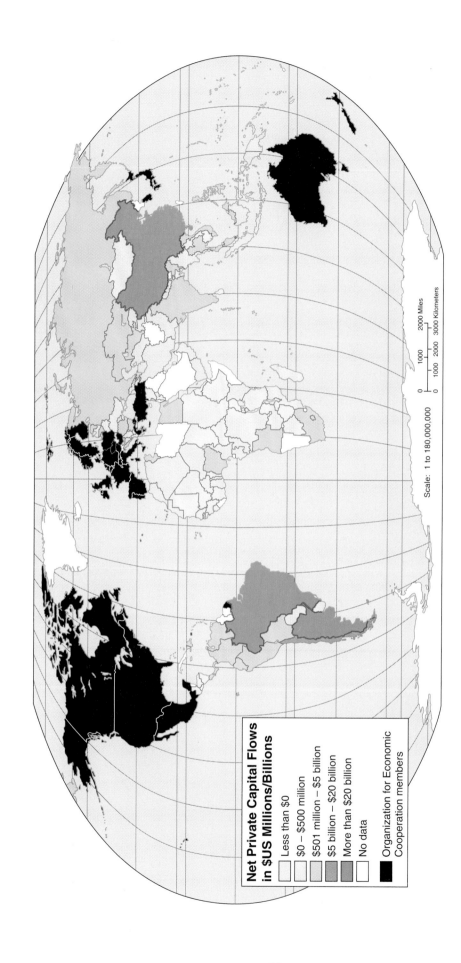

Net Private Capital Flows in $US Millions/Billions

- Less than $0
- $0 – $500 million
- $501 million – $5 billion
- $5 billion – $20 billion
- More than $20 billion
- No data
- Organization for Economic Cooperation members

Scale: 1 to 180,000,000

0   1000   2000 Miles
0   1000   2000   3000 Kilometers

International capital flows include private debt and nondebt flows from one country to another, shown on the map as flows into a country. Nearly all of the capital comes from those countries that are members of the Organization for Economic Cooperation and Development (OECD), shown in black on the map. Capital flows include commercial bank lending, bonds, other private credits, foreign direct investment, and portfolio investment. Most of these flows are indicators of the increasing influence developed countries exert over the developing economies. Foreign direct investment or FDI, for example, is a measure of the net inflow of investment monies used to acquire long-term management interest in businesses located somewhere other than in the economy of the investor. Usually this means the acquisition of at least 10% of the stock of a company by a foreign investor and is, then, a measure of what might be termed "economic colonialism": control of a region's economy by foreign investors that could, in the world of the future, be as significant as colonial political control was in the past. International capital flows have increased greatly in the last decade as the result of the increasing liberalization of developing countries, the strong economic growth exhibited by many developing countries, and the falling costs and increased efficiency of communication and transportation services.

Map 34 Economic Output Per Sector

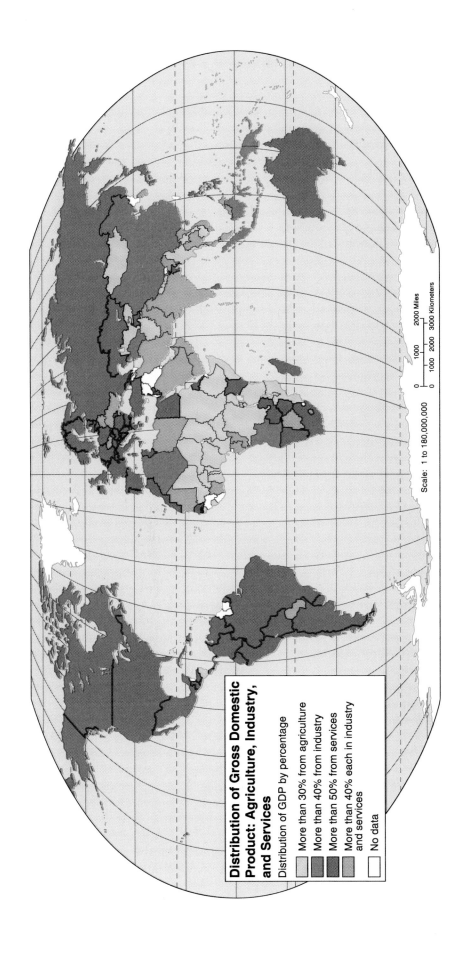

Distribution of Gross Domestic Product: Agriculture, Industry, and Services

Distribution of GDP by percentage

- More than 30% from agriculture
- More than 40% from industry
- More than 50% from services
- More than 40% each in industry and services
- No data

Scale: 1 to 180,000,000

0   1000   2000 Miles

0   1000   2000   3000 Kilometers

The percentage of the gross domestic product (the final output of goods and services produced by the domestic economy, including net exports of goods and nonfactor—nonlabor, noncapital—services) that is devoted to agricultural, industrial, and service activities is considered a good measure of the level of economic development. In general, countries with more than 40 percent of their GDP derived from agriculture are still in a "colonial dependency" economy—that is, raising agricultural goods primarily for the export market and dependent upon that market (usually the richer countries). Similarly, countries with more than 40 percent of GDP devoted to both agriculture and services often emphasize resource extractive (primarily mining and forestry) activities. These also tend to be "colonial dependency" countries, providing raw materials for for-

eign markets. Countries with more than 40 percent of their GDP obtained from industry are normally well along the path to economic development. Countries with more than half of their GDP based on service activities fall into two ends of the development spectrum. On the one hand are countries heavily dependent upon both extractive activities and tourism and other low-level service functions. On the other hand are countries that can properly be termed "postindustrial": they have already passed through the industrial stage of their economic development and now rely less on the manufacture of products than on finance, research, communications, education, and other service-oriented activities.

Map 35 Employment by Economic Activity

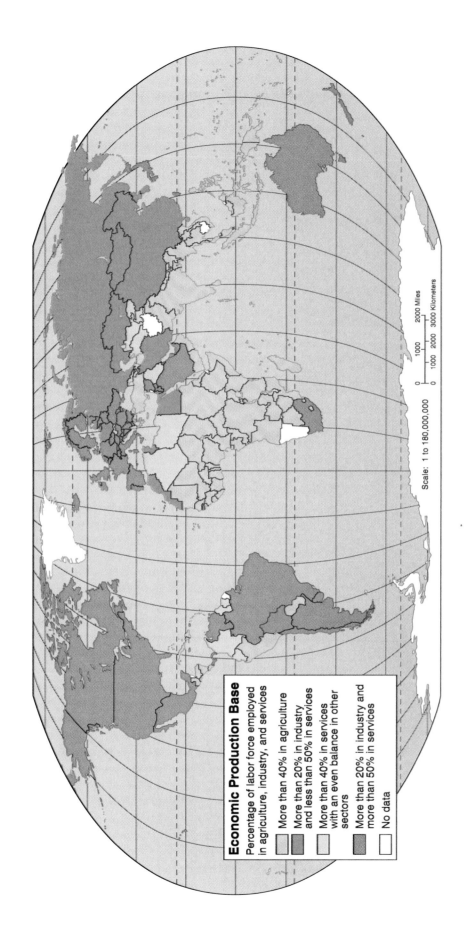

Economic Production Base

Percentage of labor force employed in agriculture, industry, and services

- More than 40% in agriculture
- More than 20% in industry and less than 50% in services
- More than 40% in services with an even balance in other sectors
- More than 20% in industry and more than 50% in services
- No data

Scale: 1 to 180,000,000

0   1000   2000 Miles
0 1000 2000 3000 Kilometers

The employment structure of a country's population is one of the best indicators of the country's position on the scale of economic development. At one end of the scale are those countries with more than 40 percent of their labor force employed in agriculture. These are almost invariably the least developed, with high population growth rates, poor human services, significant environmental problems, and so on. In the middle of the scale are two types of countries: those with more than 20 percent of their labor force employed in industry and those with a fairly even balance among agricultural, industrial, and service employment but with at least 40 percent of their labor force employed in service activities. Generally, these countries have undergone the industrial revolution fairly recently and are still developing an industrial base while building up their service activities. This category also includes countries with a disproportionate share of their economies in service activities primarily related to resource extraction. On the other end of the scale are countries with more than 20 percent of their labor force employed in industry and more than 50 percent in service activities. These countries are, for the most part, those with a highly automated industrial base and a highly mechanized agricultural system (the "postindustrial," developed countries). They also include, particularly in Middle and South America and Africa, industrializing countries that are also heavily engaged in resource extraction as a service activity.

Map 36 Central Government Expenditures Per Capita

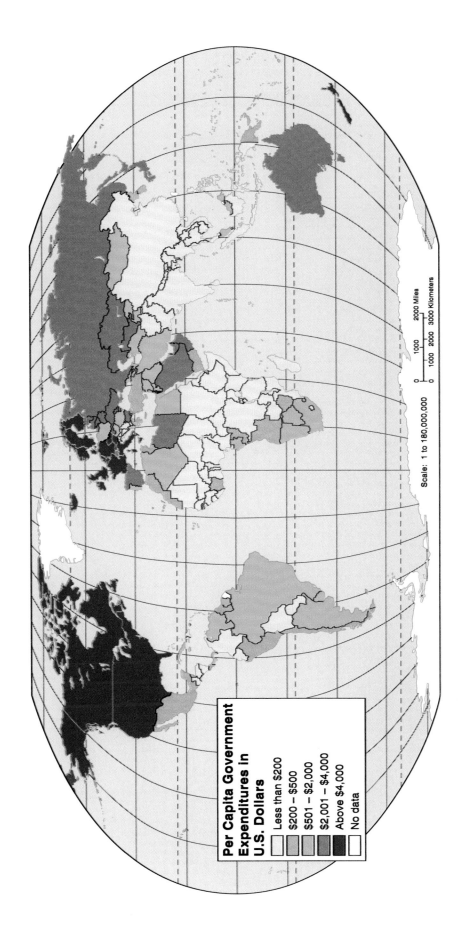

Per Capita Government Expenditures In U.S. Dollars

- Less than $200
- $200 – $500
- $501 – $2,000
- $2,001 – $4,000
- Above $4,000
- No data

Scale: 1 to 180,000,000

0 1000 2000 Miles

0 1000 2000 3000 Kilometers

The amount of money that the central government of a country spends upon a variety of essential governmental functions is a measure of relative economic development, particularly when it is viewed on a per-person basis. These functions include such governmental responsibilities as agriculture, communications, culture, defense, education, fishing and hunting, health, housing, recreation, religion, social security, transportation, and welfare. Generally, the higher the level of economic development, the greater the per capita expenditures on these services. However, the data do mask some internal variations. For example, countries that spend 20 percent or more of their central gov-

ernment expenditures on defense will often show up in the more developed category when, in fact, all that the figures really show is that a disproportionate amount of the money available to the government is devoted to purchasing armaments and maintaining a large standing military force. Thus, the fact that Libya spends $2,937 per capita—more than 10 times the average for Africa—does not suggest that the average Libyan is 10 times better off than the average Tanzanian. Nevertheless, this map—particularly when compared with Map 54, Energy Requirements Per Capita—does provide a reasonable approximation of economic development levels.

-55-

Map 37 The Indebtedness of States

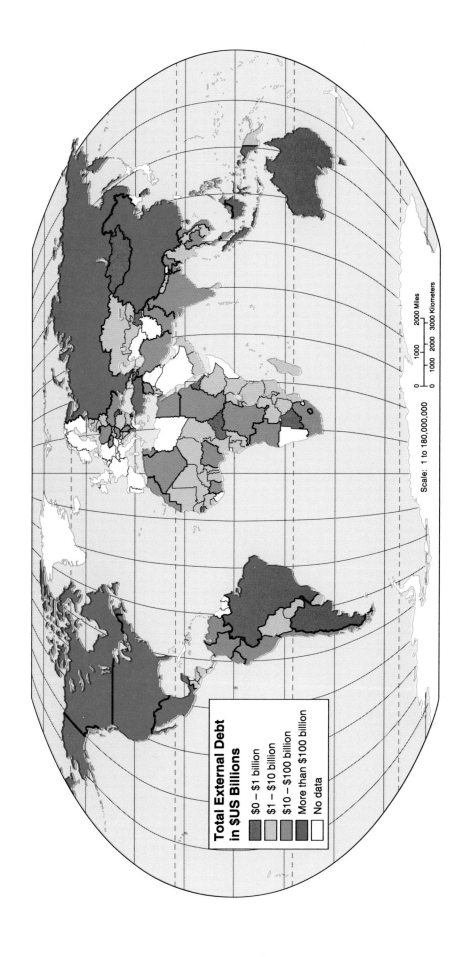

Total External Debt in $US Billions

- $0 – $1 billion
- $1 – $10 billion
- $10 – $100 billion
- More than $100 billion
- No data

Scale: 1 to 180,000,000

0   1000   2000 Miles

0   1000   2000   3000 Kilometers

Many governments spend more on a wide variety of services and activities than they collect in taxes and other revenues. In order to finance this deficit spending, governments borrow money—often from banks or other investors outside their country. Repayment of these debts, or even meeting interest payments on them, often means expending a country's export income—in other words, exchanging a country's wealth in production or, more often, resources, for debt service. Where the debt is external, as

it is in most developing countries, governments become more open to outside influence in political as well as economic terms. Even internal debt service or repayment of monies owed to investors within a country gives financial establishments a measure of influence over government decisions. The amounts of debt shown on the map indicate the total external indebtedness of states.

Map 38 Exports of Primary Products

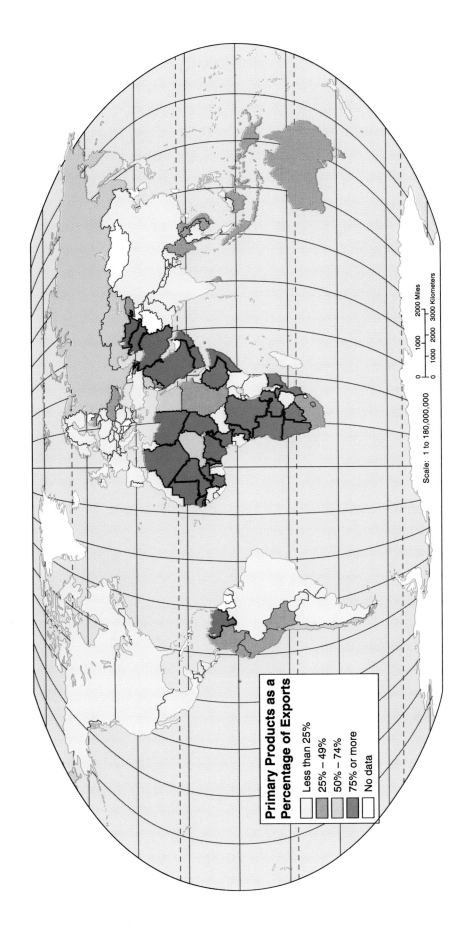

Primary Products as a Percentage of Exports

Less than 25%
25% – 49%
50% – 74%
75% or more
No data

Scale: 1 to 180,000,000

0   1000   2000 Miles
0   1000   2000   3000 Kilometers

Primary products are those that require additional processing before they enter the consumer market: metallic ores that must be converted into metals and then into metal products such as automobiles or refrigerators; forest products such as timber that must be converted to lumber before they become suitable for construction purposes; and agricultural products that require further processing before being ready for human consumption. It is an axiom in international economics that the more a country relies on primary products for its export commodities, the more vulnerable its economy is to market fluctuations. Those countries with only primary products to export are hampered in their economic growth. A country dependent on only one or two products for export revenues is unprotected from economic shifts, particularly a changing market demand for its products. Imagine what would happen to the thriving economic status of the oil-exporting states of the Persian Gulf, for example, if an alternate source of cheap energy were found. A glance at this map, together with Map 49, shows that those countries with the lowest levels of economic development tend to be concentrated on primary products and, therefore, have economies that are especially vulnerable to economic instability.

Map 39 Dependence on Trade

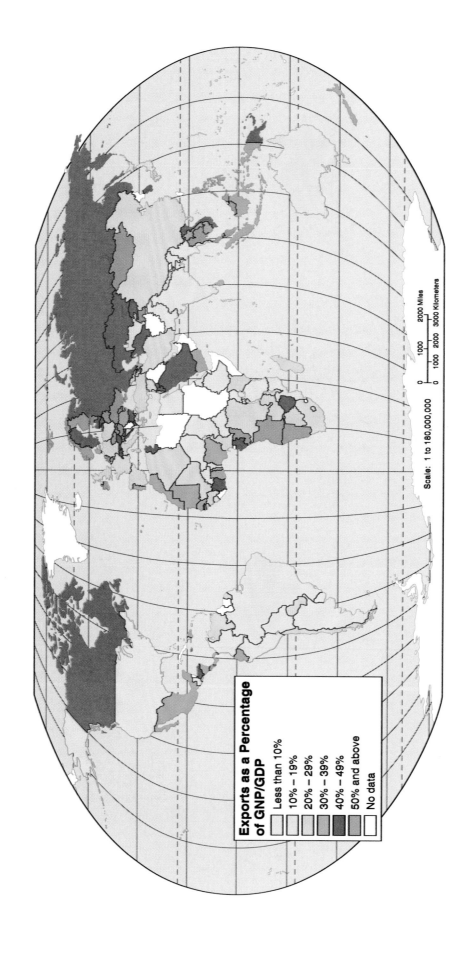

Exports as a Percentage of GNP/GDP

- Less than 10%
- 10% – 19%
- 20% – 29%
- 30% – 39%
- 40% – 49%
- 50% and above
- No data

Scale: 1 to 180,000,000

0   1000   2000 Miles

0   1000   2000   3000 Kilometers

As the global economy becomes more and more a reality, the economic strength of virtually all countries is increasingly dependent upon trade. For many developing nations, with relatively abundant resources and limited industrial capacity, exports provide the primary base upon which their economies rest. Even countries like the United States, Japan, and Germany, with huge and diverse economies, depend on exports to generate a significant percentage of their employment and wealth. Without imports, many products that consumers want would be unavailable or more expensive; without exports, many jobs would be eliminated.

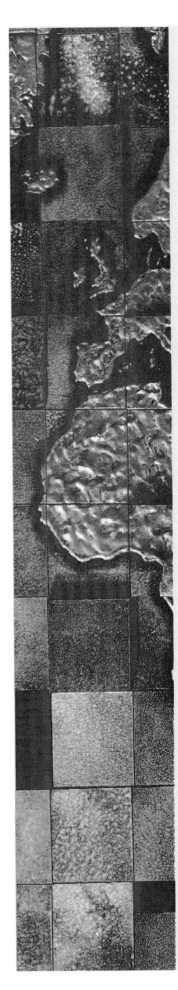

Part IV

Population and Human Development

Map 40 Population Growth Rate

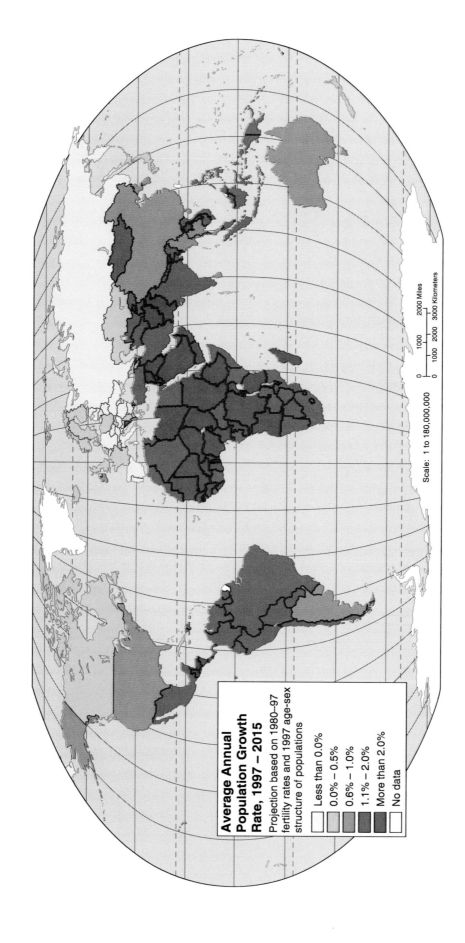

Average Annual Population Growth Rate, 1997 – 2015

Projection based on 1980–97 fertility rates and 1997 age-sex structure of populations

- Less than 0.0%
- 0.0% – 0.5%
- 0.6% – 1.0%
- 1.1% – 2.0%
- More than 2.0%
- No data

Scale: 1 to 180,000,000

0   1000   2000   3000 Kilometers

0   1000   2000 Miles

Of all the statistical measurements of human population, that of the rate of population growth is the most important. The growth rate of a population is a combination of natural change (births and deaths), in-migration, and out-migration; it is obtained by adding the number of births to the number of immigrants during a year and subtracting from that total the sum of deaths and emigrants for the same year. For a specific country, this figure will determine many things about the country's future ability to feed, house, educate, and provide medical services to its citizens. Some of the countries with the largest populations (such as India) also have high growth rates. Since these countries tend to be in developing regions, the combination of high population and high growth rates poses special problems for political stability and continuing economic development; the combination also carries heightened risks for environmental degradation. Many people believe that the rapidly expanding world population is a potential crisis that may cause environmental and human disaster by the middle of the twenty-first century.

Map 41 Infant Mortality Rate

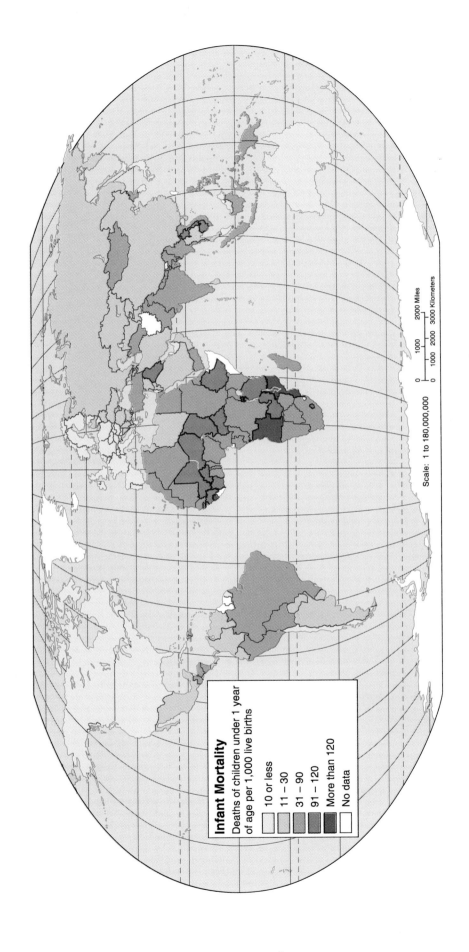

Infant Mortality

Deaths of children under 1 year
of age per 1,000 live births

- 10 or less
- 11 – 30
- 31 – 90
- 91 – 120
- More than 120
- No data

Scale: 1 to 180,000,000

0   1000   2000   3000 Kilometers
0   1000   2000 Miles

Infant mortality rates are calculated by dividing the number of children born in a given year who die before their first birthday by the total number of children born that year and then multiplying by 1,000; this shows how many infants have died for every 1,000 births. Infant mortality rates are prime indicators of economic development. In highly developed economies, with advanced medical technologies, sufficient diets, and adequate public sanitation, infant mortality rates tend to be quite low. By contrast, in less developed countries, with the disadvantages of poor diet, limited access to medical technology, and the other problems of poverty, infant mortality rates tend to be high.

Although worldwide infant mortality has decreased significantly during the last 2 decades, many regions of the world still experience infant mortality above the 10 percent level (100 deaths per 1,000 live births). Such infant mortality rates represent not only human tragedy at its most basic level, but also are powerful inhibiting factors for the future of human development. Comparing infant mortality rates in the midlatitudes and the tropics shows that children in most African countries are more than 10 times as likely to die within a year of birth as children in European countries.

Map 42 Average Life Expectancy at Birth

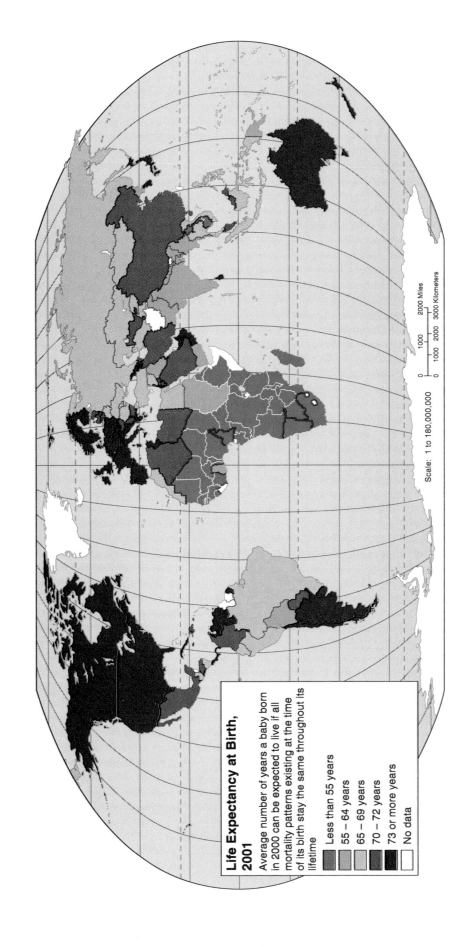

Life Expectancy at Birth, 2001

Average number of years a baby born in 2000 can be expected to live if all mortality patterns existing at the time of its birth stay the same throughout its lifetime

- Less than 55 years
- 55 – 64 years
- 65 – 69 years
- 70 – 72 years
- 73 or more years
- No data

Scale: 1 to 180,000,000

0   1000   2000 Miles

0   1000   2000   3000 Kilometers

Average life expectancy at birth is a measure of the average longevity of the population of a country. Like all average measures, it is distorted by extremes. For example, a country with a high mortality rate among children will have a low average life expectancy. Thus, an average life expectancy of 45 years does not mean that everyone can be expected to die at the age of 45. More normally, what the figure means is that a substantial number of children die between birth and 5 years of age, thus reducing the average life expectancy for the entire population. In spite of the dangers inherent in

misinterpreting the data, average life expectancy (along with infant mortality and several other measures) is a valid way of judging the relative health of a population. It reflects the nature of the health care system, public sanitation and disease control, nutrition, and a number of other key human need indicators. As such, it is a measure of well-being that is significant in indicating economic development and predicting political stability.

Map 43 Population By Age Group

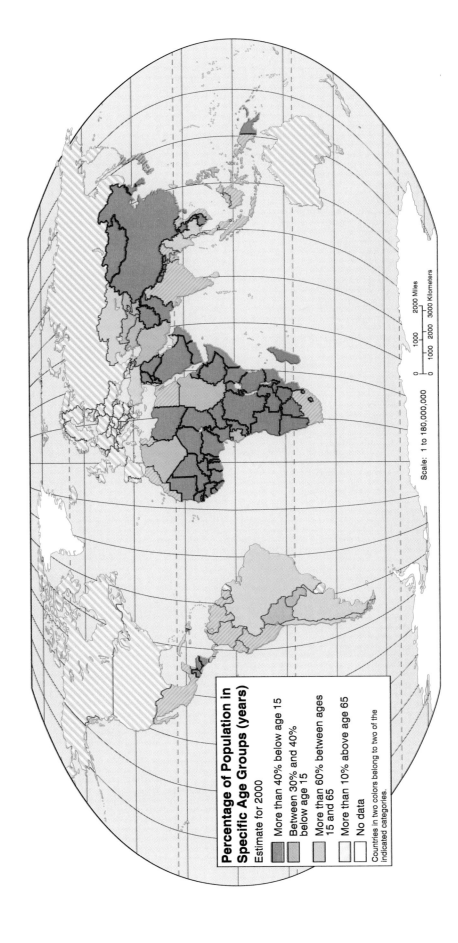

Percentage of Population in Specific Age Groups (years)

Estimate for 2000

- More than 40% below age 15
- Between 30% and 40% below age 15
- More than 60% between ages 15 and 65
- More than 10% above age 65
- No data

Countries in two colors belong to two of the indicated categories.

Scale: 1 to 180,000,000

0   1000   2000 Miles

0   1000   2000   3000 Kilometers

Of all the measurements that illustrate the dynamics of a population, age distribution may be the most significant, particularly when viewed in combination with average growth rates. The particular relevance of age distribution is that it tells us what to expect from a population in terms of growth over the next generation. If, for example, approximately 40–50 percent of a population is below the age of 15, that suggests that in the next generation about one-quarter of the total population will be women of childbearing age. When age distribution is combined with fertility rates (the average number of children born per woman in a population), an especially valid measurement of future growth potential may be derived. A simple example: Nigeria, with a 1995 population of 127 million, has 47 percent of its population below the age of 15 and a fertility rate of 6.4; the United States, with a 1995 population of 263 million, has 22 percent of its population below the age of 15 and a fertility rate of 2.1. During the period in which those women presently under the age of 15 are in their childbearing years, Nigeria can be expected to add a total of approximately 197 million persons to its total population. Over the same period, the United States can be expected to add only 61 million.

Map 44 Total Labor Force, 2000

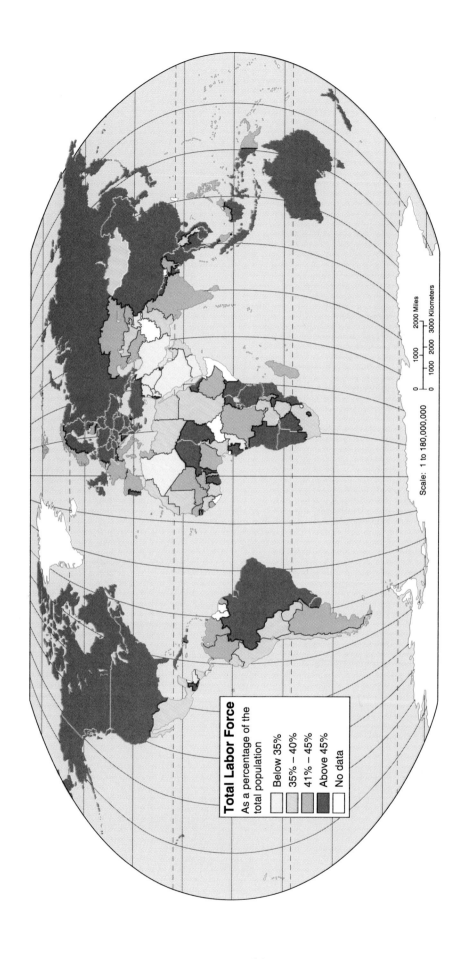

Scale: 1 to 180,000,000

0   1000   2000 Miles
0 1000 2000 3000 Kilometers

Total Labor Force
As a percentage of the
total population

Below 35%
35% – 40%
41% – 45%
Above 45%
No data

The term *labor force* refers to the economically active portion of a population, that is, all people who work or are without work but are available for and are seeking work to produce economic goods and services. The total labor force thus includes both the employed and the unemployed (as long as they are actively seeking employment). Labor force is considered a better indicator of economic potential than employment/unemployment figures, since unemployment figures will include experienced workers with considerable potential who are temporarily out of work. Unemployment figures will also incorporate persons seeking employment for the first time (many recent college graduates, for example). Generally, countries with higher percentages of total population within the labor force will be countries with higher levels of economic development. This is partly a function of levels of education and training and partly a function of the age distribution of populations. In developing countries, substantial percentages of the total population are too young to be part of the labor force.

Map 45 Urban Population

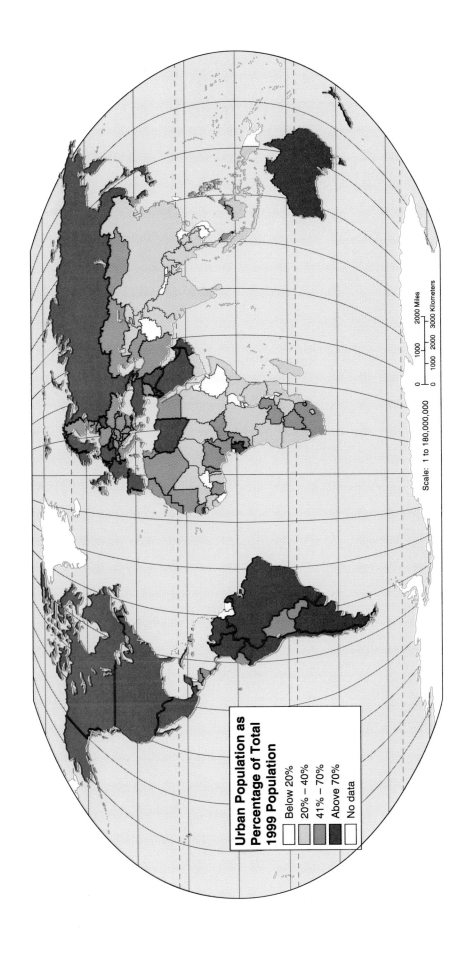

Urban Population as Percentage of Total 1999 Population

- Below 20%
- 20% — 40%
- 41% — 70%
- Above 70%
- No data

Scale: 1 to 180,000,000

0   1000   2000 Miles
0 1000 2000 3000 Kilometers

The proportion of a country's population that resides in urban areas was formerly considered a measure of relative economic development, with countries possessing a large urban population ranking high on the development scale and countries with a more rural population ranking low. Given the rapid rate of urbanization in developing countries, however, this traditional measure is no longer so valuable. What relative urbanization rates now tell us is something about levels of economic development in a negative sense. Latin American, African, and Asian countries with more than 40 percent of their populations living in urban areas generally suffer from a variety of problems: rural overpopulation and flight from the land, urban poverty and despair, high unemployment, and poor public services. The rate of urbanization in less developed nations is such that many cities in these nations will outstrip those in North America and Europe by the end of this century. It has been estimated, for example, that Mexico City—now the world's second largest metropolis—has over 27 million inhabitants. Urbanization was once viewed as an indicator of economic health and political maturity. For many countries it is instead a harbinger of potential economic and environmental disaster.

-65-

Map 46 Illiteracy Rates

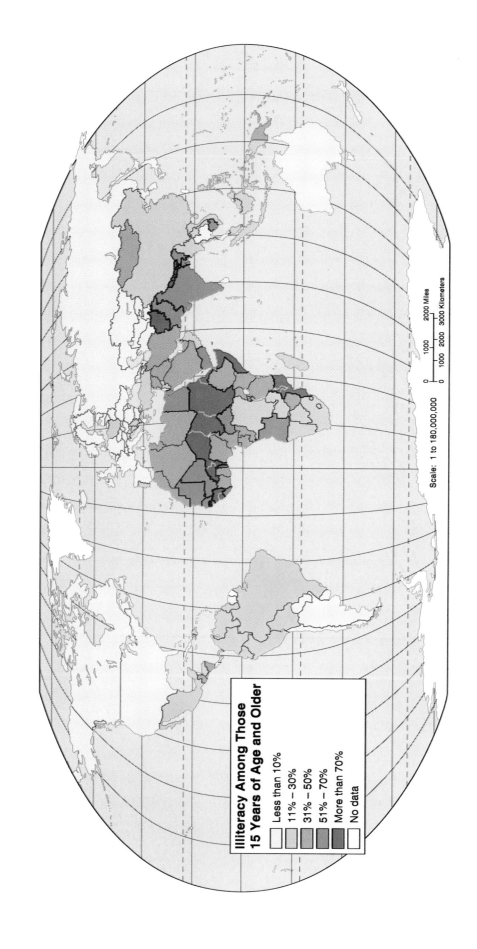

**Illiteracy Among Those
15 Years of Age and Older**

Less than 10%
11% – 30%
31% – 50%
51% – 70%
More than 70%
No data

Scale: 1 to 180,000,000

0   1000   2000 Miles

0   1000   2000   3000 Kilometers

Illiteracy rates are based on the percentages of people age 15 or above (classed as adults in most countries) who are not able to write and read, with understanding, a brief, simple statement about everyday life written in their home- or official language. As might be expected, illiteracy rates tend to be higher in the lesser-developed states, where educational systems are a low government priority. Rates of literacy or illiteracy also tend to be gender-differentiated, with women in many countries experiencing educational neglect or discrimination that makes it more likely they will be illiterate. In many developing countries, between five and ten times as many women will be illiterate as men, and the illiteracy rate for women may even exceed 90%. Both male and female illiteracy severely compromise economic development.

-66-

Map 47 Unemployment in Labor Force

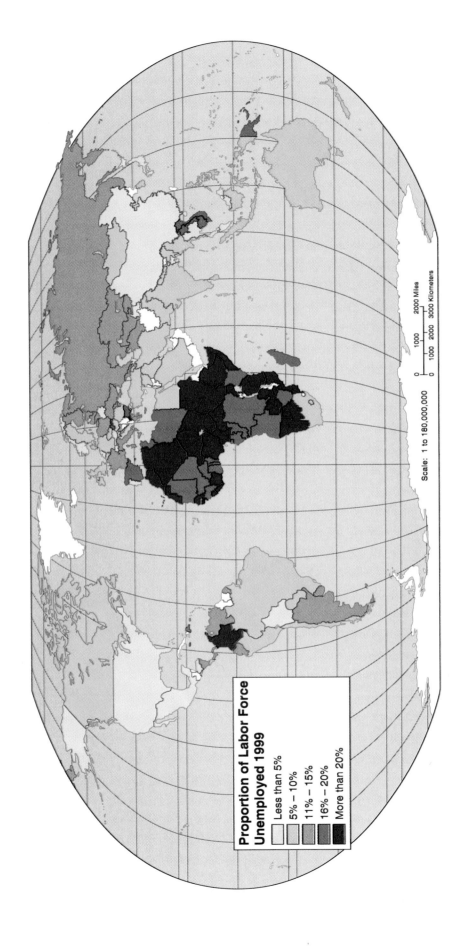

Proportion of Labor Force Unemployed 1999

- Less than 5%
- 5% – 10%
- 11% – 15%
- 16% – 20%
- More than 20%

Scale: 1 to 180,000,000

0   1000   2000 Miles
0 1000 2000 3000 Kilometers

The percentage of a country's labor force that is classified as "unemployed" include those without work but who are available for work and seeking employment. Countries may define the labor force in different ways, however. In many developing countries, for example, "employability" based on age may be more extensive than in more highly developed economies with stringent child labor laws. Generally, countries with higher percentages of their labor forces employed will be countries with higher levels of eco-nomic development. Where unemployment tends to be high, the out-migration of labor also tends to be high as workers unable to find employment at home cross international boundaries in search of work. Again, there tends to be a difference based on levels of economic development with the more developed countries experiencing inflows of labor while the reverse is true in the less developed world.

Map 48 The Gender Gap: Inequalities in Education and Employment

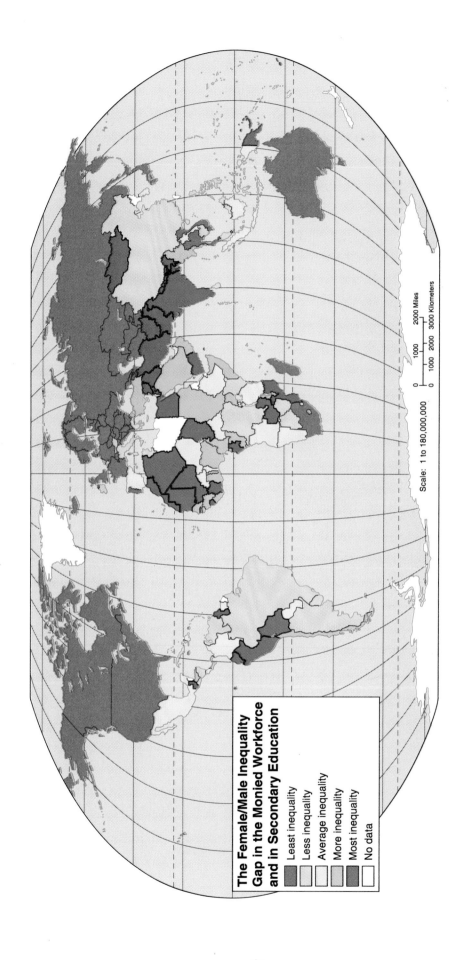

The Female/Male Inequality Gap in the Monied Workforce and in Secondary Education

- Least inequality
- Less inequality
- Average inequality
- More inequality
- Most inequality
- No data

Scale: 1 to 180,000,000

0   1000   2000 Miles

0 1000 2000 3000 Kilometers

Although women in developed countries, particularly in North America and Europe, have made significant advances in socioeconomic status in recent years, in most of the world females suffer from significant inequality when compared with their male counterparts. Women have received the right to vote in most of the world's countries, but in over 90 percent of these countries that right has only been granted in the last 50 years. In most regions, literacy rates for women still fall far short of those for men; in Africa and Asia, for example, only about half as many women are literate as are men. Women marry considerably younger than men and attend school for shorter periods of time. Inequalities in education and employment are perhaps the most telling indicators of the unequal status of women in most of the world. Lack of secondary education in comparison with men prevents women from entering the workforce with equally high-paying jobs. Even where women are employed in positions similar to those held by men, they still tend to receive less compensation. The gap between rich and poor involves not only a clear geographic differentiation, but a clear gender differentiation as well.

-68-

Map 49 The Index of Human Development

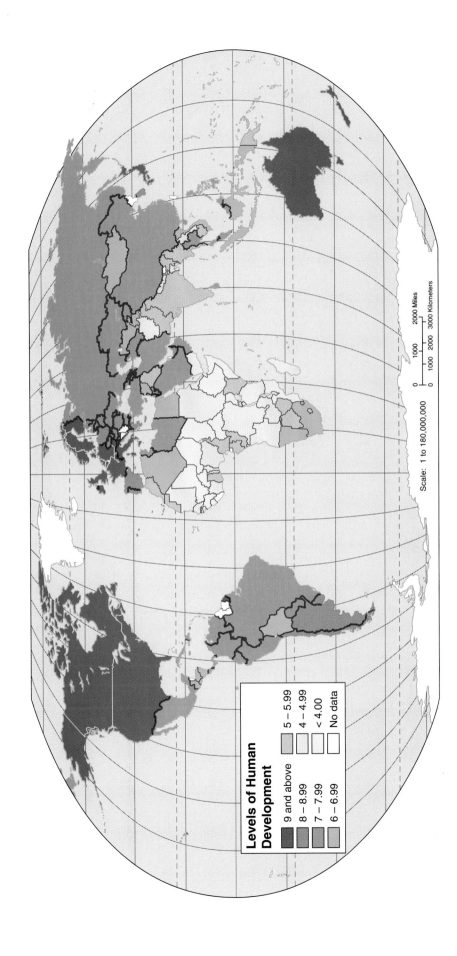

Levels of Human Development

■ 9 and above	□ 5 – 5.99
■ 8 – 8.99	□ 4 – 4.99
■ 7 – 7.99	□ < 4.00
■ 6 – 6.99	□ No data

Scale: 1 to 180,000,000

0   1000   2000 Miles

0   1000   2000   3000 Kilometers

The development index upon which this map is based takes into account a wide variety of demographic, health, and educational data, including population growth, per capita gross domestic income, longevity, literacy, and years of schooling. The map reveals significant improvement in the quality of life in Middle and South America, although it is questionable whether the gains made in those regions can be maintained in the face of the dramatic population increases expected over the next 30 years. More clearly than anything else, the map illustrates the near-desperate situation in Africa and South Asia. In those regions, the unparalleled growth in population threatens to overwhelm all efforts to improve the quality of life. In Africa, for example, the population is increasing by 20 million persons per year. With nearly 45 percent of the continent's population aged 15 years or younger, this growth rate will accelerate as the women reach childbearing age. Africa, along with South Asia, faces the very difficult challenge of providing basic access to health care, education, and jobs for a rapidly increasing population. The map also illustrates the striking difference in quality of life between those who inhabit the world's equatorial and tropical regions and those fortunate enough to live in the temperate zones, where the quality of life is significantly higher.

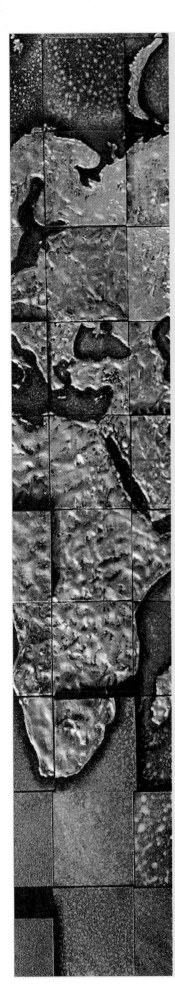

Part V

Food, Energy, and Materials

Map 50 Production of Staples–Cereals, Roots, and Tubers

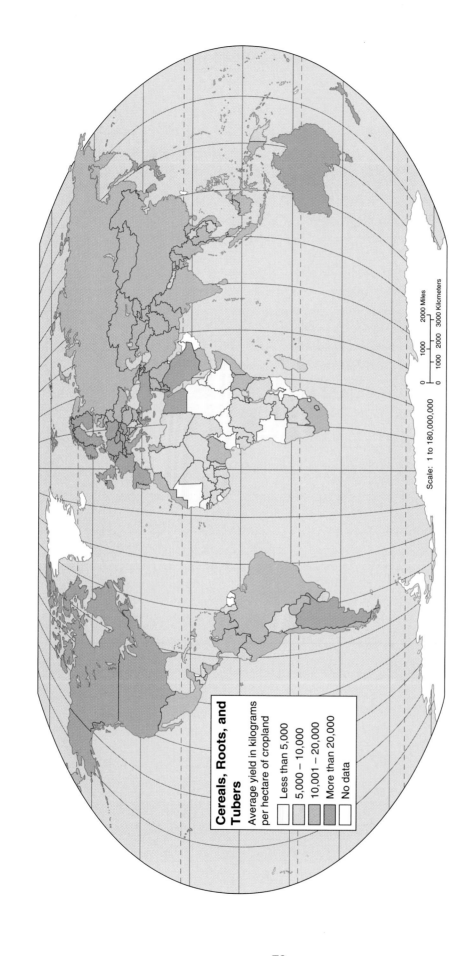

Cereals, Roots, and Tubers

Average yield in kilograms per hectare of cropland

- Less than 5,000
- 5,000 – 10,000
- 10,001 – 20,000
- More than 20,000
- No data

Scale: 1 to 180,000,000

0   1000   2000 Miles
0 1000 2000 3000 Kilometers

For most of the world's population, food crops (as opposed to livestock foods) provide the bulk of dietary intake. Good agricultural land is simply too scarce to be used for the inefficient process of raising food to feed animals, which, in turn, feed people. Global production of the staple (most important) food crops has increased over the last 10 years—but so has global population. In Africa, for example, despite a 30 percent increase in staple crop production since 1981, per capita food output has dropped more than 5 percent because of population growth that is faster than the growth in agricultural output. The map illustrates considerable regional differences in outputs of food staples per areal unit of cropland. Globally, 1 hectare (2.47 acres) of cropland in 1990 yielded, on average, about 2.6 metric tons (2,600 kilograms or about 5,700 pounds) of

cereals or about 11.8 metric tons of roots and tubers. Yet in Africa, 1 hectare yielded only 1.2 metric tons of cereals or 7.9 metric tons of roots and tubers. In Europe, on the other hand, 1 hectare yielded 4.2 tons of cereals or 21.2 metric tons of roots and tubers. Such great differences are explainable primarily in terms of agricultural inputs: different farming methods, varying levels of fertilizers, agricultural chemicals, irrigation, and machinery. The European farmer applies 2.3 times the global average of fertilizer per hectare, the African farmer only one-fifth of the global average. These conditions are not likely to change and the map may be viewed as an indicator not just of present agricultural output but of potential food production as well.

Map 51 Agricultural Production Per Capita

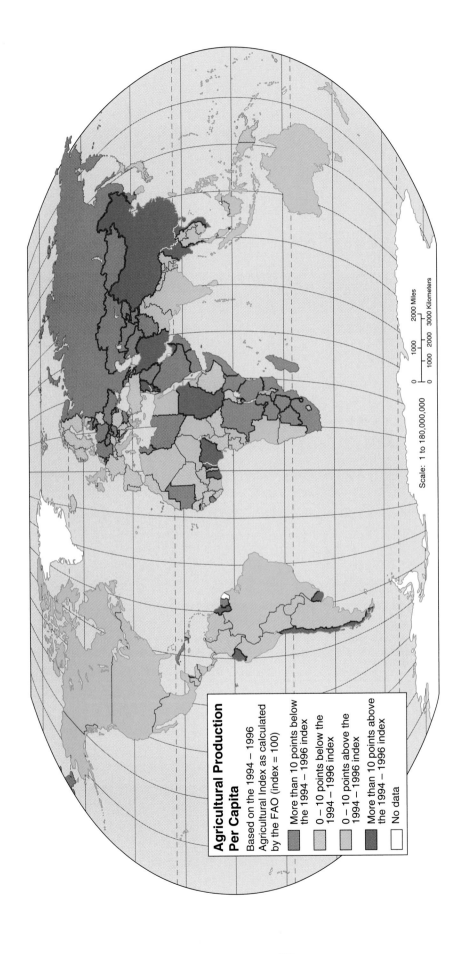

Agricultural Production Per Capita

Based on the 1994 – 1996
Agricultural Index as calculated
by the FAO (index = 100)

- More than 10 points below the 1994 – 1996 index
- 0 – 10 points below the 1994 – 1996 index
- 0 – 10 points above the 1994 – 1996 index
- More than 10 points above the 1994 – 1996 index
- No data

Scale: 1 to 180,000,000

0   1000   2000 Miles
0   1000   2000   3000 Kilometers

Agricultural production includes the value of all crop and livestock products originating within a country for the base period of 1994–1996. The index value portrays the disposable output (after deductions for livestock feed and seed for planting) of a country's agriculture in comparison with the base period 1989–1991. Thus, the production values show not only the relative ability of countries to produce food but also show whether or not that ability has increased or decreased over an 8-year period. In general, global food production has kept up with or very slightly exceeded population growth. However, there are significant regional variations in the trend of food production keeping up with or surpassing population growth. For example, agricultural production in Africa and in Middle America has fallen, while production in South America, Asia, and Europe has risen. In the case of Africa, the drop in production reflects a population

growing more rapidly than agricultural productivity. Where rapid increases in food production per capita exist (as in certain countries in South America, Asia, and Europe), most often the reason is the development of new agricultural technologies that have allowed food production to grow faster than population. In much of Asia, for example, the so-called Green Revolution of new, highly productive strains of wheat and rice made positive index values possible. Also in Asia, the cessation of major warfare allowed some countries (Cambodia, Laos, and Vietnam) to show substantial increases over the 1982–1984 index. In some cases, a drop in production per capita reflects government decisions to limit production in order to maintain higher prices for agricultural products. The United States and Japan fall into this category.

-73-

Map 52 Average Daily Per Capita Supply of Calories (Kilocalories)

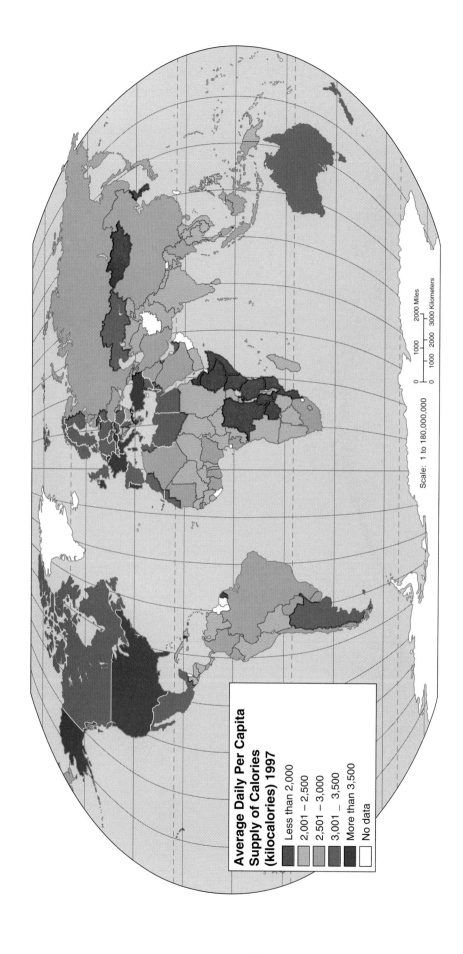

Average Daily Per Capita
Supply of Calories
(kilocalories) 1997

Less than 2,000
2,001 – 2,500
2,501 – 3,000
3,001 – 3,500
More than 3,500
No data

Scale: 1 to 180,000,000

0 1000 2000 Miles

0 1000 2000 3000 Kilometers

The data shown on this map, which indicate the presence or absence of critical food shortages, do not necessarily indicate the presence of starvation or famine. But they certainly do indicate potential problem areas for the next decade. The measurements are in calories from *all* food sources: domestic production, international trade, drawdown on stocks or food reserves, and direct foreign contributions or aid. The quantity of calories available is that amount, estimated by the UN's Food and Agriculture Organization (FAO), that reaches consumers. The calories actually consumed may be lower than the figures shown, depending on how much is lost in a variety of ways: in home storage (to pests such as rats and mice), in preparation and cooking, through consumption by pets and domestic animals, and as discarded foods, for example. The estimate of need is not a global uniform value but is calculated for each country on the basis of the age and sex distribution of the population and the estimated level of activity of the population. Compare this map with Map 51 for a good measure of potential problem areas for food shortages within the next decade.

Map 53 Commercial Energy Production

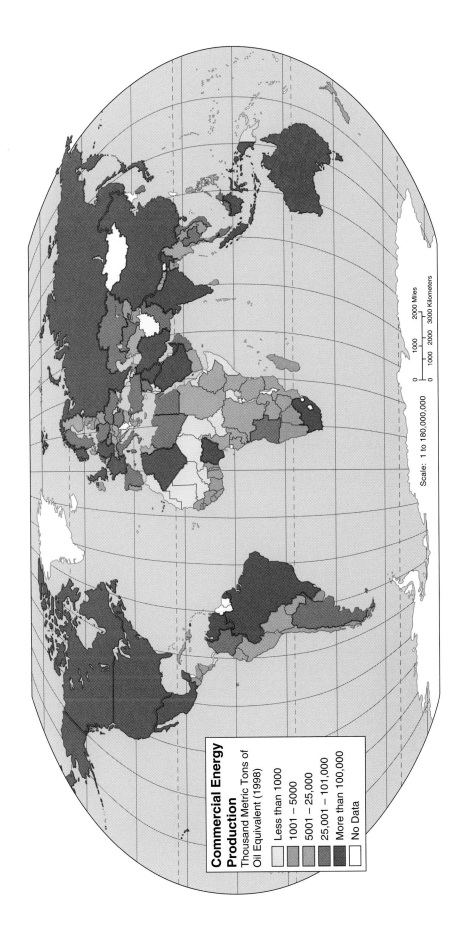

Commercial Energy Production
Thousand Metric Tons of Oil Equivalent (1998)

Less than 1000
1001 – 5000
5001 – 25,000
25,001 – 101,000
More than 100,000
No Data

Scale: 1 to 180,000,000

0   1000   2000 Miles
0   1000   2000   3000 Kilometers

The production of commercial energy in all its forms—solid fuels (primarily coal), liquid fuels (primarily petroleum), natural gas, geothermal, wind, solar, hydroelectric, and nuclear—is a good measure of a country's ability to produce sufficient quantities of energy to meet domestic demands or to provide a healthy export commodity—or, in some instances, both. Commercial energy production is also a measure of the level of economic development, although a fairly subjective one. With exceptions, wealthier countries produce more energy from all sources than do poorer countries. Countries such as Japan and many European states rank among the world's wealthiest, but are energy-poor and produce relatively little of their own energy. They have the ability, however, to pay for it. On the other hand, countries such as those of the Persian Gulf or the oil-producing states of Middle and South America may rank relatively low on the scale of economic development but rank high as producers of energy. The map does not show the enormous amounts of energy from noncommercial sources (traditional fuels like firewood and animal dung) used by the world's poor, particularly in Middle and South America, Africa, South Asia, and East Asia. In these regions, firewood and animal dung may account for more actual energy production than coal or oil. Indeed, for many in the developing world, the real energy crisis is a shortage of wood for cooking and heating.

Map 54 Energy Requirements Per Capita

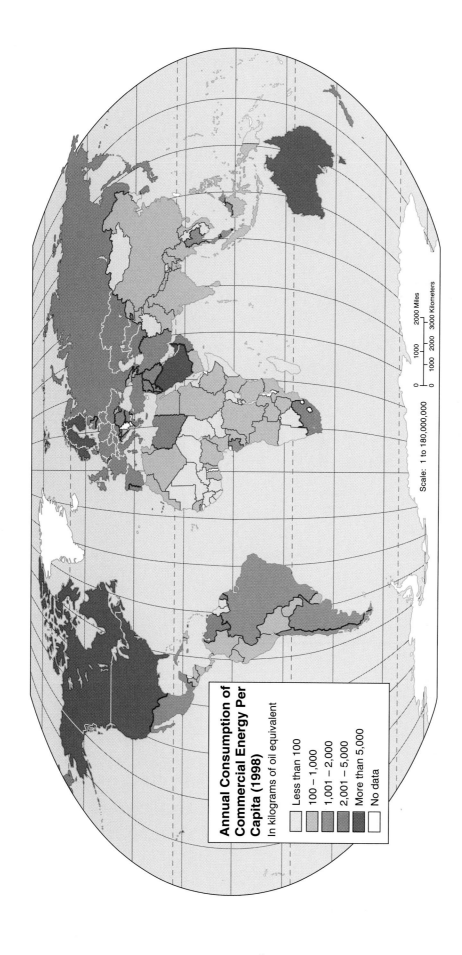

Annual Consumption of Commercial Energy Per Capita (1998)

In kilograms of oil equivalent

- Less than 100
- 100 – 1,000
- 1,001 – 2,000
- 2,001 – 5,000
- More than 5,000
- No data

Scale: 1 to 180,000,000

0   1000   2000 Miles

0   1000   2000   3000 Kilometers

Of all the quantitative measures of economic well-being, energy consumption per capita may be the most expressive. All of the countries defined by the World Bank as having high incomes consume at least 100 gigajoules of commercial energy (the equivalent of about 3.5 metric tons of coal) per person per year, with some, such as the United States and Canada, having consumption rates in the 300 gigajoule range (the equivalent of more than 10 metric tons of coal per person per year). With the exception of the oil-rich Persian Gulf states, where consumption figures include the costly "burning off" of excess energy in the form of natural gas flares at wellheads, most of the highest-consuming countries are in the Northern Hemisphere, concentrated in North America and Western Europe. At the other end of the scale are low-income countries, whose consumption rates are often less than 1 percent of those of the United States and other high consumers. These figures do not, of course, include the consumption of noncommercial energy—the traditional fuels of firewood, animal dung, and other organic matter widely used in the less developed parts of the world.

Map 55 Energy Dependency

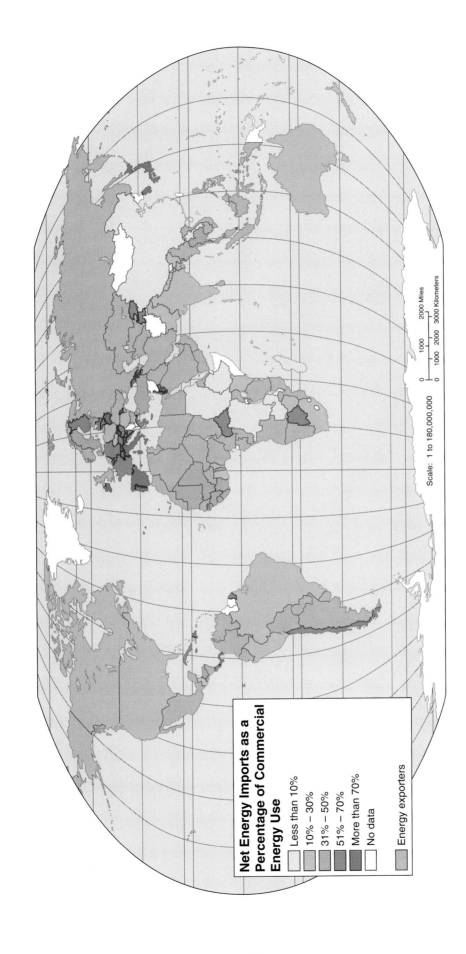

Net Energy Imports as a Percentage of Commercial Energy Use

- Less than 10%
- 10% – 30%
- 31% – 50%
- 51% – 70%
- More than 70%
- No data
- Energy exporters

Scale: 1 to 180,000,000

0   1000   2000 Miles

0   1000   2000   3000 Kilometers

The patterns on the map show dependence on commercial energy before transformation to other end-use fuels such as electricity or refined petroleum products; energy from traditional sources such as fuelwood or dried animal dung is not included. Energy dependency is the difference between domestic consumption and domestic production of commercial energy and is most often expressed as a net energy import or export. A few of the world's countries are net exporters of energy: most are importers. The growth in global commercial energy use over the last decade indicates growth in the modern sectors of the economy—industry, transportation, and urbanization—particularly in the lesser developed countries. Still, the primary consumers of energy—and those having the greatest dependence on foreign sources of energy—are the more highly developed countries of Europe, North America, and Japan.

Map 56 Flows of Oil

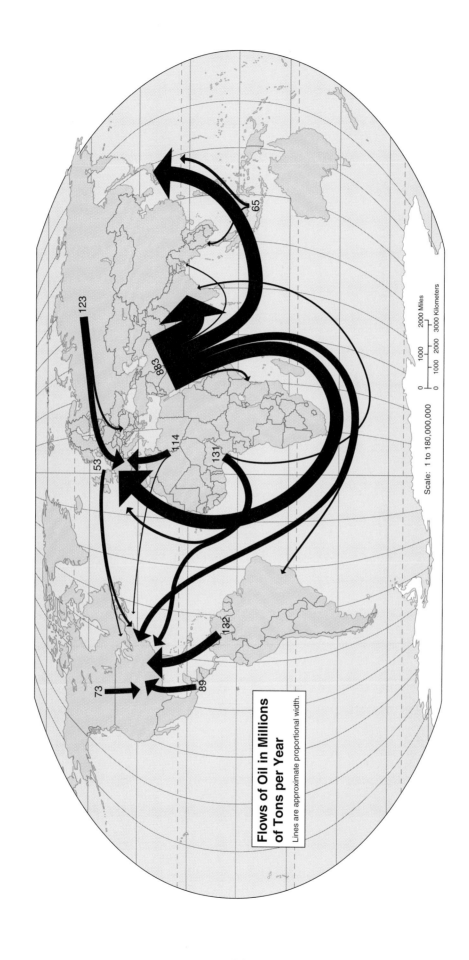

Flows of Oil in Millions of Tons per Year

Lines are approximate proportional width.

Scale: 1 to 180,000,000

0   1000   2000 Miles
0   1000   2000   3000 Kilometers

The pattern of oil movements from producing region to consuming region is one of the dominant facts of contemporary international maritime trade. Supertankers carry a million tons of crude oil and charge rates in excess of $0.10 per ton per mile, making the transportation of oil not only a necessity for the world's energy-hungry countries, but also an enormously profitable proposition. One of the major negatives of these massive oil flows is the damage done to the oceanic ecosystems—not just from the well-publicized and dramatic events like the wrecking of the *Exxon Valdez* but from the incalculable amounts of oil from leakage, scrubbings, purgings, and so on, which are a part of the oil transport technology. It is clear from the map that the primary recipients of these oil flows are the world's most highly developed economies.

Map 57 Production of Crucial Materials

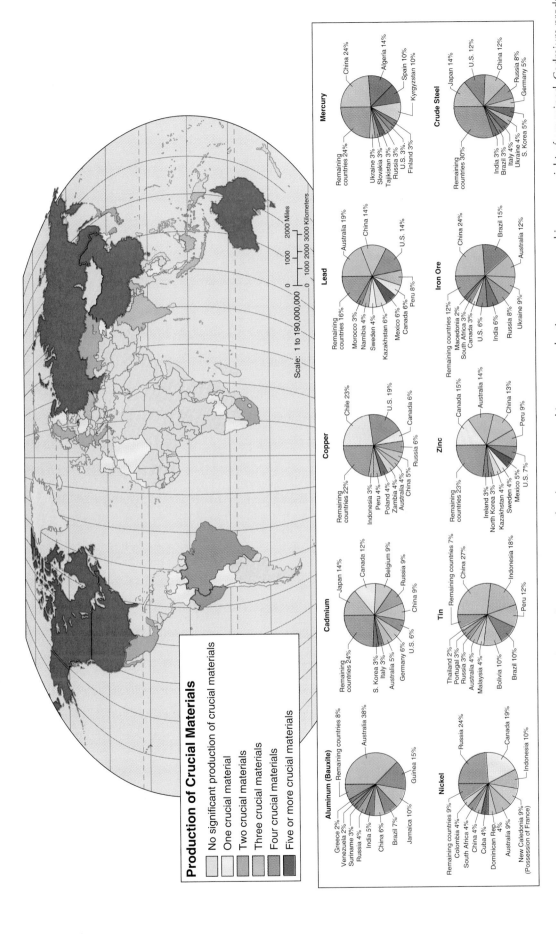

Production of Crucial Materials

- No significant production of crucial materials
- One crucial material
- Two crucial materials
- Three crucial materials
- Four crucial materials
- Five or more crucial materials

Scale: 1 to 190,000,000

0   1000   2000   3000 Kilometers
0   1000   2000 Miles

Mercury
China 24%
Algeria 14%
Spain 10%
Kyrgyzstan 10%
Finland 3%
U.S. 3%
Russia 3%
Tajikistan 3%
Slovakia 3%
Ukraine 3%
Remaining countries 24%

Crude Steel
Japan 14%
U.S. 12%
China 12%
Russia 8%
Germany 5%
S. Korea 5%
Ukraine 4%
Italy 4%
Brazil 3%
India 3%
Remaining countries 30%

Lead
Australia 19%
China 14%
U.S. 14%
Peru 8%
Canada 6%
Mexico 6%
Kazakhstan 6%
Sweden 4%
Namibia 4%
Morocco 3%
Remaining countries 16%

Iron Ore
China 24%
Brazil 15%
Australia 12%
Russia 8%
Ukraine 9%
India 6%
U.S. 6%
Canada 3%
South Africa 3%
Macedonia 2%
Remaining countries 12%

Copper
Chile 23%
U.S. 19%
Canada 6%
Russia 6%
China 5%
Australia 5%
Zambia 4%
Poland 4%
Peru 4%
Indonesia 3%
Remaining countries 22%

Zinc
Canada 15%
Australia 14%
China 13%
Peru 9%
U.S. 7%
Mexico 5%
Sweden 4%
Kazakhstan 4%
North Korea 3%
Ireland 3%
Remaining countries 23%

Cadmium
Japan 14%
Canada 12%
Belgium 9%
Russia 9%
China 9%
U.S. 6%
Germany 6%
Australia 5%
Italy 3%
S. Korea 3%
Remaining countries 24%

Tin
China 27%
Indonesia 18%
Peru 12%
Brazil 10%
Bolivia 10%
Malaysia 4%
Australia 4%
Russia 3%
Portugal 3%
Thailand 2%
Remaining countries 7%

Aluminum (Bauxite)
Australia 38%
Guinea 15%
Jamaica 10%
Brazil 7%
China 6%
India 5%
Russia 4%
Suriname 3%
Venezuela 2%
Greece 2%
Remaining countries 8%

Nickel
Russia 24%
Canada 19%
Indonesia 10%
New Caledonia 9% (Possession of France)
Australia 9%
Dominican Rep. 4%
Cuba 4%
South Africa 4%
Colombia 4%
Remaining countries 9%

The data on this map portray world production of the metals most important for the operation of a modern industrial economy. The sector graphs across the bottom of the map show the percentage of production of crucial materials by the 10 leading countries for each of 10 materials. For copper, lead, mercury, nickel, tin, and zinc, the annual production data reflect the metal content of the ore mined. Aluminum (or bauxite ore) and iron ore production are expressed in gross weight of ore mined. Cadmium production refers to the refined metal, and crude steel production to usable ingots, cast products, and liquid steel. By comparing this map with Map 58, you will discover that some of the world's top producer nations of these critical materials are also among the world's top consumer nations.

Map 58 Consumption of Crucial Materials

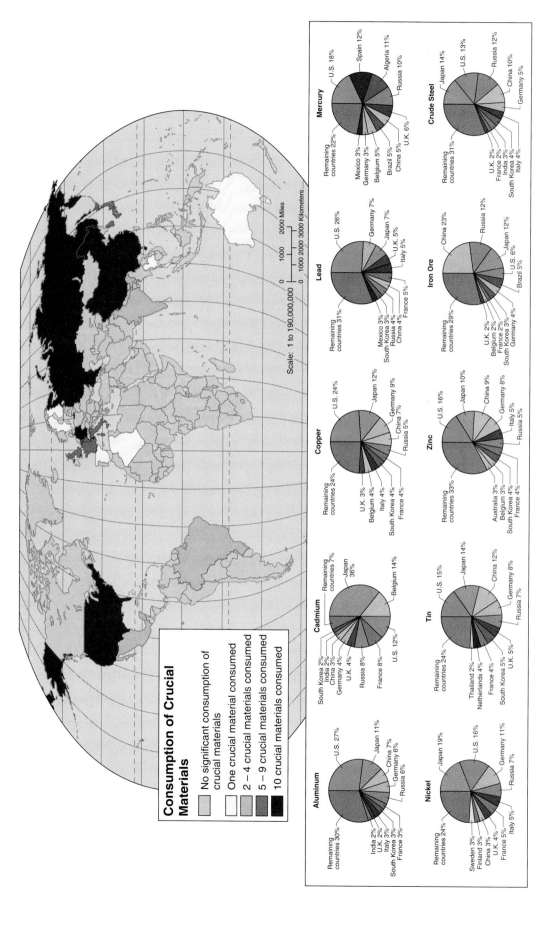

Consumption of Crucial Materials

- No significant consumption of crucial materials
- One crucial material consumed
- 2 – 4 crucial materials consumed
- 5 – 9 crucial materials consumed
- 10 crucial materials consumed

Scale: 1 to 190,000,000

0 1000 2000 3000 Kilometers
0 1000 2000 Miles

Mercury
- U.S. 18%
- Spain 12%
- Algeria 11%
- Russia 10%
- U.K. 6%
- China 5%
- Brazil 5%
- Belgium 5%
- Germany 3%
- Mexico 3%
- Remaining countries 22%

Crude Steel
- Japan 14%
- U.S. 13%
- Russia 12%
- China 10%
- Germany 5%
- Italy 4%
- South Korea 4%
- India 3%
- France 2%
- U.K. 2%
- Remaining countries 31%

Lead
- U.S. 26%
- Germany 7%
- Japan 7%
- U.K. 5%
- Italy 5%
- France 5%
- China 4%
- Russia 4%
- South Korea 3%
- Mexico 3%
- Remaining countries 31%

Iron Ore
- China 23%
- Russia 12%
- Japan 12%
- U.S. 6%
- Brazil 5%
- Germany 4%
- South Korea 3%
- France 2%
- Belgium 2%
- U.K. 2%
- Remaining countries 29%

Copper
- U.S. 24%
- Japan 12%
- Germany 9%
- China 7%
- Russia 5%
- France 4%
- South Korea 4%
- Italy 4%
- Belgium 4%
- U.K. 3%
- Remaining countries 24%

Zinc
- U.S. 16%
- Japan 10%
- China 9%
- Germany 8%
- Italy 5%
- Russia 5%
- France 4%
- South Korea 4%
- Belgium 3%
- Australia 3%
- Remaining countries 33%

Cadmium
- Japan 36%
- Belgium 14%
- U.S. 12%
- France 8%
- Russia 8%
- U.K. 4%
- Germany 4%
- China 3%
- India 2%
- South Korea 2%
- Remaining countries 7%

Tin
- Japan 14%
- China 12%
- Germany 8%
- Russia 7%
- U.K. 5%
- South Korea 4%
- France 4%
- Netherlands 4%
- Thailand 2%
- U.S. 15%
- Remaining countries 24%

Aluminum
- U.S. 27%
- Japan 11%
- China 7%
- Germany 6%
- Russia 6%
- France 3%
- South Korea 3%
- Italy 3%
- U.K. 2%
- India 2%
- Remaining countries 30%

Nickel
- Japan 19%
- U.S. 16%
- Germany 11%
- Russia 7%
- Italy 5%
- France 5%
- U.K. 4%
- Finland 3%
- Sweden 3%
- Remaining countries 24%

Consumption data refer to the domestic use of refined metals (for example, the tons of steel used in the manufacture of automobiles). Some countries rank among the top in both production and consumption, and those that do are among the most highly developed nations. The United States, for example, ranks in the top 4 consumers for each metal; but the United States also ranks in the top 10 producer countries for 7 of the metals. Many countries that rank high as producers but not as consumers have colonial dependency economies, producing raw materials for an export market, often at the mercy of the marketplace. Jamaica and Suriname, for example, depend extremely heavily upon the sale of bauxite ore (crude aluminum). When the United States, Japan, or Russia cuts its use of aluminum, the economies of Jamaica and Suriname crash.

-80-

Part VI

Environmental Conditions

Map 59 Deforestation and Desertification

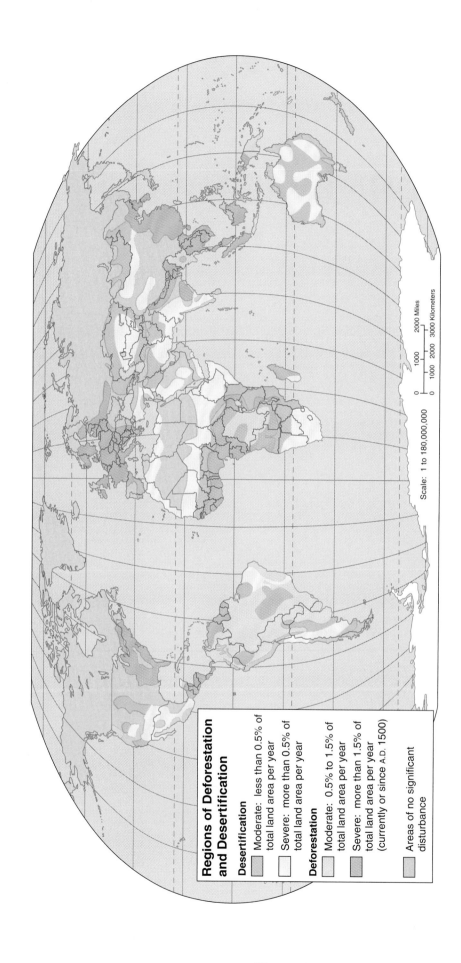

Regions of Deforestation and Desertification

Desertification

Moderate: less than 0.5% of total land area per year

Severe: more than 0.5% of total land area per year

Deforestation

Moderate: 0.5% to 1.5% of total land area per year

Severe: more than 1.5% of total land area per year (currently or since A.D. 1500)

Areas of no significant disturbance

Scale: 1 to 180,000,000

0   1000   2000 Miles

0 1000 2000 3000 Kilometers

While those of us in the developed countries of the world tend to think of environmental deterioration as the consequence of our heavily industrialized economies, in fact the worst examples of current environmental degradation are found within the world's less developed regions. There, high population growth rates and economies limited primarily to farming have forced the increasing use of more marginal (less suited to cultivation) land. In the world's grassland and arid environments, which occupy approximately 40 percent of the world's total land area, increasing cultivation pressures are turning vulnerable areas into deserts incapable of sustaining agricultural productiv-

ity. In the world's forested regions, particularly in the tropical forests of Middle and South America, Africa, and Asia, a similar process is occurring: increasing pressure for more farmland is creating a process of deforestation or forest clearing that destroys the soil, reduces the biological diversity of the forest regions, and ultimately may have the capacity to alter the global climate by contributing to an increase in carbon dioxide in the atmosphere. This increases the heat trapped in the atmosphere and enhances the greenhouse effect.

Map 60 Soil Degradation

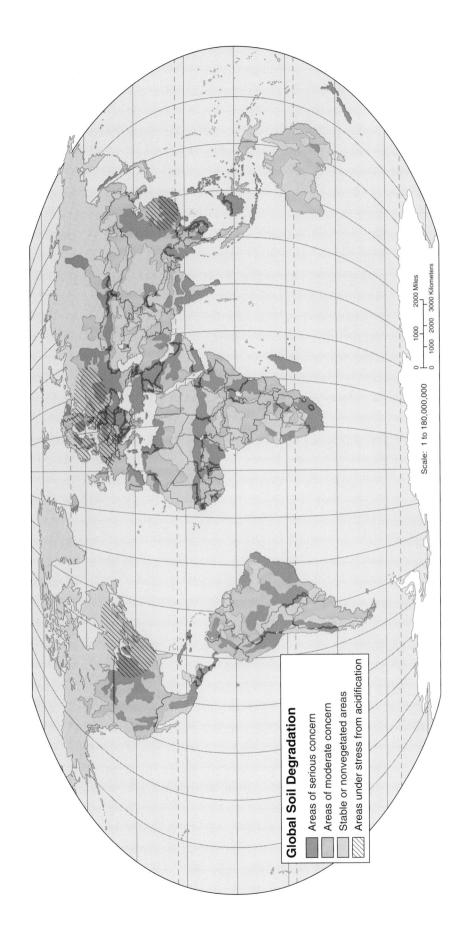

Global Soil Degradation

- Areas of serious concern
- Areas of moderate concern
- Stable or nonvegetated areas
- Areas under stress from acidification

Scale: 1 to 180,000,000

0   1000   2000 Miles

0   1000   2000   3000 Kilometers

Recent research has shown that more than 3 billion acres of the world's surface suffer from serious soil degradation, with more than 22 million acres so severely eroded or poisoned with chemicals that they can no longer support productive crop agriculture. Most of this soil damage has been caused by poor farming practices, overgrazing of domestic livestock, and deforestation. These activities strip away the protective cover of natural vegetation—forests and grasslands—allowing wind and water erosion to remove the topsoil that contains the necessary nutrients and soil microbes for plant growth. But millions of acres of topsoil have been degraded by chemicals as well. In some instances these chemicals are the result of overapplication of fertilizers, herbicides, pesticides, and other agricultural chemicals. In other instances, chemical deposition from industrial and urban wastes and from acid precipitation has poisoned millions of acres of soil. As the map shows, soil erosion and pollution are problems not just in developing countries with high population densities and increasing use of marginal lands but in the more highly developed regions of mechanized, industrial agriculture as well. While many methods for preventing or reducing soil degradation exist, they are seldom used because of ignorance, cost, or perceived economic inefficiency.

Map 61 Air and Water Quality

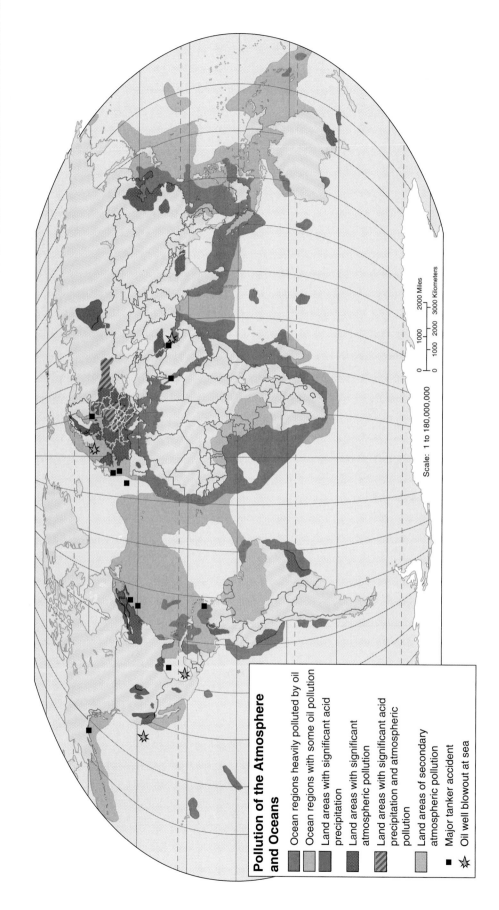

Pollution of the Atmosphere and Oceans

- Ocean regions heavily polluted by oil
- Ocean regions with some oil pollution
- Land areas with significant acid precipitation
- Land areas with significant atmospheric pollution
- Land areas with significant acid precipitation and atmospheric pollution
- Land areas of secondary atmospheric pollution
- ■ Major tanker accident
- ☆ Oil well blowout at sea

Scale: 1 to 180,000,000

0   1000   2000 Miles

0   1000   2000   3000 Kilometers

The pollution of the world's oceans and atmosphere has long been a matter of concern to environmental scientists. The great circulation systems of ocean and air are the controlling factors of the earth's natural environment, and modifications to those systems have unknown consequences. This map is based on what we can measure: (1) areas of oceans where oil pollution has been proven to have inflicted significant damage to ocean ecosystems and lifeforms (including phytoplankton—the oceans' primary food producers, the equivalent of land vegetation); (2) areas of oceans where unusually high concentrations of hydrocarbons from oil spills may have inflicted some damage to the oceans' biota; (3) land areas where the combination of sulphur and nitrogen oxides with atmospheric water vapor has produced acid precipitation at high enough levels to

have produced significant damage to terrestrial vegetation systems; (4) land areas where the emissions from industrial, transportation, commercial, residential, and other uses of fossil fuels have produced concentrations of atmospheric pollutants high enough to be damaging to human health; and (5) land areas of secondary air pollution where the primary pollutant is smoke from forest clearance. A glance at the map shows that there are few areas of the world where some form of oceanic or atmospheric pollution is not a part of our environmental system. Scientists are still debating the long-range implications of this pollution, but nearly all agree that the consequences, whatever they may be, will not be good.

Map 62 Per Capita Carbon Dioxide (CO₂) Emissions

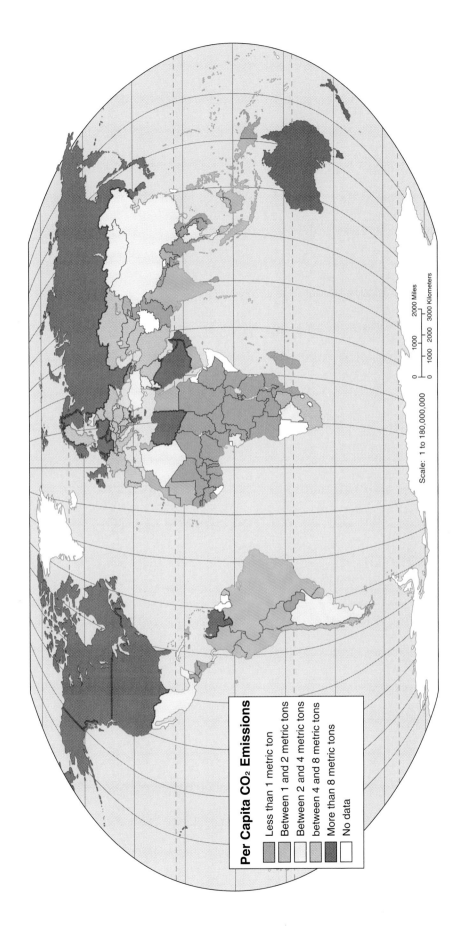

Per Capita CO₂ Emissions

- Less than 1 metric ton
- Between 1 and 2 metric tons
- Between 2 and 4 metric tons
- between 4 and 8 metric tons
- More than 8 metric tons
- No data

Scale: 1 to 180,000,000

0   1000   2000 Miles

0 1000 2000 3000 Kilometers

Carbon dioxide emissions are a major indicator of economic development, since they are generated largely by burning of fossil fuels for electrical power generation, for industrial processes, for domestic and commercial heating, and for the internal combustion engines of automobiles, trucks, buses, planes, and trains. Scientists have long known that carbon dioxide in the atmosphere increases the ability of atmosphere to retain heat, a phenomenon known as the greenhouse effect. While the greenhouse effect is a natural process (and life on earth as we know it would not be possible with-out it), many scientists are concerned that an increase in carbon dioxide in the atmosphere will augment this process, creating a global warming trend and a potential worldwide change of climate patterns. These climatological changes threaten disaster for many regions and their peoples in both the developed and less developed areas of the world. You will note from the map that the countries of the midlatitude regions generate extremely high levels of carbon dioxide per capita.

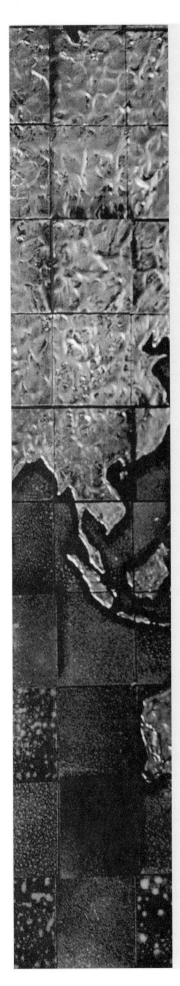

Part VII

Regions of the World

Map 63 North America: Physical

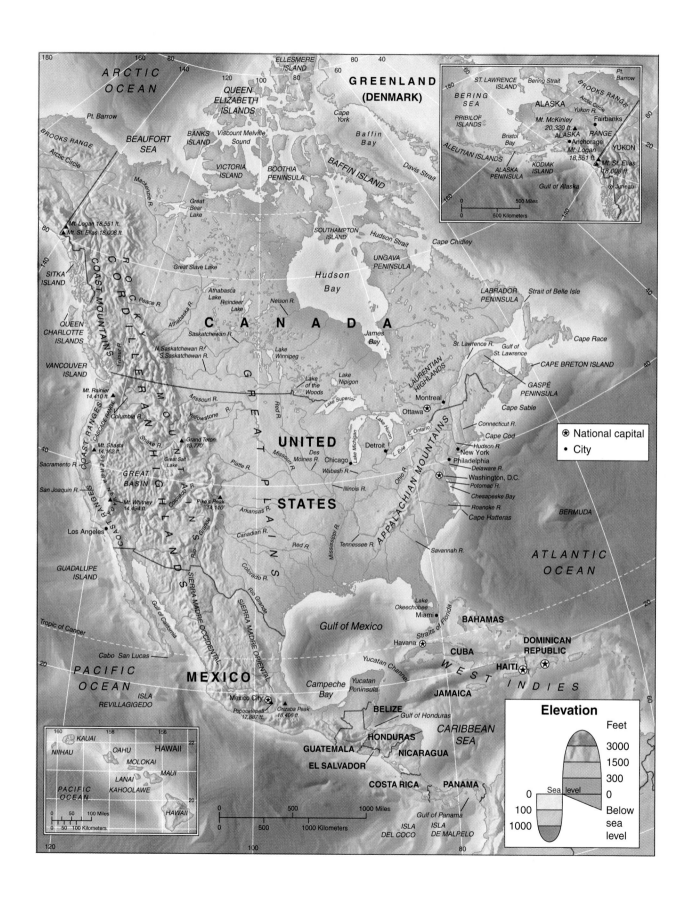

Map 64 North America: Political

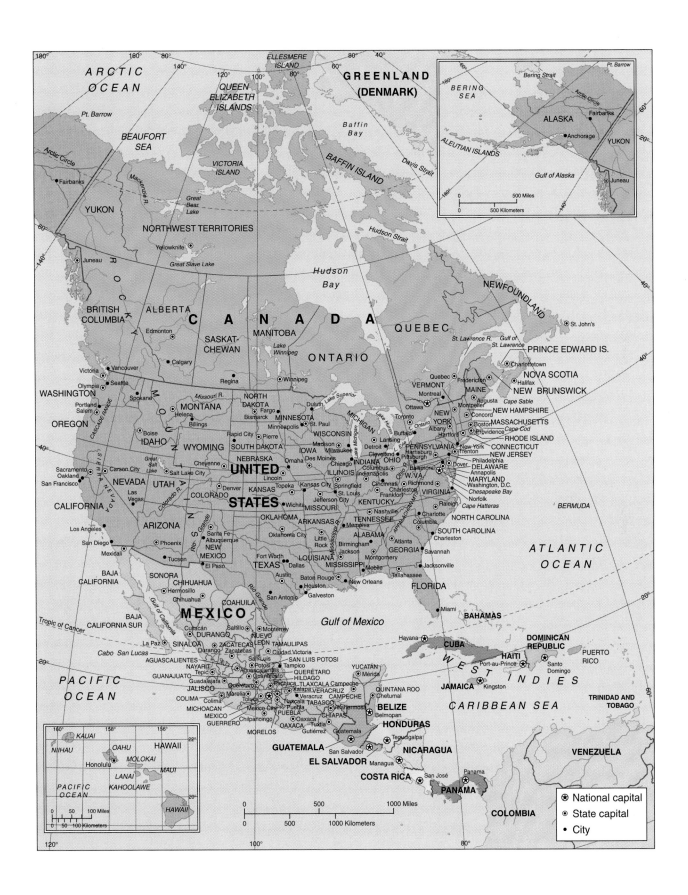

Map **65** South America: Physical

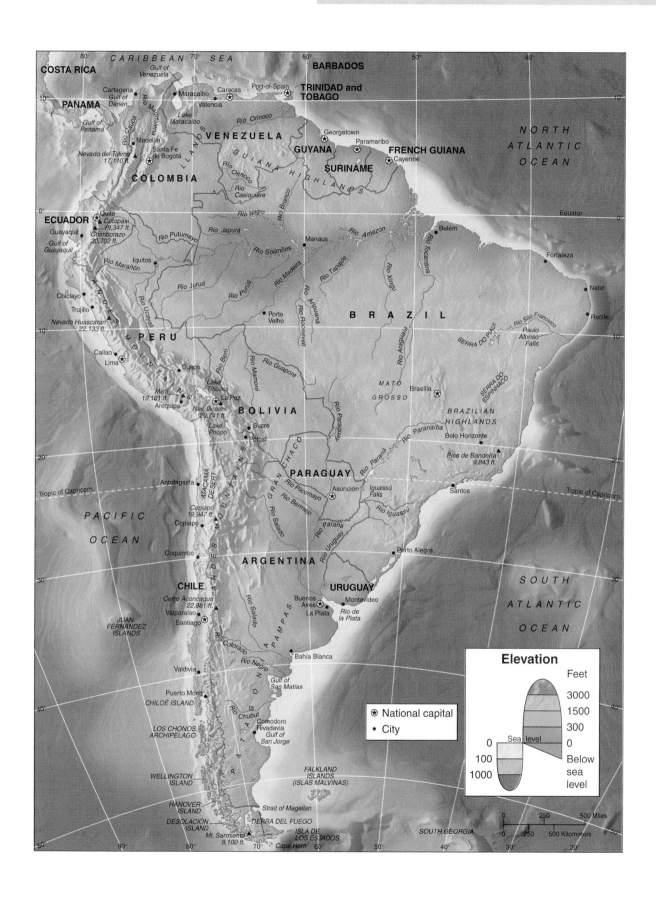

Map 66 South America: Political

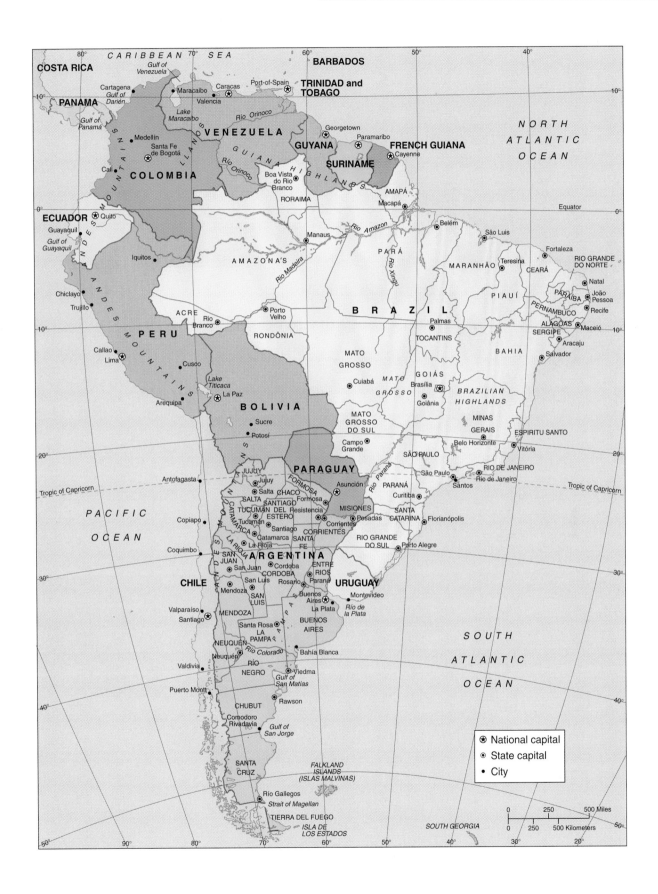

Map 67 Europe: Physical

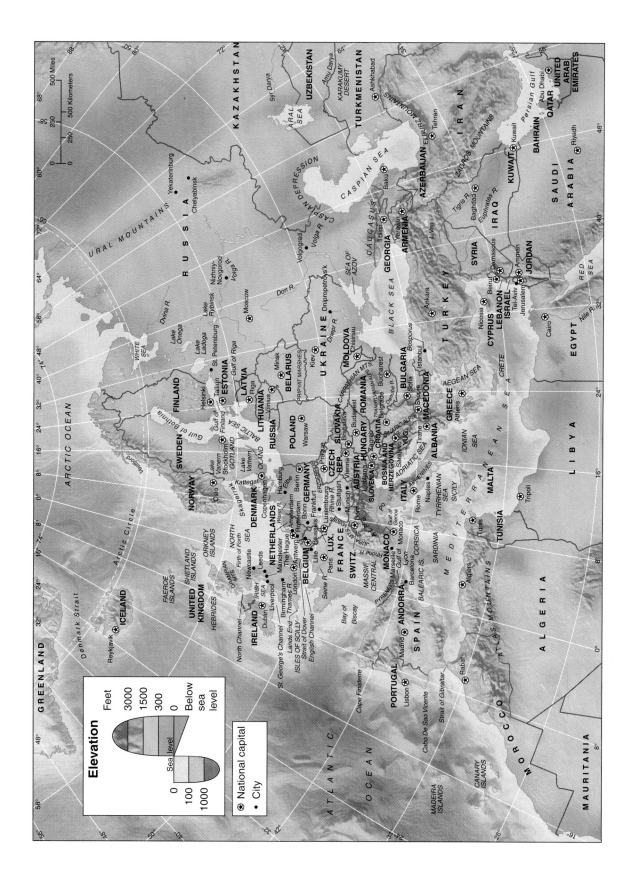

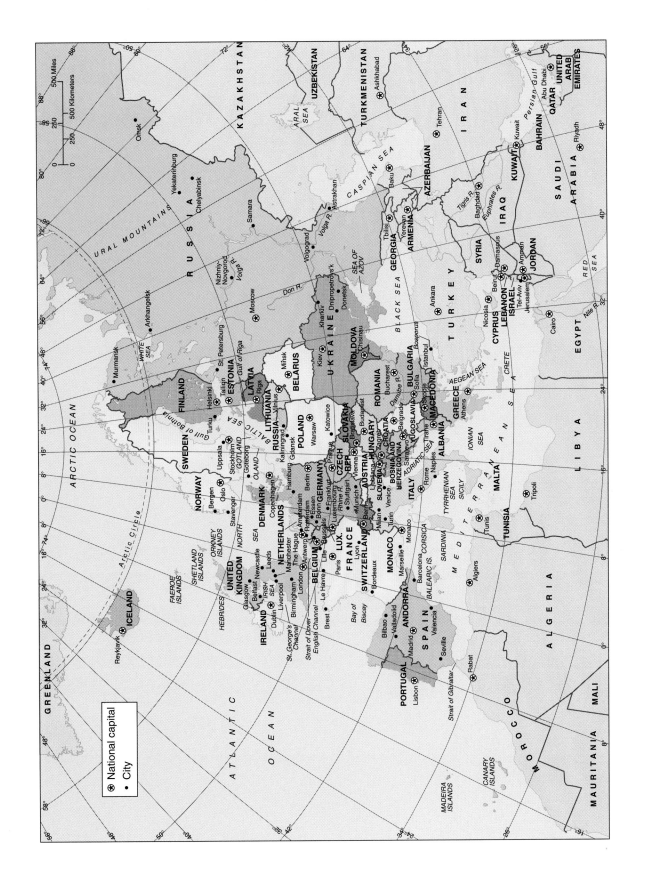

Map 68 Europe: Political

Map 69 Asia: Physical

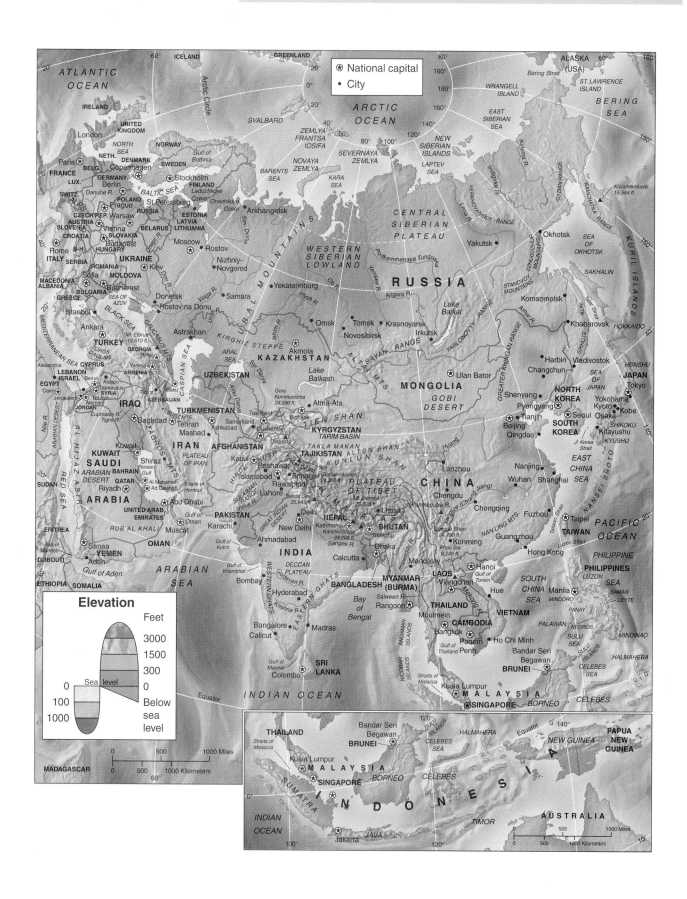

Map 70 Asia: Political

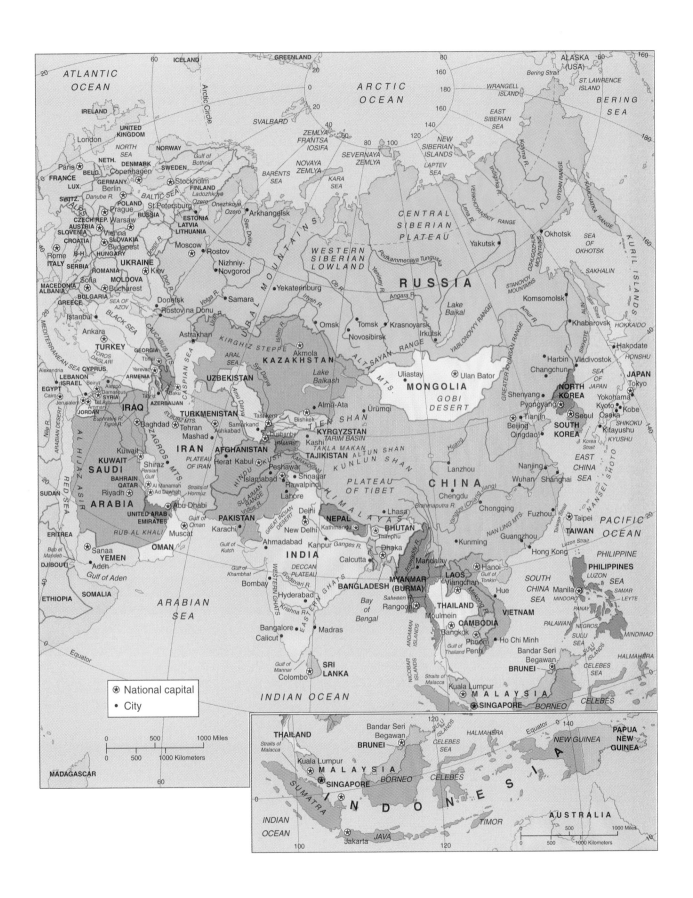

National capital
• City

Map **71** Africa: Physical

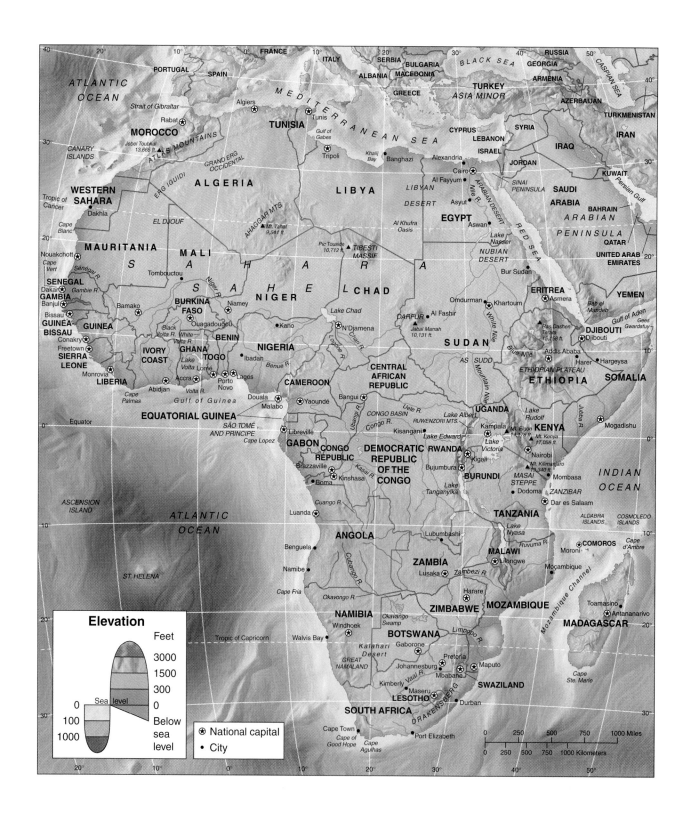

Elevation

Feet

3000
1500
300
0
Below
sea
level

0   Sea level
100
1000

⊛ National capital
• City

Map 72 Africa: Political

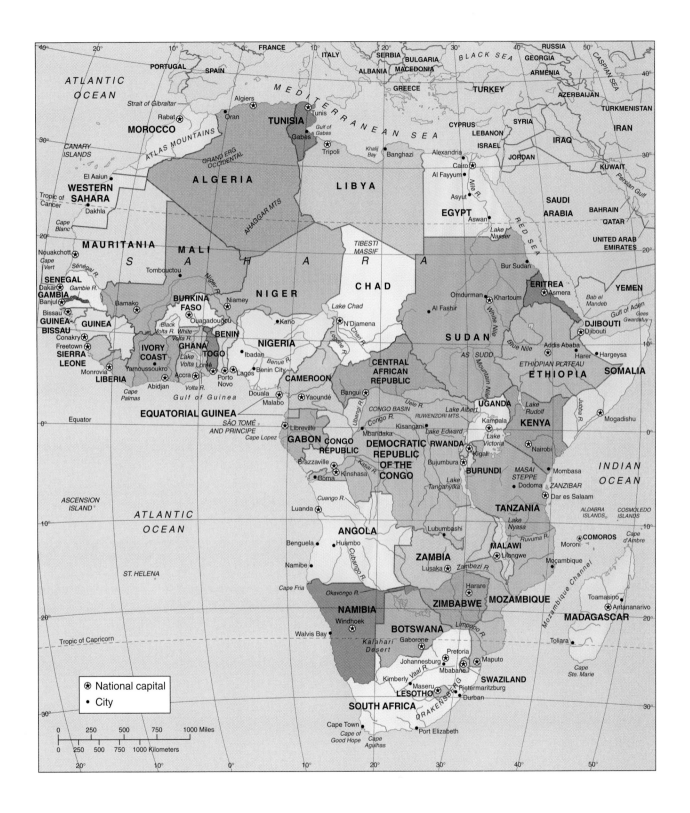

Map 73 Australia and Oceania: Physical

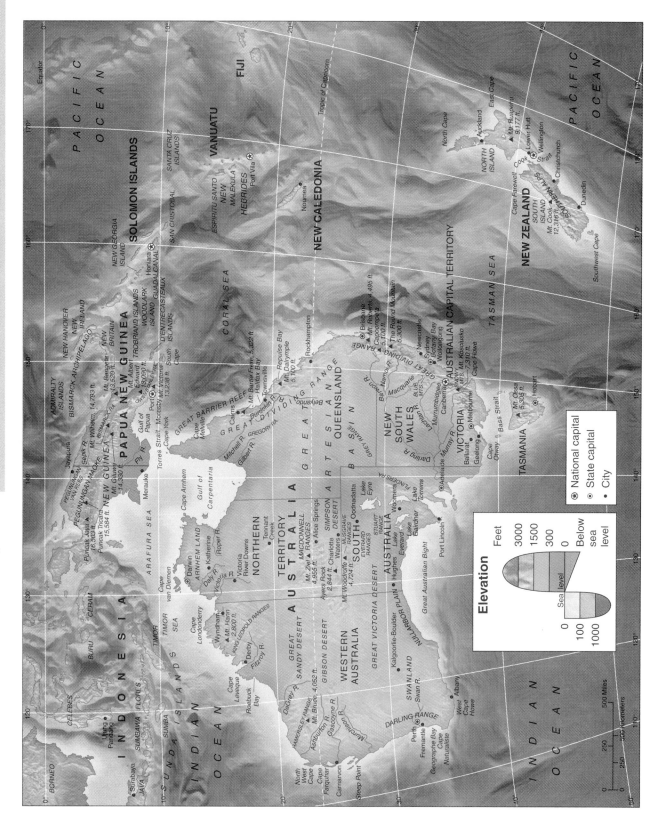

Map 74 Australia and Oceania: Political

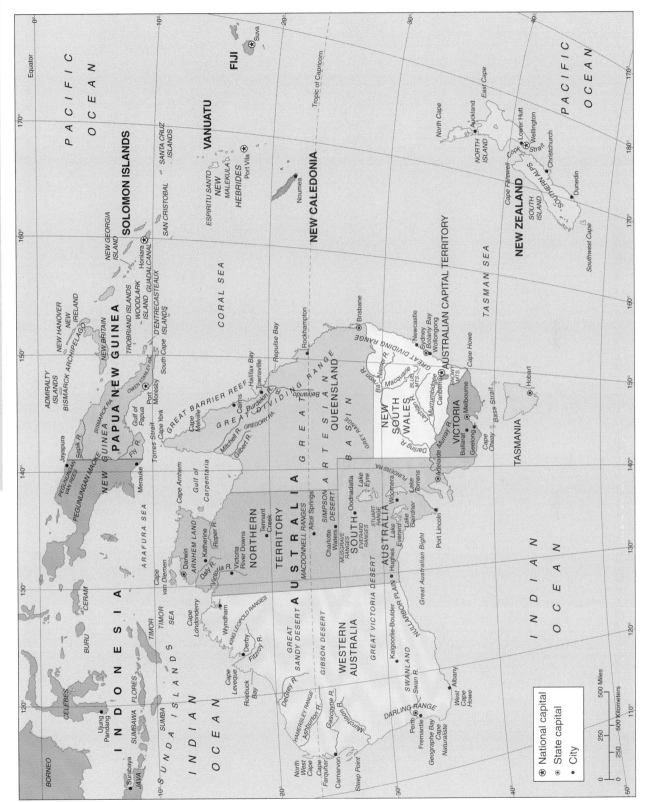

Map 74 Australia and Oceania: Political

PACIFIC OCEAN

Equator

FIJI
• Suva

SOLOMON ISLANDS

SANTA CRUZ ISLANDS

VANUATU
ESPIRITU SANTO
NEW HEBRIDES
MALEKULA
• Port Vila

NEW CALEDONIA
Noumea

NEW GEORGIA ISLAND
Honiara ⊛ GUADALCANAL
SAN CRISTOBAL

PACIFIC OCEAN

North Cape
Auckland •
NORTH ISLAND
Cook Strait
Wellington
Lower Hutt
East Cape
Cape Farewell
SOUTHERN ALPS
Christchurch
SOUTH ISLAND
Dunedin •
Southwest Cape

NEW ZEALAND

TASMAN SEA

ADMIRALTY ISLANDS
NEW HANOVER
NEW IRELAND
BISMARCK ARCHIPELAGO
NEW BRITAIN
PAPUA NEW GUINEA
TROBRIAND ISLANDS
WOODLARK ISLAND
D'ENTRECASTEAUX ISLANDS
South Cape
OWEN STANLEY RA.

CORAL SEA

NEW GUINEA
PEGUNUNGAN MAOKE
PEGUNUNGAN VAN REES
Jayapura •
Sepik R.
Fly R.
Merauke •
Gulf of Papua
Port Moresby •
Cape York

Brisbane ⊛
Newcastle •
Sydney ⊛ Botany Bay
Wollongong •

AUSTRALIAN CAPITAL TERRITORY
Canberra ⊛

GREAT DIVIDING RANGE

Rockhampton •
Repulse Bay
Halifax Bay
Townsville •
Cairns •
Cape Melville
Burdekin R.
GREAT DIVIDING RANGE
QUEENSLAND
GREAT ARTESIAN BASIN
GREY RANGE

NEW SOUTH WALES
Namoi R.
Bogan R.
Macquarie R.
Lachlan R.
Murrumbidgee
Murray R.
Darling R.
BLUE MTS.
SNOWY MTS.
Cape Howe

VICTORIA
Melbourne ⊛
Geelong •
Ballarat •
Cape Otway
Bass Strait

TASMANIA
Hobart •

GREAT BARRIER REEF
Mitchell R.
Gregory R.
Gilbert R.

Torres Strait
Gulf of Carpentaria
Cape Arnhem

ARAFURA SEA

Cape van Diemen
ARNHEM LAND
Darwin ⊛
Katherine •
Daly R.
Roper R.
Victoria R.
Victoria River Downs

NORTHERN TERRITORY
Tennant Creek •
Alice Springs •
MACDONNELL RANGES
Charlotte Waters •
SIMPSON DESERT

AUSTRALIA

SOUTH AUSTRALIA
Oodnadatta •
Lake Eyre
STUART RANGE
MUSGRAVE RANGES
EVERARD RANGES
Lake Torrens
Lake Gairdner
Lake Everard
Woomera •
Adelaide ⊛
FLINDERS RA.
Port Lincoln •

Great Australian Bight

NULLARBOR PLAIN
Hughes •

WESTERN AUSTRALIA
GREAT VICTORIA DESERT
GIBSON DESERT
GREAT SANDY DESERT
Kalgoorlie-Boulder •
SWANLAND
Swan R.
Perth ⊛
Fremantle •
DARLING RANGE
Albany •
West Cape Howe
Cape Naturaliste
Geographe Bay

KING LEOPOLD RANGES
Wyndham •
Derby •
Fitzroy R.
Roebuck Bay
Cape Leveque
Cape Londonderry
DeGrey R.
Ashburton R.
HAMERSLEY RANGE
North West Cape
Cape Farquhar
Carnarvon •
Steep Point
Gascoyne R.
Murchison R.

INDIAN OCEAN

TIMOR SEA
TIMOR

INDONESIA
CERAM
BURU
CELEBES
BORNEO
JAVA
Surabaya •
SUMBAWA
FLORES
SUMBA
SUNDA ISLANDS
Ujung Pandang •

INDIAN OCEAN

Tropic of Capricorn

National capital ⊛
State capital ⊙
City •

0   250   500 Miles
0   250   500 Kilometers

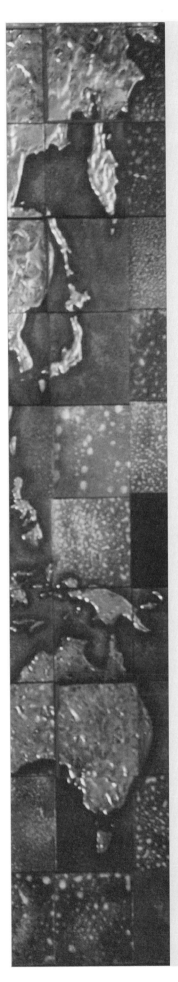

Part VIII

World Countries: Data Tables

Table A
World Countries: Area, Population, and Population Density, 2000

COUNTRY	AREA		POPULATION	DENSITY	
	(Mi^2)	(Km^2)	(2000)[a]	(Pop/Mi^2)	(Pop/Km^2)
Afghanistan	251,826	652,229	21,764,955	86	33
Albania	11,100	28,749	3,134,222	282	109
Algeria	919,595	2,381,750	30,291,341	33	13
Andorra	175	453	66,824	382	148
Angola	481,354	1,246,706	13,134,452	27	11
Antigua and Barbuda	171	443	66,422	388	150
Argentina	1,073,400	2,780,104	37,031,814	34	13
Armenia	11,506	29,801	3,786,997	329	127
Australia	2,966,155	7,682,337	19,137,645	6	2
Austria	32,377	83,856	8,079,902	250	96
Azerbaijan	33,436	86,599	8,041,278	240	93
Bahamas	5,382	13,939	304,233	57	22
Bahrain	267	692	639,753	2,396	924
Bangladesh	55,598	143,999	137,439,261	2,472	954
Barbados	166	430	267,498	1,611	622
Belarus	80,155	207,601	10,186,996	127	49
Belgium	11,783	30,518	10,249,370	870	336
Belize	8,866	22,963	226,325	26	10
Benin	43,475	112,600	6,271,732	144	56
Bhutan	18,200	47,138	2,085,136	115	44
Bolivia	424,165	1,098,587	8,328,685	20	8
Bosnia-Herzegovina	19,776	51,233	3,977,106	201	78
Botswana	231,803	600,362	1,541,256	7	3
Brazil	3,286,488	8,511,999	170,406,280	52	20
Brunei	2,228	5,770	328,305	147	57
Bulgaria	42,823	110,912	7,949,331	186	72
Burkina Faso	105,869	274,201	11,535,072	109	42
Burundi	10,745	27,830	6,356,252	592	228
Cambodia	69,898	181,036	13,104,030	187	72
Cameroon	183,569	475,443	14,875,513	81	31
Canada	3,849,674	9,970,650	30,756,698	8	3
Cape Verde	1,557	4,033	426,958	274	106
Central African Republic	240,535	622,985	3,717,293	15	6
Chad	495,755	1,284,005	7,885,299	16	6
Chile	292,259	756,950	15,211,308	52	20
China	3,705,392	9,596,960	1,275,132,866	344	133
Colombia	439,734	1,138,910	42,104,701	96	37
Comoros	838	2,170	705,929	842	325
Congo Republic	132,047	342,002	3,018,426	23	9
Costa Rica	19,730	51,101	4,023,502	204	79
Côte d'Ivoire	124,502	322,460	16,013,139	129	50
Croatia	21,824	56,538	4,653,749	213	82
Cuba	42,804	110,862	11,199,176	262	101
Cyprus	3,571	9,250	783,827	219	85
Czech Republic	30,387	78,703	10,271,830	338	131

Table A *(Continued)*
World Countries: Area, Population, and Population Density, 2000

COUNTRY	AREA		POPULATION	DENSITY	
	(Mi^2)	(Km^2)	(2000)[a]	(Pop/Mi^2)	(Pop/Km^2)
Democratic Republic of the Congo (formerly Zaire)	905,564	2,345,410	50,948,236	56	22
Denmark	16,629	43,070	5,320,065	320	124
Djibouti	8,494	22,000	632,096	74	29
Dominica	290	750	71,540	247	95
Dominican Republic	18,815	48,730	8,372,695	445	172
Ecuador	109,484	283,563	12,645,796	116	45
Egypt	386,662	1,001,454	67,884,476	176	68
El Salvador	8,124	21,041	6,277,897	773	298
Equatorial Guinea	10,831	28,052	456,703	42	16
Eritrea	46,842	121,320	3,658,777	78	30
Estonia	17,413	45,100	1,393,470	80	31
Ethiopia	435,184	1,127,127	62,907,788	145	56
Fiji	7,054	18,270	813,607	115	45
Finland	130,127	337,030	5,171,806	40	15
France	176,460	547,030	59,237,668	336	108
Gabon	103,347	267,669	1,230,088	12	5
The Gambia	4,363	11,300	1,302,723	299	115
Georgia	26,911	69,699	5,262,050	196	75
Germany	137,803	356,910	82,016,767	595	230
Ghana	92,098	238,534	19,305,633	210	81
Greece	50,942	131,940	10,609,962	208	80
Grenada	131	340	89,018	680	262
Guatemala	42,042	108,889	1,138,532	27	10
Guinea	94,926	245,858	8,154,267	86	33
Guinea-Bissau	13,948	36,125	1,199,198	86	33
Guyana	83,000	214,970	760,513	9	4
Haiti	10,714	27,749	8,142,471	760	293
Honduras	43,277	112,087	6,416,635	148	57
Hungary	35,920	93,033	9,967,555	277	107
Iceland	39,768	103,000	279,291	7	3
India	1,269,340	3,287,590	1,008,937,356	795	307
Indonesia	741,097	1,919,440	212,092,024	286	110
Iran	636,294	1,648,000	70,330,053	111	43
Iraq	168,754	437,072	22,946,245	136	52
Ireland	27,137	70,285	3,803,085	140	54
Israel[b]	8,019	20,769	6,040,427	753	291
Italy	116,305	301,230	57,529,998	495	191
Jamaica	4,244	10,992	2,576,085	607	234
Japan	145,882	377,835	127,096,314	871	336
Jordan	35,445	89,213	4,913,115	139	55
Kazakhstan	1,049,156	2,717,313	16,172,470	15	6
Kenya	224,961	582,649	30,668,697	136	53
Kiribati	277	717	91,985	332	128
Korea, North	46,540	120,539	22,268,377	478	185

Table A (Continued)
World Countries: Area, Population, and Population Density, 2000

COUNTRY	AREA		POPULATION	DENSITY	
	(Mi^2)	(Km^2)	(2000)[a]	(Pop/Mi^2)	(Pop/Km^2)
Korea, South	38,023	98,480	46,740,141	1,229	475
Kuwait	6,880	17,819	1,914,404	278	107
Kyrgyzstan	76,641	198,500	4,920,847	64	25
Laos	91,429	236,801	5,278,563	58	22
Latvia	24,749	64,100	2,420,546	98	38
Lebanon	4,015	10,399	3,496,489	871	336
Lesotho	11,720	30,355	2,034,667	174	67
Liberia	43,000	111,370	2,913,064	68	26
Libya	679,362	1,759,547	5,289,730	8	3
Liechtenstein	62	161	32,207	519	200
Lithuania	25,174	65,201	3,696,093	147	57
Luxembourg	998	2.585	436,818	438	168,982
Macedonia	9,781	25,333	2,033,975	208	80
Madagascar	226,658	587,044	15,970,364	70	27
Malawi	45,747	118,485	11,308,352	247	95
Malaysia	127,317	329,750	22,218,485	175	67
Maldives	115	298	290,959	2,530	976
Mali	478,767	1,240,006	11,350,798	24	9
Malta	124	320	389,941	3,145	1,219
Marshall Islands	70	181	68,126	973	376
Mauritania	397,954	1,030,700	2,664,528	7	3
Mauritius	718	1,860	1,161,371	1,618	624
Mexico	761,603	1,972,550	98,872,230	130	50
Micronesia	271	702	133,144	491	190
Moldova	13,012	33,701	4,295,453	330	127
Monaco	1.21	1.95	31,693	26,193	16,253
Mongolia	604,427	1,565,000	2,533,299	4	2
Morocco	172,413	446,550	29,878,403	173	67
Mozambique	309,494	801,590	18,292,382	59	23
Myanmar (Burma)	261,969	678,500	47,748,939	182	70
Namibia	318,259	824,290	1,756,597	6	2
Nauru	8	21	11,845	1,481	564
Nepal	54,363	140,800	23,042,704	424	164
Netherlands	14,413	37,330	15,863,747	1,101	425
New Zealand	103,738	268,680	3,778,004	36	14
Nicaragua	49,998	129,494	5,071,423	101	39
Niger	489,191	1,267,004	10,831,545	22	9
Nigeria	356,669	923,772	113,861,753	319	123
Norway	125,182	324,220	4,469,030	36	14
Oman	82,030	212,458	2,538,161	31	12
Pakistan	310,402	803,940	141,256,186	455	176
Palau	177	458	18,766	106	41
Panama	30,193	78,200	2,855,694	95	37
Papua New Guinea	178,259	461,690	4,809,215	27	10
Paraguay	157,048	406,754	5,496,467	35	14

Table A (Continued)
World Countries: Area, Population, and Population Density, 2000

COUNTRY	AREA		POPULATION	DENSITY	
	(Mi²)	(Km²)	(2000)[a]	(Pop/Mi²)	(Pop/Km²)
Peru	496,225	1,285,222	25,661,679	52	20
Philippines	115,831	300,002	75,653,257	653	252
Poland	120,728	312,685	38,605,447	320	123
Portugal	35,552	92,080	10,015,505	282	109
Qatar	4,247	11,000	565,439	133	51
Romania	91,699	237,500	2,243,771	24	9
Russia	6,592,745	17,075,200	145,491,166	22	9
Rwanda	10,169	26,338	7,608,928	748	289
St. Kitts and Nevis	104	269	38,819	373	144
St. Lucia	238	616	147,783	621	240
St. Vincent/Grenadines	131	340	115,461	881	340
Samoa	1,104	2,860	158,633	144	55
San Marino	23	60	26,937	1,171	449
Soã Tomé and Principe	372	963	159,883	430	166
Saudi Arabia	756,982	1,960,582	20,346,231	27	10
Senegal	75,749	196,190	9,420,518	124	48
Seychelles	175	453	79,326	453	175
Sierra Leone	27,699	71,740	4,404,740	159	61
Singapore	244	633	4,018,114	16,468	6,348
Slovakia	18,859	48,845	5,398,693	286	111
Slovenia	7,836	20,296	1,987,682	254	98
Solomon Islands	10,985	28,450	447,428	41	16
Somalia	246,201	637,660	8,777,879	36	14
South Africa	471,444	1,221,040	43,309,197	92	35
Spain	194,885	504,752	39,910,274	205	79
Sri Lanka	25,332	65,610	18,923,749	747	288
Sudan	967,500	2,505,824	31,095,162	32	12
Suriname	63,039	163,270	417,159	7	3
Swaziland	6,704	17,363	924,786	138	53
Sweden	173,732	449,966	8,842,094	51	20
Switzerland	15,943	41,292	7,170,407	450	174
Syria	71,498	185,180	16,188,760	226	87
Taiwan	13,892	35,980	22,191,087	1,597	617
Tajikistan	55,251	143,100	6,086,983	110	43
Tanzania	364,900	945,090	35,119,255	96	37
Thailand	198,456	514,000	62,805,574	316	122
Togo	21,925	56,786	4,526,972	206	80
Tonga	290	751	102,321	353	136
Trinidad and Tobago	1,980	5,128	1,294,368	654	252
Tunisia	63,170	163,610	9,458,661	150	58
Turkey	301,382	780,580	66,667,997	221	85
Turkmenistan	188,456	488,101	4,737,256	25	10
Tuvalu	10	26	10,838	1,084	417
Uganda	93,135	236,040	23,300,162	250	99
Ukraine	233,090	603,703	49,568,167	213	82

COUNTRY	AREA		POPULATION	DENSITY	
	(Mi^2)	(Km^2)	(2000)[a]	(Pop/Mi^2)	(Pop/Km^2)
United Arab Emirates	31,969	82,880	2,605,958	82	31
United Kingdom	94,525	244,820	59,414,643	629	243
United States	3,717,797	9,629,091	283,230,243	76	29
Uruguay	68,039	176,220	3,337,080	49	19
Uzbekistan	172,742	447,402	24,880,545	144	56
Vanuatu	5,699	14,760	196,803	35	13
Venezuela	352,145	912,055	24,169,742	69	27
Vietnam	127,243	329,560	78,136,913	614	237
Yemen	203,850	527,970	18,348,746	90	35
Yugoslavia (Serbia-Montenegro)	39,517	102,350	10,552,420	267	103
Zambia	290,586	752,617	10,421,339	36	14
Zimbabwe	150,803	390,580	12,627,277	84	32

[a]Primary source for population figures: United Nations Population Division.

[b]The figures for Israel do not include the West Bank and Gaza. These territories combined have a population of 3,190,943 (mid-2000), and an area of approximately 2,400 square miles. The West Bank has an estimated population density of 780 persons per square mile and Gaza an estimated population density of 8,700 persons per square mile.

Sources: *World Development Indicators 2001* (The World Bank, 2001); *The New York Times 2001 Almanac* (Penguin Putnam, Inc., New York, 2000); *World Population Prospects: The 2000 Revision* (United Nations Population Information Network, 2001).

Table B
World Countries: Form of Government, Capital City, Major Languages

Notes: Unless indicated otherwise, republics are multiparty. "Theocratic" normally refers to fundamentalist Islamic rule. "Transitional" governments are those still in the process of change from a previous form (e.g., single-party communist state to multiparty republic).

COUNTRY	GOVERNMENT	CAPITAL	MAJOR LANGUAGES
Afghanistan	Theocratic republic/transitional	Kabul	Dari, Pashtu, Uzbek, Turkmen
Albania	Multiparty democracy	Tiranë	Albanian, Greek
Algeria	Military-transitional	Algiers	Arabic, Berber, dialects, French
Andorra	Parliamentary democracy	Andorra	Catalán, French, Spanish
Angola	Multiparty democracy/ transitional	Luanda	Portugese; Bantu and other African
Antigua and Barbuda	Parliamentary democracy	St. John's	English, local dialects
Argentina	Federal republic	Buenos Aires	Spanish, English, Italian, German
Armenia	Republic	Yerevan	Armenian, Azerbaijani, Russian
Australia	Federal parliamentary democracy	Canberra	English, indigenous
Austria	Federal republic	Vienna	German
Azerbaijan	Republic	Baku	Azerbaijani, Russian, Armenian
Bahamas	Parliamentary democracy; independent commonwealth	Nassau	English
Bahrain	Traditional monarchy	Al Manamah	Arabic, English, Farsi, Urdu
Bangladesh	Republic	Dhaka	Bangla, English
Barbados	Parliamentary democracy	Bridgetown	English
Belarus	Republic	Minsk	Byelorussian, Russian
Belgium	Constitutional monarchy	Brussels	Dutch (Flemish), French, German
Belize	Parliamentary state	Belmopan	English, Spanish, Garifuna, Mayan
Benin	Multiparty republic	Porto-Novo	French, Fon, Yoruba
Bhutan	Monarchy; special treaty relationship with India	Timphu	Dzongha, Tibetan, Nepalese
Bolivia	Republic	La Paz	Spanish, Quechua, Aymara
Bosnia-Herzegovina	Republic/transitional	Sarajevo	Croatian, Serbian, Bosnian
Botswana	Parliamentary republic	Gaborone	English, Setswana
Brazil	Federal republic	Brasília	Portugese, Spanish, English, French
Brunei	Constitutional monarchy	Bandar Seri Begawan	Malay, English, Chinese
Bulgaria	Parliamentary republic	Sofia	Bulgarian
Burkina Faso	Provisional military	Ouagadougou	French, indigenous
Burundi	Republic/transitional	Bujumbura	French, Kirundi, Swahili
Cambodia	Multiparty democracy/ transitional (under UN supervision)	Phnom Penh	Khmer, French
Cameroon	Multiparty republic	Yaoundé	English, French, indigenous
Canada	Federal parliamentary	Ottawa	English, French
Cape Verde	Republic	Cidade de Praia	Portugese, Crioulu
Central African Republic	Republic	Bangui	French, Sangho, Arabic, Hunsa, Swahili
Chad	Republic	N'Djamena	French, Arabic, Sara, Sango, other indigenous
Chile	Republic	Santiago	Spanish
China	Single-party communist state	Beijing	Various Chinese dialects
Colombia	Republic	Bogotá	Spanish
Comoros	Republic	Moroni	Arabic, French, Comoran
Congo Republic	Multiparty republic	Brazzaville	French, Lingala, Kikongo
Costa Rica	Republic	San José	Spanish
Côte d'Ivoire	Multiparty republic	Abidjan	French, indigenous

Table B *(Continued)*
World Countries: Form of Government, Capital City, Major Languages

Notes: Unless indicated otherwise, republics are multiparty. "Theocratic" normally refers to fundamentalist Islamic rule. "Transitional" governments are those still in the process of change from a previous form (e.g., single-party communist state to multiparty republic).

COUNTRY	GOVERNMENT	CAPITAL	MAJOR LANGUAGES
Croatia	Parliamentary democracy	Zaghreb	Serbo-Croatian
Cuba	Single-party communist state	Havana	Spanish
Cyprus	Republic	Nicosia	Greek, Turkish, English
Czech Republic	Federal republic	Prague	Czech, Slovak, Hungarian
Democratic Republic of the Congo (formerly Zaire)	Republic/transitional from military dictatorship	Kinshasa	French, Lingala, Kingwana, Kikongo, Tshuliba
Denmark	Constitutional monarchy	Copenhagen	Danish, Faroese, German
Djibouti	Republic	Djibouti	French, Somali, Afar, Arabic
Dominica	Republic	Roseau	English, French
Dominican Republic	Republic	Santo Domingo	Spanish
Ecuador	Republic	Quito	Spanish, Quechua, indigenous
Egypt	Republic	Cairo	Arabic
El Salvador	Republic	San Salvador	Spanish, Nahua
Equatorial Guinea	Republic	Malabo	Spanish, indigenous, English
Eritrea	Transitional government	Asmara	Afar, Amharic, Arabic, Tigre, other indigenous
Estonia	Parliamentary democracy	Tallinn	Estonian, Russian, Ukranian, Finnish
Ethiopia	Federal republic	Addis Ababa	Amharic, Tigrinya, Orominga, Somali, Arabic, English
Fiji	Republic	Suva	English, Fijian, Hindustani
Finland	Republic	Helsinki	Finnish, Swedish
France	Republic	Paris	French
Gabon	Multiparty presidential republic	Libreville	French, Fang, indigenous
The Gambia	Multiparty democratic republic	Banjul	English, Mandinka, Wolof, Fula
Georgia	Republic	Tbilisi	Georgian, Russian, Armenian
Germany	Federal republic	Berlin	German
Ghana	Parliamentary democracy	Accra	English, Akan, indigenous
Greece	Parliamentary democratic republic	Athens	Greek
Grenada	Parliamentary state	St. George's	English, French
Guatemala	Republic	Guatemala City	Spanish, Quiche, Cakchiquel, other indigenous
Guinea	Republic	Conakry	French, indigenous
Guinea-Bissau	Multiparty republic	Bissau	Portuguese, Crioulo, indigenous
Guyana	Republic (within U.K. Commonwealth)	Georgetown	English, indigenous
Haiti	Republic	Port-au-Prince	Creole, French
Honduras	Republic	Tegucigalpa	Spanish, indigenous
Hungary	Republic	Budapest	Hungarian
Iceland	Republic	Reykjavík	Icelandic
India	Federal republic	New Delhi	English, Hindi
Indonesia	Republic	Jakarta	Bahasa Indonesian, English, Dutch, Javanese
Iran	Theocratic republic	Tehran	Farsi, Turkish, Kurdish, Arabic
Iraq	Single-party republic/ dictatorship	Baghdad	Arabic, Kurdish, Assyrian, Armenian
Ireland	Republic	Dublin	English, Irish Gaelic
Israel	Parliamentary democracy	Jerusalem	Hebrew, Arabic, Yiddish
Italy	Republic	Rome	Italian
Jamaica	Parliamentary state	Kingston	English, Creole

Notes: Unless indicated otherwise, republics are multiparty. "Theocratic" normally refers to fundamentalist Islamic rule. "Transitional" governments are those still in the process of change from a previous form (e.g., single-party communist state to multiparty republic).

COUNTRY	GOVERNMENT	CAPITAL	MAJOR LANGUAGES
Japan	Constitutional monarchy	Tokyo	Japanese
Jordan	Constitutional monarchy	Amman	Arabic
Kazakhstan	Republic/transitional	Alma-Ata	Kazakh, Russian, German, Ukranian
Kenya	Republic	Nairobi	English, Swahili, indigenous
Kiribati	Republic	Tarawa	English, Gilbertese
Korea, North	Single-party communist state	Pyongyang	Korean
Korea, South	Republic	Seoul	Korean
Kuwait	Constitutional monarchy	Kuwait	Arabic, English
Kyrgyzstan	Republic	Bishkek	Kirghiz, Russian, Uzbek, Ukranian
Laos	Single-party communist state	Vientiane	Lao, French, Thai, indigenous
Latvia	Multiparty republic	Riga	Lettish, Lithuanian, Russian
Lebanon	Republic	Beirut	Arabic, French, Armenian, English
Lesotho	Constitutional monarchy	Maseru	English, Sesotho, Zulu, Xhosa
Liberia	Republic/transitional	Monrovia	English, indigenous
Libya	Single party/military dictatorship	Tripoli	Arabic
Liechtenstein	Constitutional monarchy	Vaduz	German
Lithuania	Republic	Vilnius	Lithuanian, Russian, Polish
Luxembourg	Constitutional monarchy	Luxembourg	French, Luxembourgian, German
Macedonia	Republic/transitional	Skopje	Macedonian, Albanian, Turkish, Serbo-Croatian
Madagascar	Republic	Antananarivo	Malagasy, French
Malawi	Multiparty republic	Lilongwe	Chichewa, English, Tombuka
Malaysia	Constitutional monarchy	Kuala Lumpur	Malay, Chinese, English
Maldives	Republic	Male	Divehi
Mali	Single-party republic	Bamako	French, Bambara, indigenous
Malta	Parliamentary democracy	Valletta	English, Maltese
Marshall Islands	Constitutional government (free association with U.S.)	Majuro	English, Polynesian dialects, Japanese
Mauritania	Republic/transitional	Nouakchott	Arabic, Wolof, Pular, French
Mauritius	Parliamentary state	Port Louis	English, Creole, French, Hindi, Urdu, Bojpoori
Mexico	Federal republic	Mexico City	Spanish, indigenous
Micronesia	Constitutional government (free association with U.S.)	Palikir	English, Trukese, Pohnpeian, Yapese
Moldova	Republic	Kishinev	Moldavian, Russian, Gagauz
Monaco	Constitutional monarchy	Monaco	French, English, Italian, Monegasque
Mongolia	Republic	Ulan Bator	Khalkha Mongol, Turkic, Russian, Chinese
Morocco	Constitutional monarchy	Rabat	Arabic, Berber dialects, French
Mozambique	Republic	Maputo	Portuguese, indigenous
Myanmar (Burma)	Provisional military	Rangoon	Burmese, indigenous
Namibia	Republic	Windhoek	Afrikaans, English, German, indigenous
Nauru	Republic	Yaren district	Nauruan, English
Nepal	Parliamentary democracy	Kathmandu	Nepali, Maithali, Bhojpuri, indigenous
Netherlands	Constitutional monarchy	Amsterdam	Dutch
New Zealand	Parliamentary democracy	Wellington	English, Maori
Nicaragua	Republic	Managua	Spanish, English, indigenous
Niger	Provisional military	Niamey	French, Hausa, Djerma, indigenous
Nigeria	Military/transitional	Abuja	English, Hausa, Fulani, Yorbua, Ibo

Notes: Unless indicated otherwise, republics are multiparty. "Theocratic" normally refers to fundamentalist Islamic rule. "Transitional" governments are those still in the process of change from a previous form (e.g., single-party communist state to multiparty republic).

COUNTRY	GOVERNMENT	CAPITAL	MAJOR LANGUAGES
Norway	Constitutional monarchy	Oslo	Norwegian, Lapp
Oman	Monarchy	Muscat	Arabic, English, Baluchi, Urdu
Pakistan	Federal Islamic republic	Islamabad	Punjabi, Sindhi, Siraiki, Pashtu, Urbu, English, others
Palau	Constitutional government (free association with U.S.)	Koror	English, Palauan
Panama	Democratic republic	Panama	Spanish, English, indigenous
Papua New Guinea	Parliamentary democracy	Port Moresby	Various indigenous, English, Motu
Paraguay	Republic/transitional	Asunción	Spanish, Guarani
Peru	Republic	Lima	Quechua, Spanish, Aymara
Philippines	Republic	Manila	English, Pilipino, Tagalog
Poland	Republic	Warsaw	Polish
Portugal	Republic	Lisbon	Portuguese
Qatar	Traditional monarchy	Doha	Arabic, English
Romania	Republic	Bucharest	Romanian, Hungarian, German
Russia	Federational republic	Moscow	Russian, numerous other
Rwanda	Republic/transitional	Kigali	French, Kinyarwanda, English, Kiswahili
St. Kitts and Nevis	Constitutional monarchy	Basseterre	English
St. Lucia	Parliamentary democracy	Castries	English, French
St. Vincent/Grenadines	Parliamentary monarchy	Kingstown	English, French
Samoa	Constitutional monarchy	Apia	Samoan, English
San Marino	Republic	San Marino	Italian
São Tomé and Príncipe	Republic	São Tomé	Portuguese, Fang
Saudi Arabia	Islamic monarchy	Riyadh	Arabic
Senegal	Republic	Dakar	French, Wolof, indigenous
Seychelles	Republic	Victoria	English, French, Creole
Sierra Leone	Transitional government	Freetown	English, Krio, indigenous
Singapore	Republic	Singapore	Mandarin Chinese, English, Malay
Slovakia	Parliamentary democracy	Bratislava	Slovak, Hungarian, Polish
Slovenia	Republic	Ljubljana	Slovenian, Serbo-Croatian
Solomon Islands	Parliamentary state	Honiara	Mostly indigenous, English
Somalia	Transitional	Mogadishu	Arabic, Somali, English, Italian
South Africa	Republic	Pretoria	Afrikaans, English, Zulu, Xhosa, other
Spain	Parliamentary monarchy	Madrid	Castilian Spanish, Catalan, Galician, Basque
Sri Lanka	Republic	Colombo	English, Sinhala, Tamil
Sudan	Provisional military	Khartoum	Arabic, Nubian, various others
Suriname	Constitutional democracy	Paramaribo	Dutch, Sranang Tongo, English
Swaziland	Monarchy	Mbabane	English, siSwati
Sweden	Constitutional monarchy	Stockholm	Swedish
Switzerland	Federal republic	Bern	German, French, Italian, Romansch
Syria	Republic (authoritarian)	Damascus	Arabic, Kurdish, Armenian, Aramaic
Taiwan	Multiparty democracy	Taipei	Chinese dialects
Tajikistan	Republic	Dushanbe	Tajik, Uzbek, Russian
Tanzania	Republic	Dar es Salaam	Kiswahili, Swahili, English, indigenous
Thailand	Constitutional monarchy	Bangkok	Thai, English
Togo	Republic/transitional	Lomé	French, indigenous

Table B *(Continued)*
World Countries: Form of Government, Capital City, Major Languages

Notes: Unless indicated otherwise, republics are multiparty. "Theocratic" normally refers to fundamentalist Islamic rule. "Transitional" governments are those still in the process of change from a previous form (e.g., single-party communist state to multiparty republic).

COUNTRY	GOVERNMENT	CAPITAL	MAJOR LANGUAGES
Tonga	Constitutional monarchy	Nuku'alofa	Tongan, English
Trinidad and Tobago	Parliamentary democracy	Port of Spain	English, Hindi, French, Spanish
Tunisia	Republic	Tunis	Arabic, French
Turkey	Parliamentary republic	Ankara	Turkish, Kurdish, Arabic
Turkmenistan	Republic	Ashkhabad	Turkmen, Russian, Uzbek, Kazakh
Tuvalu	Constitutional monarchy	Funafuti	Tuvaluan, English
Uganda	Republic	Kampala	English, Luganda, Swahili, indigenous
Ukraine	Republic	Kiev	Ukranian, Russian
United Arab Emirates	Federated monarchy	Abu Dhabi	Arabic, English, Farsi, Hindi, Urdu
United Kingdom	Constitutional monarchy	London	English, Welsh, Gaelic
United States	Federal republic	Washington, D.C.	English, Spanish
Uruguay	Republic	Montevideo	Spanish, Portunol/Brazilero
Uzbekistan	Republic	Tashkent	Uzbek, Russian, Kazakh, Tajik, Tatar
Vanatu	Republic	Port Vila	English, French, Bislama (pidgin)
Venezuela	Federal republic	Caracas	Spanish, indigenous
Vietnam	Single-party communist state	Hanoi	Vietnamese, French, Chinese, English
Yemen	Republic	San'aa	Arabic
Yugoslavia (Serbia-Montenegro)	Republic	Belgrade	Serb, Albanian, Hungarian
Zambia	Single-party republic	Lusaka	English, Tonga, Lozi, other indigenous
Zimbabwe	Republic	Harare	English, Shona, Sindebele

Sources: The New York Times 2001 Almanac (Penguin Putnam, New York, 2000); *The World Factbook 2000* (CIA, Washington, DC, 2000).

Table C
Defense Expenditures, Armed Forces, Refugees, and the Arms Trade

COUNTRY	MILITARY EXPENDITURES	NUMBERS IN ARMED FORCES	REFUGEE POPULATION	ARMS TRADE	
	(% of GNP)	(in thousands)		Exports (% of Total Exports)	Imports (% of Total Imports)
Albania	1.4	52	3,900	0.0	1.3
Algeria	3.9	124	165,200	0.0	5.6
Angola	20.5	95	13,100	0.0	3.5
Argentina	1.2	65	2,300	0.0	0.2
Armenia	3.5	60	296,200	2.1	0.0
Australia	2.2	65	59,700	0.0	1.4
Austria	0.9	48	82,500	0.0	0.3
Azerbaijan	1.9	75	221,600	1.3	0.0
Bangladesh	1.4	110	22,200	0.0	0.7
Belarus	1.7	65	260	6.7	0.0
Belgium	1.5	46	17,900	0.1	0.2
Benin	1.3	8	3,700	0.0	0.0
Bolivia	1.9	33	350	0.0	1.6
Bosnia-Herzegovina	5.9	40	65,600	0.0	6.5
Botswana	5.1	8	1,300	0.0	0.9
Brazil	1.8	296	2,400	0.1	0.7
Bulgaria	3.0	80	550	2.4	0.2
Burkina Faso	2.8	9	680	0.0	0.0
Burundi	6.1	35	22,100	0.0	16.5
Cambodia	4.1	60	20	0.0	0.9
Cameroon	3.0	13	49,200	0.0	0.7
Canada	1.3	61	123,300	0.3	0.2
Central African Republic	3.9	5	49,300	0.0	0.0
Chad	2.7	35	23,500	0.0	2.1
Chile	3.9	102	320	0.0	0.3
China	2.2	2,600	293,300	0.6	0.4
Hong Kong, China	–	–	970	–	–
Colombia	3.7	149	230	0.0	0.8
Congo Republic	4.1	10	39,900	0.0	1.1
Costa Rica	0.6	10	22,900	0.0	0.1
Côte d'Ivoire	1.1	15	138,400	0.0	0.0
Croatia	6.3	58	28,400	0.0	0.1
Cuba	2.3	55	970	0.0	0.0
Czech Republic	1.9	55	1,200	0.4	0.5
Democratic Republic of Congo (formerly Zaire)	5.0	50	285,300	0.0	2.4
Denmark	1.7	29	69,000	0.0	0.5
Dominican Republic	1.1	22	630	0.0	0.1
Ecuador	4.0	58	310	0.0	3.2
Egypt	2.8	430	6,600	0.1	12.1
El Salvador	0.9	15	20	0.0	0.3
Eritrea	7.8	55	3,000	0.0	0.0
Estonia	1.5	7	–	0.0	0.2
Ethiopia	1.9	100	257,700	0.0	0.0

Table C (*Continued*)
Defense Expenditures, Armed Forces, Refugees, and the Arms Trade

COUNTRY	MILITARY EXPENDITURES	NUMBERS IN ARMED FORCES	REFUGEE POPULATION	ARMS TRADE	
	(% of GNP)	(in thousands)		Exports (% of Total Exports)	Imports (% of Total Imports)
Finland	1.7	35	12,800	0.1	1.2
France	3.0	475	129,700	2.0	0.1
Gabon	2.0	10	15,100	0.0	0.0
The Gambia	3.7	1	17,200	0.0	11.9
Georgia	1.4	11	5,200	0.0	1.1
Germany	1.6	335	975,500	0.1	0.2
Ghana	0.7	7	13,300	0.0	0.0
Greece	4.6	206	6,300	0.3	3.1
Guatemala	1.4	30	730	0.0	0.1
Guinea	1.5	12	501,500	0.0	3.7
Guinea-Bissau	3.2	7	7,100	0.0	0.0
Haiti	–	0	–	0.0	0.8
Honduras	1.3	10	10	0.0	0.5
Hungary	1.9	50	5,000	0.0	0.5
India	2.8	1,260	180,000	0.3	1.0
Indonesia	2.3	280	162,500	0.0	1.0
Iran	3.0	575	1,835,700	0.1	5.8
Iraq	4.9	400	128,900	0.0	0.0
Ireland	1.2	17	1,100	0.0	0.1
Israel	9.7	185	130	1.6	3.6
Italy	2.0	419	22,900	0.3	0.2
Jamaica	0.9	3	40	0.0	0.2
Japan	1.0	250	4,200	0.0	0.8
Jordan	9.0	102	1,000	0.0	3.2
Kazakhstan	1.3	34	14,800	0.0	3.3
Kenya	2.1	24	223,700	0.0	1.2
Korea, North	27.5	1,100	–	8.1	2.1
Korea, South	3.4	670	10	0.0	0.8
Kuwait	7.5	28	4,300	0.0	24.3
Kyrgyzstan	1.6	14	10,800	0.0	0.0
Laos	3.4	50	–	0.0	1.4
Latvia	0.9	5	10	0.0	0.0
Lebanon	3.0	57	4,200	0.0	0.5
Lesotho	2.5	2	–	0.0	0.0
Libya	6.1	70	10,500	0.0	0.1
Lithuania	0.8	12	40	0.0	0.1
Macedonia	2.5	15	21,200	0.0	0.0
Madagascar	1.5	21	–	0.0	0.0
Malawi	1.0	8	1,700	0.0	0.0
Malaysia	2.2	110	50,500	0.0	0.9
Mali	1.7	10	8,300	0.0	1.5
Mauritania	2.3	11	220	0.0	0.0
Mauritius	0.3	1	–	0.0	0.4
Mexico	1.1	250	24,500	0.0	0.1

Table C *(Continued)*
Defense Expenditures, Armed Forces, Refugees, and the Arms Trade

COUNTRY	MILITARY EXPENDITURES	NUMBERS IN ARMED FORCES	REFUGEE POPULATION	ARMS TRADE	
	(% of GNP)	(in thousands)		Exports (% of Total Exports)	Imports (% of Total Imports)
Moldova	1.0	11	10	7.9	0.0
Mongolia	1.9	20	–	0.0	0.0
Morocco	4.3	195	900	0.0	1.9
Mozambique	2.8	14	220	0.0	0.0
Myanmar (Burma)	7.6	322	–	0.0	13.6
Namibia	2.7	8	7,400	0.0	0.3
Nepal	0.8	35	127,900	0.0	0.0
Netherlands	1.9	57	139,200	0.3	0.3
New Zealand	1.3	10	4,800	0.0	0.7
Nicaragua	1.5	14	470	0.0	0.0
Niger	1.1	5	350	0.0	1.4
Nigeria	1.4	76	6,900	0.0	0.7
Norway	2.1	33	47,900	0.0	0.7
Oman	26.1	38	–	0.0	3.2
Pakistan	5.7	610	1,202,000	0.0	5.2
Panama	1.4	12	1,300	0.0	0.3
Papua New Guinea	1.3	5	–	0.0	0.0
Paraguay	1.3	16	20	0.0	0.1
Peru	2.1	115	700	0.0	3.0
Philippines	1.5	105	170	0.0	0.3
Poland	2.3	230	940	0.2	0.4
Portugal	2.4	72	410	0.0	0.3
Romania	2.4	200	1,200	0.1	2.2
Russia	5.8	1,300	80,100	2.6	0.0
Rwanda	4.4	40	34,400	0.0	6.7
Saudi Arabia	14.5	180	5,600	0.0	40.4
Senegal	1.6	14	21,500	0.0	0.0
Sierra Leone	5.9	5	6,600	0.0	0.0
Singapore	5.7	55	–	0.1	0.3
Slovakia	2.1	44	440	0.5	0.1
Slovenia	1.7	10	4,400	0.0	0.2
South Africa	1.8	75	14,500	1.2	0.1
Spain	1.5	107	6,400	0.5	0.4
Sri Lanka	5.1	110	20	0.0	1.5
Sudan	4.6	105	391,000	0.0	1.3
Sweden	2.5	60	159,900	1.1	0.5
Switzerland	1.4	39	82,300	0.1	0.4
Syria	5.6	320	6,500	0.0	1.7
Tajikistan	1.7	10	4,500	0.0	0.0
Tanzania	1.3	35	622,200	0.0	1.5
Thailand	2.3	288	100,100	0.0	1.5
Togo	2.0	12	12,100	0.0	1.3
Trinidad and Tobago	1.5	2	–	0.0	0.2
Tunisia	2.0	35	450	0.0	0.3

Table C *(Continued)*
Defense Expenditures, Armed Forces, Refugees, and the Arms Trade

COUNTRY	MILITARY EXPENDITURES	NUMBERS IN ARMED FORCES	REFUGEE POPULATION	ARMS TRADE	
	(% of GNP)	(in thousands)		Exports (% of Total Exports)	Imports (% of Total Imports)
Turkey	4.0	820	2,800	0.0	3.3
Turkmenistan	4.6	21	18,500	0.0	0.0
Uganda	4.2	50	218,200	0.0	2.3
Ukraine	3.7	450	2,700	3.5	0.0
United Arab Emirates	6.9	60	500	0.1	4.7
United Kingdom	2.7	218	137,000	2.3	0.7
United States	3.3	1,530	513,000	4.6	0.2
Uruguay	1.4	25	90	0.0	0.3
Uzbekistan	2.5	65	1,000	1.7	0.1
Venezuela	2.2	75	190	0.0	1.8
Vietnam	2.8	650	15,000	0.0	1.1
West Bank and Gaza	–	–	–	–	–
Yemen	8.1	69	60,500	0.0	5.5
Yugoslavia (Serbia-Montenegro)	4.9	115	500,700	1.6	0.4
Zambia	1.1	21	206,400	0.0	0.0
Zimbabwe	3.8	40	2,100	0.0	0.5

Sources: Refugees and Others of Concern to UNHCR: 1999 Statistical Overview (UN High Commissioner on Refugees, 2000).
Note: Data for some countries are based on partial or uncertain data or rough estimates; see U.S. Department of State (2000).

Table D
Major Armed Conflicts, 1990–2001

COUNTRY	TYPE OF WAR	LOCATION OF WAR	ADVERSARIES (in interstate wars)	DATE WAR BEGAN	COMBAT STATUS (1/1/2001)
Afghanistan	civil war	general		1978	continuing
	interstate war	general	United States and allies against Taliban/terrorism	2001	continuing
Albania	civil war	southern regions		1996	order restored by UN peacekeepers 1997
Algeria	civil war	general		1992	continuing
Angola	civil war	general		1975	continuing
	regional civil war	Cabinda enclave		1978	continuing
Armenia	interstate war	Nagorno-Karabakh	Azerbaijan	1990	suspended by agreement 1994
Azerbaijan	interstate war	Nagorno-Karabakh	Armenia	1990	suspended by agreement 1994
Bangladesh	regional civil war	Chittagong		1973	suspended by agreement 1992
Bosnia-Herzegovina	civil and interstate war	general		1992	suspended by agreement 1995
Burundi	civil war	general		1988	continuing
Cambodia	civil war	general		1970	suspended by agreement 1992; fighting terminated by 1997–98
Cameroon	interstate war	Bakassi border region	Nigeria	1996	continuing
Chad	civil war	general		1965	continuing
Colombia	civil war	general		1986	continuing
Congo, Republic	civil war	general		1993	suspended by agreement 1994
	civil war	general		1997	continuing
Croatia	civil and interstate war	Slavonia/Krajina	Yugoslavia (Serbia-Montenegro)	1991	suspended by agreement 1992
	regional civil war	Western Slavonia/Krajina		1995	suspended by agreement 1995
Democratic Republic of the Congo (formerly Zaire)	civil war	general		1996	suspended by agreement 1997
	interstate war	general	Uganda, Rwanda, Burundi	1998	continuing
Djibouti	regional civil war	Afar		1991	suspended by agreement 2000
Ecuador	interstate war	border region	Peru	1995	suspended by agreement 1995
Egypt	civil war	general		1992	continuing
El Salvador	civil war	general		1979	suspended by agreement 1979
Eritrea	war of independence	Eritrea	Ethiopia	1962	suspended by agreement 1991
	interstate war	Hanish Islands	Yemen	1997	suspended by agreement 1998
	interstate war	border region with Ethiopia	Ethiopia	1998	suspended by agreement 2000
Ethiopia	against war of independence	Eritrea	Eritrea	1962	suspended by agreement 1991
	civil war	general		1974	suspended by agreement 1991

COUNTRY	TYPE OF WAR	LOCATION OF WAR	ADVERSARIES (in interstate wars)	DATE WAR BEGAN	COMBAT STATUS (1/1/2001)
Ethiopia *(continued)*	interstate war	border region with Eritrea	Eritrea	1998	suspended by agreement 2000
France	interstate war	Kuwait/Iraq		1991	suspended by agreement 1991
Georgia	regional civil war	western region		1991	break in action 1993
	regional civil war	South Ossetia		1991	suspended by agreement 1996
	regional civil war	Abkhazia		1992	suspended by agreement 1994
Ghana	regional civil war	northern regions		1994	break in action 1995
Guatemala	civil war	general		1965	suspended by agreement 1996
Haiti	civil war	general		1991	suspended by U.S./UN intervention 1994
India	interstate war	Jammu-Kashmir	Pakistan	1982	continuing
	regional civil war	Jammu-Kashmir		1990	continuing
	regional civil war	Andhra Pradesh		1969	continuing
	regional civil war	Punjab		1981	break in action 1993
	regional civil war	Assam		1987	continuing
Indonesia	regional civil war	Irian Jaya/West Papua		1963	continuing
	regional civil war	East Timor		1975	suspended by agreement/UN peacekeeping mission 1999
	regional civil war	Ambon		1999	continuing
	regional civil war	Borneo		1999	continuing
	regional civil war	Sumatra (Aceh)		1989	continuing
Iran	civil war	general		1978	break in action 1993
	regional civil war	northwestern Kurdish regions		1979	break in action 1995
Iraq	regional civil war	northern regions/ Kurdistan		1974	continuing
	interstate war	Iraq/Kuwait	Kuwait, France, Saudi Arabia, Syria, United Kingdom, United States	1990	suspended by agreement 1991
	regional civil war	southern Shia regions		1991	continuing
	interstate war	central Iraq	United States and United Kingdom	1998	continuing
Israel	civil war	general, including occupied territories		1948	continuing
Kurdistan	regional civil war	Turkish border region		1991	continuing
	civil war	general		1993	continuing
Kuwait	interstate war	Kuwait/Iraq	Iraq	1990	suspended by agreement 1991
Laos	civil war	general		1975	break in action 1990
	civil war	border region		2000	continuing

Table D (Continued)
Major Armed Conflicts, 1990–2001

COUNTRY	TYPE OF WAR	LOCATION OF WAR	ADVERSARIES (in interstate wars)	DATE WAR BEGAN	COMBAT STATUS (1/1/2001)
Lebanon	general, then regional civil war	southern zone, from 1990		1975	continuing
Liberia	civil war; possibly interstate	general, especially northern regions	Guinea	1989	continuing
Libya	civil war	general		1995	continuing
Mali	regional civil war	northern Tuareg regions		1990	suspended by agreement 1995
Mauritania	interstate war	border regions	Senegal	1989	suspended by agreement 1991
Mexico	regional civil war	Chiapas and other southern states		1994	continuing
Moldova	regional civil war	Trans-Dniestr		1991	suspended by agreement 1997
Morocco	against war of independence	western Sahara	Polisario Front (western Sahara)	1975	break in action 1991
Mozambique	civil war	general		1976	suspended by agreement 1992
Myanmar (Burma)	regional civil war	Kachin		1948	suspended by agreement 1994
	regional civil war	Shan		1948	continuing
	regional civil war	Karen		1949	continuing
	civil war	general		1991	break in action 1992
	regional civil war	Arakan		1992	suspended by agreement 1994
	regional civil war	Kaya		1992	continuing
Nicaragua	civil war	general		1970	suspended by agreement 1992
Niger	regional civil war	northern Tuareg regions		1991	continuing
	regional civil war	eastern region		1994	continuing
Nigeria	interstate war	Bakassi border region	Cameroon	1996	continuing
	regional civil war	Kaduna state		1997	continuing
	interstate war	Sierra Leone	Sierra Leone	1997	suspended by agreement 1999
Pakistan	interstate war	Kashmir	India	1982	continuing
	regional civil war	Karachi/Sind		1992	continuing
Papua New Guinea	regional civil war	Bougainville		1988	cease-fire and break in action 1998
Peru	civil war	general		1980	continuing
	interstate war	border region	Ecuador	1940's (?)	suspended by agreement 1998
Philippines	civil war	general		1969	continuing
	regional civil war	Mindanao		1974	suspended by agreement 2001
Russia	regional civil war	North Ossetia/ Ingushetia		1992	break in action 1992
	regional civil war	Moscow		1993	break in action 1993
	regional civil war	Chechnya		1994	ongoing
Rwanda	civil war	general		1990	break in action 1998

Major Armed Conflicts, 1990–2001

COUNTRY	TYPE OF WAR	LOCATION OF WAR	ADVERSARIES (in interstate wars)	DATE WAR BEGAN	COMBAT STATUS (1/1/2001)
Rwanda, *(continued)*	interstate war	general	Dem. Republic of the Congo, Angola, Namibia, Chad, Zimbabwe	1998	suspended by agreement 1999
Saudi Arabia	interstate war	Kuwait/Iraq	Iraq	1991	suspended by agreement 1991
Senegal	interstate war	border regions	Mauritania	1989	suspended by agreement 1991
	regional civil war	Casamance region		1984	suspended by agreement 2001
Sierra Leone	civil war	general		1991	suspended by agreement 1999; sporadic fighting continues
Slovenia	interstate war	Slovenia	Yugoslavia (Serbia-Montenegro)	1991	suspended by agreement 1991
Somalia	civil war	general		1991	continuing
	regional civil war	Somaliland		1991	break in action 1995
South Africa	civil war	general		1948	suspended by agreement 1994
Spain	regional civil war	Basque region		1968	ongoing
Sri Lanka	regional civil war	Tamil areas/northeast		1977	continuing
Sudan	regional civil war	southern regions		1983	continuing
	regional civil war	Kassala		2000	ongoing
Suriname	civil war	general		1986	suspended by agreement 1992
Syria	interstate war	Kuwait/Iraq	Iraq	1991	suspended by agreement 1991
Tajikistan	civil war	general		1992	continuing
Togo	civil war	general		1991	break in action 1991
Trinidad and Tobago	civil war	general		1990	break in action 1990
Turkey	regional civil war	southeastern Kurdish region/northern Iraq		1977	continuing
	regional civil war	western region		1991	break in action 1992
Uganda	regional civil war	northern region		early 1980's	continuing
	regional civil war	central region		1994	break in action 1995
	regional civil war	southeastern region		1995	break in action 1995
	interstate war	general	Dem. Republic of the Congo, Angola, Namibia, Chad, Zimbabwe	1998	suspended by agreement 1999
United Kingdom	regional civil war	Northern Ireland		1969	suspended by agreement 1994
	interstate war	Kuwait/Iraq	Iraq	1991	suspended by agreement 1991
United States	interstate war	Kuwait/Iraq	Iraq	1991	suspended by agreement 1991
Venezuela	civil war	general		1992	break in action 1992

COUNTRY	TYPE OF WAR	LOCATION OF WAR	ADVERSARIES (in interstate wars)	DATE WAR BEGAN	COMBAT STATUS (1/1/2001)
Yemen	civil war	general		1994	suspended by agreement 1994
Yugoslavia (Serbia-Montenegro)	interstate war	Slovenia	Slovenia	1991	suspended by agreement 1991
	interstate war	Croatia	Croatia	1991	suspended by agreement 1992
	interstate war	Kosovo	NATO countries	1999	suspended by agreement 1999

Sources: The World Factbook 2000 (U.S. CIA, 2001); The Federation of American Scientists Military Analysis Network (2001).

Table E
World Countries: Basic Economic Indicators, 1999

COUNTRY	GROSS NATIONAL INCOME (GNI) 1999 [a, b]		PURCHASING POWER PARITY GNI 1999			AVERAGE ANNUAL % GROWTH IN GDP		STRUCTURE OF ECONOMIC OUTPUT (GDP) 1999 (value added in % of GDP)			
	Total ($US billions)	Per Capita ($US)	Total ($US billions)	Per Capita ($US)	Rank	1980-1990	1990-1999	Agriculture	Industry	Manufacturing	Services
Albania	3.1	930	11	3,240	137	1.5	3.2	53	26	12	21
Algeria	46.5	1,550	145[c]	4,840[c]	105	2.7	1.6	11	51	10	38
Angola	3.3	270	14[c]	1,100[c]	183	3.7	0.4	7	77	4	16
Argentina	276.1	7,550	437	11,940	57	−0.4	4.9	5	28	18	67
Armenia	1.9	490	9	2,360	–	–	−3.2	29	33	23	39
Australia	397.3	20,950	452	23,850	20	3.4	4.1	3	25	13	72
Austria	205.7	25,430	199	24,600	16	2.2	1.9	2	29	19	69
Azerbaijan	3.7	460	20	2,450	145	–	−9.6	23	35	5	41
Bangladesh	47.1	370	196	1,530	167	4.3	4.7	25	24	15	50
Belarus	26.3	2,620	69	6,880	83	–	−3.0	13	42	35	45
Belgium	252.1	24,650	263	25,710	12	2.0	1.7	1	25	18	73
Benin	2.3	380	6	920	189	2.9	4.7	38	14	8	48
Bolivia	8.1	990	19	2,300	150	−0.2	4.2	18	18	15	64
Bosnia-Herzegovina	4.7	1,210	–	–	–	–	35.2	15	27	21	58
Botswana	5.1	3,240	10	6,540	85	10.3	4.3	4	45	5	51
Brazil	730.4	4,350	1,148	6,840	84	2.7	3.0	9	31	23	61
Bulgaria	11.6	1,410	42	5,070	102	3.4	−2.7	15	23	15	62
Burkina Faso	2.6	240	11[c]	960[c]	187	3.6	3.8	31	28	22	40
Burundi	0.8	120	4[c]	570[c]	203	4.4	−2.9	52	17	9	30
Cambodia	3.0	260	16	1,350	174	–	4.8	51	15	6	35
Cameroon	8.8	600	22	1,490	168	3.4	1.3	44	19	10	38
Canada	614.0	20,140	776	25,440	14	3.3	2.7	–	–	–	–
Central African Republic	1.0	290	4[c]	1150[c]	181	1.4	1.8	55	20	9	25
Chad	1.6	210	6[c]	840[c]	191	3.7	2.1	36	15	12	49
Chile	69.6	4,630	126	8,410	72	4.2	7.2	8	34	16	57
China	979.9	780	4,452	3,550	127	10.2	10.7	18	49	38	33
Colombia	90.0	2,170	232	5,580	93	3.6	3.3	13	26	14	61
Congo Republic	1.6	550	2	540	205	3.3	−0.5	10	49	7	41
Costa Rica	12.8	3,570	28	7,880	76	3.0	5.1	11	37	30	53
Côte d'Ivoire	10.4	670	24	1,540	166	0.7	3.7	26	26	21	48
Croatia	20.2	4,530	32	7,260	80	–	0.2	9	32	20	59
Cuba	–	_[g]	–	–	–	–	–	–	–	–	–
Czech Republic	51.6	5,020	132	12,840	54	1.7	0.8	4	43	–	53
Democratic Republic of the Congo (formerly Zaire)	–	_[d]	–	–	–	1.6	−5.1	58	17	–	25
Denmark	170.7	32,050	136	25,600	13	2.3	2.4	2	21	14	76
Dominican Republic	16.1	1,920	44	5,210	100	3.1	5.8	11	34	17	54
Ecuador	16.8	1,360	35	2,820	140	2.0	2.2	12	37	21	50
Egypt	86.5	1,380	217	3,460	128	5.4	4.4	17	32	20	51
El Salvador	11.8	1,920	26	4,260	117	0.2	5.0	10	29	23	60
Eritrea	0.8	200	4	1,040	185	–	5.0	17	29	15	54
Estonia	4.9	3,400	12	8,190	74	2.2	−1.3	6	26	15	69
Ethiopia	6.5	100	39	620	201	2.3	4.6	52	11	7	37
Finland	127.8	24,730	117	22,600	25	3.3	2.4	3	28	21	68
France	1,453.2	24,170	1,349	23,020	23	2.3	1.5	3	23	–	74
Gabon	4.0	3,300	6	5,280	98	0.9	3.2	8	41	5	51
The Gambia	0.4	330	2[c]	1550[c]	164	3.6	2.8	31	13	6	56
Georgia	3.4	620	14	2,540	144	0.4	–	36	13	8	51

-121-

COUNTRY	GROSS NATIONAL INCOME (GNI) 1999 [a, b]		PURCHASING POWER PARITY GNI 1999			AVERAGE ANNUAL % GROWTH IN GDP		STRUCTURE OF ECONOMIC OUTPUT (GDP) 1999 (value added in % of GDP)			
	Total ($US billions)	Per Capita ($US)	Total ($US billions)	Per Capita ($US)	Rank	1980-1990	1990-1999	Agriculture	Industry	Manufacturing	Services
Germany	2,103.8	25,620	1,930	23,510	21	2.2	1.3	1	28	21	71
Ghana	7.5	400	35[c]	1850[c]	161	3.0	4.3	36	25	9	39
Greece	127.6	12,110	166	15,800	48	1.8	2.2	7	20	11	72
Guatemala	18.6	1,680	40	3,630	126	0.8	4.2	23	20	13	57
Guinea	3.6	490	14	1,870	158	–	4.2	24	37	4	39
Guinea-Bissau	0.2	160	1	630	200	4.0	0.3	62	12	10	26
Haiti	3.6	460	11[c]	1470[c]	169	−0.2	−1.3	29	22	7	48
Honduras	4.8	760	14	2,270	151	2.7	3.3	16	32	20	52
Hong Kong, China	165.1	24,570	152	22,570	26	6.9	3.9	0	15	6	85
Hungary	46.8	4,640	111	11,050	60	1.3	1.0	6	34	25	61
India	441.8	440	2,226	2,230	153	5.8	6.0	28	26	16	46
Indonesia	125.0	600	550	2,660	143	6.1	4.7	19	43	25	37
Iran	113.7	1,810	347	5,520	95	1.7	3.6	21	31	17	48
Iraq	–	_g	–	–	–	−6.8	–	–	–	–	–
Ireland	80.6	21,470	84	22,460	27	3.2	6.9	5	34	–	62
Israel	99.6	16,310	110	18,070	40	3.5	5.2	–	–	–	–
Italy	1,162.9	20,170	1,268	22,000	32	2.4	1.4	3	26	19	71
Jamaica	6.3	2,430	9	3,390	130	2.0	0.3	7	32	14	61
Japan	4,054.5	32,030	3,186	25,170	15	4.0	1.3	2	36	24	62
Jordan	7.7	1,630	18	3,880	122	2.5	5.3	2	26	16	72
Kazakhstan	18.7	1,250	71	4,790	106	–	−5.9	11	32	–	57
Kenya	10.7	360	30	1,010	186	4.2	2.2	23	16	11	61
Korea, North	–	_d	–	–	–	–	–	–	–	–	–
Korea, South	397.9	8,490	728	15,530	49	9.4	5.7	5	44	32	51
Kuwait	–	_h	–	–	–	1.3	–	–	–	–	–
Kyrgyzstan	1.5	300	12	2,420	147	–	−5.4	38	27	12	36
Laos	1.5	290	7c	1430[c]	170	–	6.6	53	22	17	25
Latvia	5.9	2,430	15	6,220	89	3.5	−4.8	4	28	15	68
Lebanon	15.8	3,700	–	–	–	–	7.7	12	27	17	61
Lesotho	1.2	550	5[c]	2350[c]	149	4.4	4.4	18	38	–	44
Libya	–	_i	–	–	–	−5.7	–	–	–	–	–
Lithuania	9.8	2,640	24	6,490	86	–	−4.0	9	32	18	59
Macedonia	3.3	1,660	9	4,590	109	–	−0.8	12	35	–	53
Madagascar	3.7	250	12	790	193	1.1	1.7	30	14	11	56
Malawi	2.0	180	6	570	203	2.5	3.6	38	18	14	45
Malaysia	76.9	3,390	173	7,640	78	5.3	7.3	11	46	32	43
Mali	2.6	240	8	740	195	2.8	3.6	47	17	4	37
Mauritania	1.0	390	4	1,550	164	1.8	4.2	25	29	10	46
Mauritius	4.2	3,540	11	8,950	68	6.2	5.1	6	33	25	61
Mexico	428.9	4,440	780	8,070	75	0.7	2.7	5	28	21	67
Moldova	1.5	410	9	2,100	155	3.0	−11.0	25	22	15	53
Mongolia	0.9	390	4	1,610	163	5.4	0.7	32	30	–	39
Morocco	33.7	1,190	94	3,320	134	4.2	2.3	15	33	17	53
Mozambique	3.8	220	14[c]	810[c]	192	−0.1	6.2	33	25	13	42
Myanmar (Burma)	–	_d	–	–	–	0.6	6.3	60	9	7	31
Namibia	3.2	1,890	9[c]	5580[c]	93	0.9	3.4	13	33	15	55
Nepal	5.2	220	30	1,280	176	4.6	4.9	42	21	9	37
Netherlands	397.4	25,140	386	24,410	17	2.3	2.7	3	24	16	74
New Zealand	53.3	13,990	67	17,630	43	1.8	3.1	–	–	–	–

COUNTRY	GROSS NATIONAL INCOME (GNI) 1999 [a, b]		PURCHASING POWER PARITY GNI 1999			AVERAGE ANNUAL % GROWTH IN GDP		STRUCTURE OF ECONOMIC OUTPUT (GDP) 1999 (value added in % of GDP)			
	Total ($US billions)	Per Capita ($US)	Total ($US billions)	Per Capita ($US)	Rank	1980-1990	1990-1999	Agriculture	Industry	Manufacturing	Services
Nicaragua	2.0	410	10c	2060c	156	−2.0	3.2	32	23	14	46
Niger	2.0	190	8c	740c	195	−0.1	2.4	41	17	6	42
Nigeria	31.6	260	95	770	194	1.6	2.4	39	33	5	28
Norway	149.3	33,470	126	28,140	8	2.8	3.8	2	31	–	67
Oman	_i	–	–	8.4	5.9	–	–	–	–		
Pakistan	62.9	470	250	1,860	159	6.3	3.8	27	23	16	49
Panama	8.7	3,080	15c	5450c	96	0.5	4.2	7	17	8	76
Papua New Guinea	3.8	810	11c	2260c	152	1.9	4.7	30	46	8	24
Paraguay	8.4	1,560	23c	4380c	113	2.5	2.4	29	26	14	45
Peru	53.7	2,130	113	4,480	111	−0.3	5.0	7	38	24	55
Philippines	78.0	1,050	296	3,990	120	1.0	3.2	18	30	21	52
Poland	157.4	4,070	324	8,390	73	1.8	4.5	3	31	18	65
Portugal	110.2	11,030	158	15,860	47	3.1	2.5	4	27	–	69
Puerto Rico	–	_i	–	–	–	4.0	3.1	–	–	–	–
Romania	33.0	1,470	134	5,970	90	0.5	−0.8	16	31	22	53
Russia	329.0	2,250	1,022	6,990	82	–	−6.1	7	38	–	56
Rwanda	2.0	250	7	880	190	2.2	−1.5	46	20	12	34
Saudi Arabia	139.4	6,900	223	11,050	60	0.0	1.6	7	48	10	45
Senegal	4.7	500	13	1,400	172	3.1	3.3	18	26	17	56
Sierra Leone	0.7	130	2	440	207	0.3	−4.7	43	27	4	31
Singapore	95.4	24,150	88	22,310	28	6.6	8.0	0	36	26	64
Slovakia	20.3	3,770	56	10,430	64	2.0	1.8	4	32	22	64
Slovenia	19.9	10,000	32	16,050	46	–	2.4	4	38	28	58
South Africa	133.6	3,170	367c	8710c	70	1.2	1.9	4	32	19	64
Spain	583.1	14,800	704	17,850	42	3.0	2.2	4	28	–	69
Sri Lanka	15.6	820	61	3,230	138	4.0	5.3	21	27	16	52
Sudan	9.4	330	–	–	–	0.4	8.2	40	18	9	42
Sweden	236.9	26,750	196	22,150	31	2.3	1.6	–	–	–	–
Switzerland	273.9	38,380	205	28,760	7	2.0	0.6	–	–	–	–
Syria	15.2	970	54	3,450	129	1.5	5.7	–	–	–	–
Tajikistan	1.7	280	–	–	–	–	–	19	25	21	57
Tanzania[j]	8.5[j]	260[j]	16	500	206	_j	2.8	45	15	7	40
Thailand	121.1	2,010	358	5,950	91	7.6	4.7	10	40	32	50
Togo	1.4	310	6	1,380	173	1.7	2.4	41	21	9	38
Trinidad and Tobago	6.1	4,750	10	7,690	77	−0.8	2.7	2	40	8	58
Tunisia	19.8	2,090	54	5,700	92	3.3	4.6	13	28	18	59
Turkey	186.5	2,900	415	6,440	87	5.4	3.8	16	24	15	60
Turkmenistan	3.2	670	16	3,340	132	–	−6.8	27	45	34	28
Uganda	6.8	320	25c	1160c	180	2.9	7.2	44	18	9	38
Ukraine	42.0	840	168	3,360	131	–	−10.7	13	38	33	49
United Arab Emirates	–	–	–	–	–	−3.5	2.9	–	–	–	–
United Kingdom	1,403.8	23,590	1,322	22,220	29	3.2	2.5	1	25	–	74
United States	8,879.5	31,910	8,878	31,910	4	3.0	3.3	–	–	–	–
Uruguay	20.6	6,220	29	8,750	69	0.4	3.8	6	27	17	67
Uzbekistan	17.6	720	54	2,230	153	–	−1.2	33	24	11	43
Venezuela	87.3	3,680	129	5,420	97	1.1	1.7	5	36	14	59
Vietnam	28.7	370	144	1,860	159	4.6	8.1	25	34	18	40
West Bank and Gaza	5.1	1,780	–	–	–	–	3.7	9	29	16	62

COUNTRY	GROSS NATIONAL INCOME (GNI) 1999 [a, b]		PURCHASING POWER PARITY GNI 1999			AVERAGE ANNUAL % GROWTH IN GDP		STRUCTURE OF ECONOMIC OUTPUT (GDP) 1999 (value added in % of GDP)			
	Total ($US billions)	Per Capita ($US)	Total ($US billions)	Per Capita ($US)	Rank	1980-1990	1990-1999	Agriculture	Industry	Manufacturing	Services
Yemen	6.1	360	12	730	197	–	3.2	17	40	11	42
Yugoslavia (Serbia-Montenegro)	_g	–	–	–	–	–	–	–	–	–	
Zambia	3.2	330	7	720	199	1.0	0.2	25	24	12	51
Zimbabwe	6.3	530	32	2,690	141	3.6	2.8	20	25	17	55

a. Calculated using the World Bank Atlas method.
b. Gross National Income (GNI) has replaced GNP in the World Bank Atlas Method's estimate of national income.
c. The estimate is based on regression; others are extrapolated from the latest International Comparison Programme benchmark estimates.
d. Estimated to be low income ($755 or less).
f. GNP data refer to GDP.
g. Estimated to be lower middle income ($756 to $2,995).
h. Estimated to be high income ($9266 or more).
i. Estimated to be upper middle income ($2,996-9,265 to $9,655).
j. Data refer to mainland Tanzania only.

Source: World Development Indicators (World Bank, 2001)

Table F
World Countries: Population Growth, 1950-2025

COUNTRY	POPULATION (thousands)			AVERAGE ANNUAL POPULATION CHANGE (percent)		AVERAGE ANNUAL INCREMENT TO THE POPULATION (mid-year population, in thousands)		
	1950	2000ª	2025ª	1975-1980	1995-00ª	1985-90	1995-2000	2005-2010
WORLD	**2,521,495.0**	**6,055,049.0**	**7,823,703.0**	**1.7**	**1.3**	**85,831.0**		
AFRICA						359.8		
Algeria	8,753	31,471	46,611	3.1	2.3	631.8	566.0	539.3
Angola	4,131	12,878	25,107	2.7	3.2	130.2	187.2	267.5
Benin	2,046	6,097	11,109	2.5	2.7	135.6	184.8	204.6
Botswana	389	1,622	2,242	3.5	1.9	43.3	21.5	−15.4
Burkina Faso	3,654	11,937	23,321	2.5	2.7	233.8	307.0	360.3
Burundi	2,456	6,695	11,569	2.3	1.7	95.2	123.0	166.5
Cameroon	4,466	15,085	26,484	2.8	2.7	326.5	370.9	374.8
Central African Republic	1,314	3,615	5,704	2.3	1.9	57.5	62.0	60.0
Chad	2,658	7,651	13,908	2.1	2.6	171.2	259.8	340.4
Congo (Zaire)	12,184	51,654	104,788	3.0	2.6	1,146.2	1,234.4	1,907.8
Congo Republic	808	2,943	5,689	2.9	2.8	56.3	62.4	67.2
Côte d'Ivoire	2,776	14,786	23,345	3.9	1.8	411.1	350.2	394.2
Egypt	21,834	68,470	95,615	2.4	1.9	1,318.5	1,199.9	1,125.0
Equatorial Guinea	226	453	795	−0.7	2.5	8.7	11.1	13.6
Eritrea	1,140	3,850	6,681	2.6	3.8	35.4	134.9	153.2
Ethiopia	18,434	62,565	115,382	2.4	2.4	1,530.7	1,670.9	1,848.4
Gabon	469	1,226	1,981	3.1	2.6	11.6	13.9	8.6
The Gambia	294	1,305	2,151	3.1	3.2	33.0	42.3	48.0
Ghana	4,900	20,212	36,876	1.9	2.7	435.4	380.2	285.2
Guinea	2,550	7,430	12,497	1.5	0.8	173.7	63.1	193.9
Guinea-Bissau	505	1,213	1,946	4.7	2.2	22.1	28.4	35.1
Kenya	6,265	30,080	41,756	3.8	2.0	723.5	604.9	206.8
Lesotho	734	2,153	3,506	2.5	2.2	41.5	39.6	11.5
Liberia	824	3,154	6,618	3.1	8.2	−2.9	236.3	107.3
Libya	1,029	5,605	8,647	4.4	2.4	92.8	92.2	136.3
Madagascar	4,230	15,942	28,964	2.5	3.0	308.1	433.2	590.5
Malawi	2,881	10,925	19,958	3.3	2.4	416.6	169.9	103.8
Mali	3,520	11,234	21,295	2.1	2.4	164.0	305.1	390.7
Mauritania	825	2,670	4,766	2.5	2.7	47.5	65.2	94.9
Morocco	8,953	28,351	38,670	2.3	1.8	565.7	535.1	515.0
Mozambique	6,198	19,680	30,612	2.8	2.5	78.7	359.2	75.1
Namibia	511	1,726	2,338	2.7	2.2	58.6	33.5	7.5
Niger	2,400	10,730	21,495	3.2	3.2	207.6	259.7	322.0
Nigeria	30,703	111,506	183,041	2.8	2.4	2,530.7	3,225.5	3,161.6
Rwanda	2,120	7,733	12,427	3.3	7.7	187.9	311.1	49.1
Senegal	2,500	9,481	16,743	2.8	2.6	191.6	278.9	336.2
Sierra Leone	1,944	4,854	8,085	2.0	3.0	106.3	143.8	162.5
Somalia	2,264	10,097	21,211	7.0	4.2	45.8	192.4	266.1
South Africa	13,683	40,377	46,015	2.2	1.5	943.4	383.4	−419.6
Sudan	9,190	29,490	46,264	3.1	2.1	634.6	902.5	1,059.5
Tanzania	7,886	33,517	57,918	3.1	2.3	799.7	832.1	970.9
Togo	1,329	4,629	8,482	2.7	2.6	122.0	160.9	115.3
Tunisia	3,530	9,586	12,843	2.6	1.4	168.9	124.3	104.8
Uganda	4,762	21,778	44,435	3.2	2.8	590.9	598.7	877.5

Table F (Continued)
World Countries: Population Growth, 1950-2025

COUNTRY	POPULATION (thousands)			AVERAGE ANNUAL POPULATION CHANGE (percent)		AVERAGE ANNUAL INCREMENT TO THE POPULATION (mid-year population, in thousands)		
	1950	2000^a	2025^a	1975-1980	1995-00^a	1985-90	1995-2000	2005-2010
Zambia	2,440	9,169	15,616	3.4	2.2	210.9	174.1	190.9
Zimbabwe	2,730	11,669	15,092	3.0	1.4	308.9	78.1	−58.6
NORTH AND CENTRAL AMERICA						353.9		
Belize	69	241	370	1.7	2.4	5.0	6.3	7.2
Canada	13,737	31,147	37,896	1.2	1.0	369.8	331.8	289.5
Costa Rica	862	4,023	5,929	3.0	2.5	76.6	65.4	58.0
Cuba	5,850	11,201	11,798	0.9	0.4	93.2	48.4	37.3
Dominican Republic	2,353	8,495	11,164	2.4	1.6	141.1	136.4	147.1
El Salvador	1,951	6,276	9,062	2.1	2.0	87.1	110.8	117.7
Guatemala	2,969	11,385	19,816	2.5	2.6	255.9	317.6	366.3
Haiti	3,261	8,222	11,988	2.1	1.7	111.8	89.1	114.6
Honduras	1,380	6,485	10,656	3.4	2.7	117.2	151.1	134.9
Jamaica	1,403	2,583	3,245	1.2	0.9	18.3	16.8	23.9
Mexico	27,737	98,881	130,196	2.7	1.6	1,594.3	1,572.4	1,425.0
Nicaragua	1,134	5,074	8,696	3.1	2.7	91.0	107.6	100.9
Panama	860	2,856	3,779	2.5	1.6	44.8	39.8	32.5
Trinidad and Tobago	636	1,295	1,493	1.3	0.5	6.5	−4.9	−6.1
United States	157,813	278,357	325,573	0.9	0.8	2,296.3	2,503.8	2,429.2
SOUTH AMERICA								
Argentina	17,150	37,032	47,160	1.5	1.3	445.4	427.4	401.1
Bolivia	2,714	8,329	13,131	2.4	2.3	127.7	155.2	128.3
Brazil	53,975	170,115	217,930	2.4	1.3	2,756.3	1,975.6	1,285.4
Chile	6,082	15,211	19,548	1.5	1.4	212.2	189.7	148.3
Colombia	12,568	42,321	59,758	2.3	1.9	636.0	681.0	630.9
Ecuador	3,387	12,646	17,796	2.8	2.0	262.0	264.1	257.2
Guyana	423	861	1,045	0.7	0.7	−3.2	−3.5	4.1
Paraguay	1,488	5,496	9,355	3.2	2.6	113.5	141.6	162.8
Peru	7,632	25,662	35,518	2.7	1.7	472.9	491.4	432.4
Suriname	215	417	525	−0.5	0.4	3.9	3.3	1.4
Uruguay	2,239	3,337	3,907	0.6	0.7	19.4	23.7	26.7
Venezuela	5,094	24,170	34,775	3.4	2.0	465.5	397.3	351.7
ASIA								
Afghanistan	8,958	22,720	44,934	0.9	2.9	170.3	879.9	724.7
Armenia	1,354	3,520	3,946	1.8	−0.3	−0.7	−13.8	7.6
Azerbaijan	2,896	7,734	9,403	1.6	0.4	103.6	23.6	61.8
Bangladesh	41,783	129,155	178,751	2.8	1.7	2,028.8	2,001.0	2,119.6
Bhutan	734	2,124	3,904	2.3	2.8	34.7	42.4	48.8
Cambodia	4,346	11,168	16,526	−1.8	2.2	313.1	271.6	314.6
China	554,760	1,277,558	1,480,412	1.5	0.9	16,833.4	11,408.3	8,726.8
Georgia	3,527	4,968	5,178	0.7	−1.1	49.9	−53.5	−14.4
India	357,561	1,013,662	1,330,449	2.1	1.6	16,448.0	16,317.4	15,140.5
Indonesia	79,538	212,107	273,442	2.1	1.4	3,283.4	3,702.8	3,388.7
Iran	16,913	67,702	94,463	3.3	1.7	1,632.8	818.3	1,000.3
Iraq	5,158	23,115	41,014	3.3	2.8	488.2	623.7	719.5

COUNTRY	POPULATION (thousands)			AVERAGE ANNUAL POPULATION CHANGE (percent)		AVERAGE ANNUAL INCREMENT TO THE POPULATION (mid-year population, in thousands)		
	1950	2000[a]	2025[a]	1975-1980	1995-00[a]	1985-90	1995-2000	2005-2010
Israel	1,258	6,217	8,277	2.3	2.2	87.4	107.5	73.6
Japan	83,625	126,714	121,150	0.9	0.2	556.6	252.5	−30.4
Jordan	1,237	6,669	12,063	2.3	3.0	126.9	159.4	145.2
Kazakhstan	6,703	16,223	17,698	1.1	−0.3	148.5	−42.0	85.9
Korea, North	9,488	24,039	29,388	1.6	1.6	307.4	27.2	4,294.4
Korea, South	20,357	46,844	52,533	1.6	0.8	943.5	459.2	322.0
Kuwait	152	1,972	2,974	6.2	3.1	81.8	70.6	90.4
Kyrgyzstan	1,740	4,699	6,096	1.9	0.6	76.8	30.0	80.9
Laos	1,755	5,433	9,653	1.2	2.6	110.7	130.3	155.3
Lebanon	1,443	3,282	4,400	−0.7	1.7	11.8	48.7	46.0
Malaysia	6,110	22,244	30,968	2.3	2.0	391.7	436.4	438.2
Mongolia	761	2,662	3,709	2.8	1.6	62.1	37.4	44.4
Myanmar (Burma)	17,832	45,611	58,120	2.1	1.2	452.8	317.4	162.3
Nepal	7,862	23,930	38,010	2.5	2.4	457.5	559.0	616.3
Oman	456	2,542	5,352	5.0	3.3	58.3	80.5	104.3
Pakistan	39,513	156,483	263,000	2.6	2.8	2,984.4	2,984.8	2,936.8
Philippines	20,988	75,967	108,251	2.3	2.1	1,450.5	1,658.1	1,666.1
Saudi Arabia	3,201	21,607	39,965	5.6	3.4	527.8	678.3	922.2
Singapore	1,022	3,567	4,168	1.3	1.4	56.1	134.2	169.1
Sri Lanka	7,678	18,827	23,547	1.7	1.0	234.4	186.9	153.5
Syria	3,495	16,125	26,292	3.1	2.5	391.1	399.2	431.5
Tajikistan	1,532	6,188	8,857	2.8	1.5	149.0	115.3	168.7
Thailand	20,010	61,399	72,717	2.4	0.9	755.5	598.8	468.5
Turkey	20,809	66,591	87,869	2.1	1.7	1,083.1	895.5	732.4
Turkmenistan	1,211	4,459	6,287	2.5	1.8	85.4	83.3	95.8
United Arab Emirates	70	2,441	3,284	14.0	2.0	76.1	38.6	40.0
Uzbekistan	6,314	24,318	33,355	2.6	1.6	473.1	381.7	485.8
Vietnam	29,954	79,832	108,037	2.2	1.6	1,321.7	1,178.3	1,123.4
Yemen	4,316	18,112	38,985	3.2	3.7	436.3	524.0	782.1
EUROPE								
Albania	1,230	3,113	3,820	1.9	−0.4	60.3	50.7	34.4
Austria	6,935	8,211	8,186	−0.1	0.5	32.1	17.8	11.3
Belarus	7,745	10,236	9,496	0.6	−0.3	46.7	−7.5	−1.4
Belgium	8,639	10,161	9,918	0.1	0.1	22.2	20.9	5.3
Bosnia-Herzegovina	2,661	3,972	4,324	0.9	3.0	29.7	96.0	15.5
Bulgaria	7,251	8,225	7,023	0.3	−0.7	−9.9	−95.1	−74.3
Croatia	3,850	4,473	4,193	0.5	−0.1	10.1	−34.6	11.2
Czech Republic	8,925	10,244	9,512	0.6	−0.2	−0.1	−10.6	−14.7
Denmark	4,271	5,293	5,238	0.2	0.3	5.5	20.8	12.0
Estonia	1,101	1,396	1,131	0.6	−1.2	7.0	−10.5	−4.9
Finland	4,009	5,176	5,254	0.3	0.3	16.9	12.3	4.8
France	41,829	59,080	61,662	0.4	0.4	312.8	236.0	142.8
Germany	68,376	82,220	80,238	−0.1	0.1	339.1	229.8	152.4
Greece	7,566	10,645	9,863	1.3	0.3	44.5	22.4	11.0
Hungary	9,338	10,036	8,900	0.3	−0.4	−55.4	−31.4	−31.1
Iceland	143	281	328	0.9	0.9	2.7	1.8	1.1

COUNTRY	POPULATION (thousands)			AVERAGE ANNUAL POPULATION CHANGE (percent)		AVERAGE ANNUAL INCREMENT TO THE POPULATION (mid-year population, in thousands)		
	1950	2000[a]	2025[a]	1975-1980	1995-00[a]	1985-90	1995-2000	2005-2010
Ireland	2,969	3,730	4,404	1.4	0.7	−6.4	37.2	31.9
Italy	47,104	57,298	51,270	0.4	0.0	4.0	74.2	−67.5
Latvia	1,949	2,357	1,936	0.4	−1.5	12.3	−23.5	−12.9
Lithuania	2,567	3,670	3,399	0.7	−0.3	22.2	−10.4	−3.6
Macedonia	1,230	2,024	2,258	1.4	0.6	6.9	11.0	7.2
Moldova	2,341	4,380	4,547	0.9	0.0	49.9	−5.8	16.0
Netherlands	10,114	15,786	15,782	0.7	0.4	92.0	86.6	62.5
Norway	3,265	4,465	4,817	0.4	0.5	17.9	24.4	18.2
Poland	24,824	38,765	39,069	0.9	0.1	178.7	8.5	11.2
Portugal	8,405	9,875	9,348	1.4	0.0	5.1	15.9	9.6
Romania	16,311	22,327	19,945	0.9	−0.4	69.0	−56.3	−49.8
Russia	102,192	146,934	137,933	0.6	−0.2	820.8	−422.7	−281.7
Slovakia	3,463	5,387	5,393	1.0	0.1	23.6	9.3	6.1
Slovenia	1,473	1,986	1,818	1.0	0.0	4.6	3.6	1.2
Spain	28,009	39,630	36,658	1.1	0.0	163.2	49.1	−2.8
Sweden	7,014	8,910	9,097	0.3	0.2	40.5	9.5	0.5
Switzerland	4,694	7,386	7,587	−0.1	0.7	54.8	19.2	7.9
Ukraine	36,906	50,456	45,688	0.4	−0.4	142.7	−432.6	−264.4
United Kingdom	50,616	58,830	59,961	0.0	0.2	189.0	178.9	94.6
Yugoslavia (Serbia-Montenegro)	7,131	10,640	10,844	0.9	0.1	21.0	−5.2	−4.6
OCEANIA								
Australia	8,219	18,886	23,098	0.9	1.0	246.8	209.7	167.0
Fiji	289	817	1,104	1.9	1.2	7.8	11.3	12.8
New Zealand	1,908	3,862	4,695	0.2	1.0	12.3	50.8	38.5
Papua New Guinea	1,613	4,807	7,460	2.5	2.2	89.3	116.4	125.1
Solomon Islands	90	444	817	3.5	3.1	11.0	13.8	14.3
DEVELOPING COUNTRIES	**1,667,848**	**4,746,022**	**6,459,163**	**2.1**	**1.6**			
DEVELOPED COUNTRIES	**852,572**	**1,306,083**	**1,359,258**	**0.6**	**0.3**			

a. Data include projections based on 1990 base year population data.

Sources: United Nations Population Division and International Labour Organisation; *World Resources 2000–2001* (World Resources Institute, Washington, D.C.); U.S. Bureau of the Census International Data Base (2000).

<table>
<tr><th colspan="13" align="center">Table G
World Countries: Basic Demographic Data, 1975–2000</th></tr>
<tr>
<td rowspan="3">COUNTRY</td>
<td colspan="2">CRUDE BIRTHRATE (births per 1,000 population)</td>
<td colspan="2">LIFE EXPECTANCY AT BIRTH (years)</td>
<td colspan="2">LIFE EXPECTANCY OF FEMALES AS A PERCENTAGE OF MALES (years)</td>
<td colspan="2">TOTAL FERTILITY RATE</td>
<td colspan="5">PERCENTAGE OF POPULATION IN SPECIFIC AGE GROUPS</td>
</tr>
<tr>
<td colspan="8"></td>
<td colspan="3">1980</td>
<td colspan="2">2000</td>
</tr>
<tr>
<td>1975–80</td><td>1995-00</td>
<td>1975-80</td><td>1995-00</td>
<td>1975-80</td><td>1995-00</td>
<td>1975-80</td><td>1995-00</td>
<td><15</td><td>15-65</td><td>65</td>
<td><15</td><td>15-65</td><td>>65</td>
</tr>
<tr><td>WORLD</td><td>28.3</td><td>21.6</td><td>59.7</td><td>63.7</td><td>106.0</td><td>107.9</td><td>3.9</td><td>2.8</td><td>35.2</td><td>58.9</td><td>5.9</td><td>30.0</td><td>63.2</td><td>7.0</td></tr>
<tr><td colspan="15"></td></tr>
<tr><td>AFRICA</td><td>46.0</td><td>37.6</td><td>47.9</td><td>50.5</td><td>106.7</td><td>105.6</td><td>6.5</td><td>5.3</td><td>44.7</td><td>52.2</td><td>3.1</td><td></td><td></td><td></td></tr>
<tr><td>Algeria</td><td>45.0</td><td>23.1</td><td>57.5</td><td>69.7</td><td>103.5</td><td>102.9</td><td>7.2</td><td>3.8</td><td>46.5</td><td>49.6</td><td>3.9</td><td>37.0</td><td>60.0</td><td>4.0</td></tr>
<tr><td>Angola</td><td>50.2</td><td>46.9</td><td>40.0</td><td>38.3</td><td>108.1</td><td>106.6</td><td>6.8</td><td>6.7</td><td>44.7</td><td>52.4</td><td>2.9</td><td>48.0</td><td>50.0</td><td>3.0</td></tr>
<tr><td>Benin</td><td>51.4</td><td>44.8</td><td>47.0</td><td>50.2</td><td>108.2</td><td>105.7</td><td>7.1</td><td>5.8</td><td>45.1</td><td>50.8</td><td>4.1</td><td>46.5</td><td>50.7</td><td>2.8</td></tr>
<tr><td>Botswana</td><td>46.6</td><td>29.6</td><td>56.5</td><td>39.3</td><td>106.6</td><td>104.3</td><td>6.4</td><td>4.5</td><td>48.7</td><td>49.3</td><td>2.0</td><td>41.9</td><td>55.6</td><td>2.4</td></tr>
<tr><td>Burkina Faso</td><td>50.8</td><td>45.3</td><td>42.9</td><td>46.7</td><td>106.0</td><td>102.2</td><td>7.8</td><td>6.6</td><td>47.4</td><td>49.8</td><td>2.8</td><td>47.0</td><td>50.3</td><td>2.7</td></tr>
<tr><td>Burundi</td><td>44.7</td><td>40.5</td><td>46.0</td><td>46.2</td><td>107.2</td><td>107.3</td><td>6.8</td><td>6.3</td><td>44.7</td><td>51.8</td><td>3.4</td><td>45.0</td><td>52.3</td><td>2.7</td></tr>
<tr><td>Cameroon</td><td>45.5</td><td>36.6</td><td>48.5</td><td>54.8</td><td>106.4</td><td>105.6</td><td>6.5</td><td>5.3</td><td>44.4</td><td>52.0</td><td>3.6</td><td>43.5</td><td>52.9</td><td>3.6</td></tr>
<tr><td>Central African Republic</td><td>44.1</td><td>37.5</td><td>44.5</td><td>44.0</td><td>111.9</td><td>109.3</td><td>5.9</td><td>5.0</td><td>41.7</td><td>54.4</td><td>4.0</td><td>41.6</td><td>54.4</td><td>4.0</td></tr>
<tr><td>Chad</td><td>44.1</td><td>48.8</td><td>41.0</td><td>50.5</td><td>108.1</td><td>106.5</td><td>5.9</td><td>5.5</td><td>41.9</td><td>54.5</td><td>3.6</td><td>43.0</td><td>53.4</td><td>3.6</td></tr>
<tr><td>Congo Republic</td><td>45.8</td><td>38.6</td><td>48.7</td><td>47.4</td><td>111.3</td><td>110.8</td><td>6.3</td><td>5.9</td><td>45.1</td><td>51.5</td><td>3.4</td><td>45.7</td><td>51.1</td><td>3.3</td></tr>
<tr><td>Cote d'Ivoire</td><td>50.7</td><td>40.8</td><td>47.9</td><td>45.1</td><td>107.1</td><td>102.0</td><td>7.4</td><td>5.1</td><td>46.6</td><td>51.0</td><td>2.5</td><td>43.0</td><td>54.0</td><td>3.0</td></tr>
<tr><td>Dem. Republic of the Congo (formerly Zaire)</td><td>47.8</td><td>46.4</td><td>48.0</td><td>48.8</td><td>107.1</td><td>106.1</td><td>6.5</td><td>6.2</td><td>46.0</td><td>51.1</td><td>2.8</td><td>48.0</td><td>49.1</td><td>2.9</td></tr>
<tr><td>Egypt</td><td>38.9</td><td>25.4</td><td>54.1</td><td>63.3</td><td>104.5</td><td>104.6</td><td>5.3</td><td>3.4</td><td>39.5</td><td>56.5</td><td>4.0</td><td>35.0</td><td>60.5</td><td>4.5</td></tr>
<tr><td>Equatorial Guinea</td><td>42.7</td><td>38.1</td><td>42.0</td><td>53.6</td><td>107.9</td><td>108.3</td><td>5.7</td><td>5.5</td><td>41.0</td><td>54.8</td><td>4.1</td><td>43.1</td><td>52.9</td><td>4.0</td></tr>
<tr><td>Eritrea</td><td>45.1</td><td>42.7</td><td>45.3</td><td>55.8</td><td>106.8</td><td>106.1</td><td>6.1</td><td>5.3</td><td>44.2</td><td>53.1</td><td>2.6</td><td>43.6</td><td>53.3</td><td>3.1</td></tr>
<tr><td>Ethiopia</td><td>49.0</td><td>45.1</td><td>42.0</td><td>45.2</td><td>107.9</td><td>104.7</td><td>6.8</td><td>7.0</td><td>46.1</td><td>51.2</td><td>2.7</td><td>47.1</td><td>50.2</td><td>2.8</td></tr>
<tr><td>Gabon</td><td>32.9</td><td>27.6</td><td>47.0</td><td>50.1</td><td>107.3</td><td>105.8</td><td>4.4</td><td>5.4</td><td>34.4</td><td>59.5</td><td>6.1</td><td>39.8</td><td>54.6</td><td>5.7</td></tr>
<tr><td>The Gambia</td><td>48.8</td><td>42.3</td><td>39.0</td><td>53.2</td><td>108.3</td><td>108.8</td><td>6.5</td><td>5.2</td><td>42.6</td><td>54.4</td><td>2.8</td><td>41.2</td><td>55.5</td><td>3.1</td></tr>
<tr><td>Ghana</td><td>45.1</td><td>29.8</td><td>51.0</td><td>57.4</td><td>106.9</td><td>106.9</td><td>6.5</td><td>5.3</td><td>44.9</td><td>52.3</td><td>2.8</td><td>43.4</td><td>53.6</td><td>3.0</td></tr>
<tr><td>Guinea</td><td>51.6</td><td>40.1</td><td>38.8</td><td>45.6</td><td>102.6</td><td>102.1</td><td>7.0</td><td>6.6</td><td>45.8</td><td>51.6</td><td>2.6</td><td>47.0</td><td>50.4</td><td>2.6</td></tr>
<tr><td>Guinea-Bissau</td><td>42.4</td><td>39.6</td><td>37.5</td><td>49.0</td><td>108.6</td><td>106.9</td><td>5.6</td><td>5.4</td><td>39.0</td><td>57.0</td><td>4.0</td><td>41.7</td><td>54.2</td><td>4.2</td></tr>
<tr><td>Kenya</td><td>53.6</td><td>29.4</td><td>53.4</td><td>48.0</td><td>107.8</td><td>103.9</td><td>8.1</td><td>4.9</td><td>50.1</td><td>46.5</td><td>3.4</td><td>43.4</td><td>53.7</td><td>2.9</td></tr>
<tr><td>Lesotho</td><td>41.9</td><td>31.7</td><td>51.8</td><td>50.8</td><td>107.0</td><td>103.9</td><td>5.7</td><td>4.9</td><td>41.9</td><td>53.9</td><td>4.2</td><td>41.0</td><td>55.0</td><td>4.1</td></tr>
<tr><td>Liberia</td><td>47.4</td><td>47.2</td><td>49.5</td><td>51.0</td><td>106.3</td><td>106.5</td><td>6.8</td><td>6.3</td><td>44.3</td><td>52.0</td><td>3.7</td><td>43.7</td><td>52.7</td><td>3.6</td></tr>
<tr><td>Libya</td><td>47.3</td><td>27.7</td><td>55.8</td><td>75.5</td><td>106.3</td><td>105.8</td><td>7.4</td><td>5.9</td><td>46.7</td><td>51.1</td><td>2.2</td><td>44.7</td><td>52.4</td><td>2.9</td></tr>
<tr><td>Madagascar</td><td>46.9</td><td>42.9</td><td>49.5</td><td>55.0</td><td>106.3</td><td>105.3</td><td>6.6</td><td>5.7</td><td>45.9</td><td>51.4</td><td>2.7</td><td>45.8</td><td>51.6</td><td>2.6</td></tr>
<tr><td>Malawi</td><td>57.2</td><td>38.5</td><td>43.1</td><td>37.6</td><td>103.3</td><td>102.5</td><td>7.6</td><td>6.7</td><td>47.5</td><td>50.3</td><td>2.3</td><td>46.4</td><td>50.9</td><td>2.7</td></tr>
<tr><td>Mali</td><td>50.7</td><td>49.2</td><td>40.0</td><td>46.7</td><td>108.1</td><td>105.8</td><td>7.1</td><td>6.6</td><td>46.8</td><td>50.7</td><td>2.5</td><td>47.2</td><td>50.2</td><td>2.5</td></tr>
<tr><td>Mauritania</td><td>44.7</td><td>43.4</td><td>45.5</td><td>50.8</td><td>107.3</td><td>105.8</td><td>6.5</td><td>5.0</td><td>43.7</td><td>53.3</td><td>3.0</td><td>41.5</td><td>55.2</td><td>3.3</td></tr>
<tr><td>Mauritius</td><td>26.7</td><td>16.7</td><td>64.9</td><td>71.0</td><td>108.3</td><td>..</td><td>3.1</td><td>2.3</td><td>35.6</td><td>60.8</td><td>3.6</td><td>26.6</td><td>67.3</td><td>6.0</td></tr>
<tr><td>Morocco</td><td>39.4</td><td>24.6</td><td>55.8</td><td>69.1</td><td>106.3</td><td>106.1</td><td>5.9</td><td>3.1</td><td>43.2</td><td>52.7</td><td>4.1</td><td>33.8</td><td>61.9</td><td>4.3</td></tr>
<tr><td>Mozambique</td><td>45.4</td><td>38.0</td><td>43.5</td><td>37.5</td><td>107.6</td><td>106.8</td><td>6.5</td><td>6.1</td><td>43.4</td><td>53.4</td><td>3.2</td><td>44.7</td><td>52.1</td><td>3.2</td></tr>
<tr><td>Namibia</td><td>41.9</td><td>35.2</td><td>51.3</td><td>42.5</td><td>105.0</td><td>101.9</td><td>6.0</td><td>4.9</td><td>43.1</td><td>53.4</td><td>3.5</td><td>41.6</td><td>54.6</td><td>3.8</td></tr>
<tr><td>Niger</td><td>59.7</td><td>51.5</td><td>40.5</td><td>41.3</td><td>108.2</td><td>106.4</td><td>8.1</td><td>7.1</td><td>46.8</td><td>50.8</td><td>2.5</td><td>48.6</td><td>49.0</td><td>2.4</td></tr>
<tr><td>Nigeria</td><td>46.6</td><td>40.2</td><td>45.0</td><td>51.6</td><td>107.4</td><td>106.1</td><td>6.5</td><td>6.0</td><td>44.3</td><td>3.1</td><td>2.6</td><td>45.0</td><td>52.1</td><td>2.9</td></tr>
<tr><td>Rwanda</td><td>52.8</td><td>34.8</td><td>45.0</td><td>39.3</td><td>107.4</td><td>107.7</td><td>8.5</td><td>6.0</td><td>48.8</td><td>48.8</td><td>2.4</td><td>44.7</td><td>53.0</td><td>2.4</td></tr>
<tr><td>Senegal</td><td>49.3</td><td>37.9</td><td>42.8</td><td>62.2</td><td>104.8</td><td>105.8</td><td>7.0</td><td>5.6</td><td>45.3</td><td>51.8</td><td>2.8</td><td>43.6</td><td>53.4</td><td>3.0</td></tr>
<tr><td>Sierra Leone</td><td>48.8</td><td>45.6</td><td>35.2</td><td>45.2</td><td>108.9</td><td>108.3</td><td>6.5</td><td>6.1</td><td>43.0</td><td>53.9</td><td>3.1</td><td>43.9</td><td>53.1</td><td>3.0</td></tr>
<tr><td>Somalia</td><td>50.4</td><td>47.7</td><td>42.0</td><td>46.2</td><td>107.9</td><td>108.8</td><td>7.0</td><td>7.0</td><td>46.0</td><td>51.0</td><td>3.0</td><td>48.0</td><td>49.5</td><td>2.6</td></tr>
<tr><td>South Africa</td><td>37.3</td><td>21.6</td><td>55.9</td><td>51.1</td><td>111.3</td><td>111.5</td><td>5.1</td><td>3.8</td><td>40.3</td><td>55.9</td><td>3.9</td><td>36.2</td><td>59.3</td><td>4.5</td></tr>
<tr><td>Sudan</td><td>47.1</td><td>38.6</td><td>46.7</td><td>56.5</td><td>106.2</td><td>103.7</td><td>6.7</td><td>4.6</td><td>44.9</td><td>52.4</td><td>2.7</td><td>38.7</td><td>58.1</td><td>3.2</td></tr>
<tr><td>Swaziland</td><td>46.2</td><td>40.6</td><td>49.9</td><td>40.4</td><td>109.9</td><td>..</td><td>6.5</td><td>4.5</td><td>45.9</td><td>51.3</td><td>2.9</td><td>41.7</td><td>55.6</td><td>2.7</td></tr>
<tr><td>Tanzania</td><td>47.5</td><td>40.2</td><td>49.0</td><td>52.3</td><td>107.2</td><td>104.2</td><td>6.8</td><td>5.5</td><td>47.6</td><td>50.1</td><td>2.3</td><td>45.1</td><td>52.3</td><td>2.6</td></tr>
<tr><td>Togo</td><td>45.2</td><td>38.0</td><td>48.0</td><td>54.7</td><td>107.1</td><td>104.1</td><td>6.6</td><td>6.1</td><td>44.6</td><td>52.3</td><td>3.2</td><td>45.6</td><td>51.3</td><td>3.1</td></tr>
<tr><td>Tunisia</td><td>36.4</td><td>17.4</td><td>60.0</td><td>73.7</td><td>101.7</td><td>104.4</td><td>5.7</td><td>2.9</td><td>41.6</td><td>54.6</td><td>3.8</td><td>32.2</td><td>62.9</td><td>4.9</td></tr>
</table>

COUNTRY	CRUDE BIRTHRATE (births per 1,000 population)		LIFE EXPECTANCY AT BIRTH (years)		LIFE EXPECTANCY OF FEMALES AS A PERCENTAGE OF MALES (years)		TOTAL FERTILITY RATE		PERCENTAGE OF POPULATION IN SPECIFIC AGE GROUPS					
									1980			2000		
	1975–80	1995-00	1975-80	1995-00	1975-80	1995-00	1975-80	1995-00	<15	15-65	65	<15	15-65	>65
Uganda	50.3	48.0	47.0	42.9	107.0	102.5	6.9	7.1	47.8	49.7	2.5	49.1	48.6	2.2
Zambia	51.6	41.9	49.3	37.2	106.9	102.5	7.2	5.5	49.4	48.2	2.4	46.3	51.4	2.3
Zimbabwe	44.2	25.0	53.8	37.8	106.9	102.3	6.6	4.7	47.9	49.5	2.6	43.6	53.7	2.7
NORTH AMERICA	15.1	12.8	73.3	78.3	111.2	108.7	1.8	1.9	22.5	66.4	11.0	21.2	66.4	12.4
Canada	15.4	11.3	74.2	79.4	110.8	107.8	1.8	1.6	22.7	67.9	9.4	19.3	68.1	12.6
United States	15.1	14.2	73.2	77.1	111.2	109.6	1.8	2.0	22.5	66.3	11.2	21.4	66.2	12.4
CENTRAL AMERICA	38.2	24.8	63.7	70.0	110.2	106.7	5.4	3.0	45.1	51.2	3.6	34.8	60.7	4.5
Belize	40.9	32.3	69.7	70.9	102.5	104.1	6.2	3.7	47.2	48.6	4.8	39.7	55.8	4.1
Costa Rica	31.7	20.7	71.0	75.8	106.4	106.7	3.9	3.0	38.9	57.5	3.6	33.1	61.8	5.1
Cuba	17.2	12.7	73.0	76.2	104.8	105.4	2.1	1.6	32.9	60.5	7.6	21.2	69.2	9.6
Dominican Republic	34.9	25.1	62.0	73.2	106.1	105.8	4.7	2.8	42.3	54.6	3.1	33.1	62.5	4.5
El Salvador	41.5	29.0	57.2	69.7	119.5	108.9	5.7	3.1	46.1	50.8	3.1	35.6	59.7	4.7
Guatemala	44.3	35.0	56.4	66.2	107.2	109.8	6.4	4.9	45.9	51.3	2.8	42.9	53.3	3.7
Haiti	36.8	32.0	50.7	49.2	106.3	109.8	5.4	4.6	40.7	54.8	4.4	40.0	56.2	3.8
Honduras	44.9	32.6	57.7	69.9	107.7	105.9	6.6	4.3	47.2	50.1	2.7	41.6	54.9	3.4
Jamaica	28.8	18.5	70.1	75.2	106.3	105.5	4.0	2.4	40.2	53.0	6.8	30.2	53.4	6.4
Mexico	37.1	23.1	65.3	71.5	110.3	107.1	5.3	2.8	45.1	51.1	3.8	33.1	62.1	4.7
Nicaragua	45.7	28.3	57.6	68.7	108.5	107.6	6.4	3.9	47.7	49.8	2.5	40.8	56.0	3.2
Panama	31.0	19.5	69.0	75.5	105.8	105.5	4.1	2.6	40.5	55.0	4.5	31.3	63.7	5.5
Trinidad and Tobago	29.3	13.8	68.3	68.0	107.6	105.5	3.4	2.1	34.2	60.2	5.5	26.1	67.4	6.5
SOUTH AMERICA	32.0	22.1	62.9	70.5	108.8	109.0	4.3	2.5	37.8	57.6	4.6	30.2	64.2	5.6
Argentina	25.7	18.6	68.7	75.0	110.4	110.0	3.4	2.6	30.5	61.4	8.1	27.7	62.6	9.7
Bolivia	41.0	28.1	50.1	63.7	108.8	105.0	5.8	4.4	42.6	53.9	3.5	30.5	56.4	4.0
Brazil	32.6	18.8	61.8	62.9	108.1	112.7	4.3	2.2	38.1	57.8	4.2	28.4	66.4	5.2
Chile	24.0	17.2	67.2	75.7	110.5	108.3	3.0	2.4	33.5	60.9	5.6	28.5	64.4	7.2
Colombia	31.7	22.9	64.0	70.3	107.3	110.4	4.1	2.7	40.0	56.2	3.7	32.5	62.8	4.6
Ecuador	38.2	26.5	61.4	71.1	105.9	107.5	5.4	3.1	42.8	53.2	4.0	33.8	61.5	4.7
Guyana	31.5	17.9	60.7	64.0	108.4	111.4	3.9	2.3	40.8	55.2	4.0	29.9	65.9	4.2
Paraguay	35.9	31.3	66.6	73.7	106.7	107.4	5.2	4.2	42.2	53.3	4.5	39.5	57.0	3.5
Peru	38.0	24.5	58.5	70.0	106.7	107.6	5.4	3.0	41.9	54.5	3.6	33.4	61.8	4.8
Suriname	29.5	21.1	65.1	71.4	107.8	107.3	4.2	2.4	39.7	55.8	4.5	32.3	62.4	5.5
Uruguay	20.3	17.4	69.6	75.2	110.2	111.4	2.9	2.3	26.9	62.5	10.5	23.9	63.5	12.7
Venezuela	34.2	21.1	67.6	73.1	109.1	108.6	4.5	3.0	40.7	56.1	3.2	34.0	61.5	4.4
ASIA	29.6	24.7	58.5	66.4	102.6	106.2	4.2	2.7	37.6	58.0	4.4	30.1	64.1	5.8
Afghanistan	50.8	41.8	40.0	45.9	100.0	102.2	7.2	6.9	43.0	54.5	2.5	41.7	55.6	2.7
Armenia	20.9	11.0	72.3	66.4	109.0	110.0	2.5	1.7	30.4	63.6	6.0	24.5	66.8	8.7
Azerbaijan	24.7	18.1	68.5	62.9	112.1	110.4	3.6	2.3	34.5	60.0	5.4	29.5	63.6	6.9
Bangladesh	47.2	25.4	46.6	60.2	97.9	100.0	6.7	3.1	46.0	50.5	3.4	35.6	61.2	3.3
Bhutan	42.8	36.2	42.6	52.4	104.8	103.3	5.9	5.9	41.3	55.6	3.1	43.0	53.8	3.2
Cambodia	30.0	33.5	31.2	56.5	108.3	107.8	4.1	4.5	39.2	57.9	2.9	40.4	56.6	3.0
China	21.5	16.1	65.3	71.4	103.0	105.8	3.3	1.8	35.5	59.7	4.7	24.9	68.4	6.7
Georgia	18.1	10.9	70.7	64.5	111.9	111.6	2.4	1.9	25.7	65.1	9.1	22.0	65.4	12.6
India	34.7	24.8	52.9	62.5	96.3	101.6	4.8	3.1	38.5	57.4	4.0	32.7	62.3	5.0
Indonesia	35.4	22.6	52.8	68.0	104.9	106.3	4.7	2.6	41.0	55.6	3.3	30.8	64.6	4.7

COUNTRY	CRUDE BIRTHRATE (births per 1,000 population)		LIFE EXPECTANCY AT BIRTH (years)		LIFE EXPECTANCY OF FEMALES AS A PERCENTAGE OF MALES (years)		TOTAL FERTILITY RATE		PERCENTAGE OF POPULATION IN SPECIFIC AGE GROUPS					
									1980			2000		
	1975–80	1995-00	1975-80	1995-00	1975-80	1995-00	1975-80	1995-00	<15	15-65	65	<15	15-65	>65
Iran	44.7	18.3	58.6	69.7	101.4	101.4	6.5	4.8	44.9	51.8	3.3	43.1	52.8	4.1
Iraq	41.9	35.0	61.4	66.5	103.0	104.9	6.6	5.3	46.0	51.3	2.7	41.4	55.5	3.1
Israel	26.0	19.3	73.1	78.6	104.9	105.2	3.4	2.8	33.2	58.2	8.6	28.1	62.4	9.5
Japan	15.2	10.0	75.5	80.7	107.4	107.8	1.8	1.5	23.6	67.4	9.0	15.2	68.3	16.5
Jordan	45.0	26.2	61.2	77.4	106.1	104.3	7.4	5.1	49.4	47.5	3.1	43.3	53.8	2.9
Kazakhstan	24.9	16.8	65.4	63.2	117.1	114.2	3.1	2.3	32.4	61.5	6.1	27.5	65.4	7.1
Korea, North	22.2	20.4	65.8	70.7	110.3	108.7	3.3	2.1	39.5	57.0	3.5	27.3	57.4	5.3
Korea, South	23.9	15.1	64.8	74.4	111.6	110.1	2.9	1.7	34.0	62.2	3.8	21.4	72.0	6.7
Kuwait	40.1	22.0	69.6	76.1	106.2	105.4	5.9	2.8	40.2	58.3	1.4	33.2	64.8	2.0
Kyrgyzstan	29.9	26.3	64.2	63.4	114.2	114.2	4.1	3.2	37.1	57.1	5.8	35.0	59.0	6.0
Laos	45.1	38.3	43.5	53.1	106.9	105.7	6.7	6.7	42.0	55.2	2.8	45.4	51.7	3.0
Lebanon	30.1	20.3	65.0	71.2	106.2	105.8	4.3	2.8	40.1	54.5	5.4	32.9	61.3	5.8
Malaysia	30.4	25.3	65.3	70.8	105.7	105.7	4.2	3.2	39.3	57.0	3.7	35.3	60.6	4.1
Mongolia	39.2	21.8	56.3	63.9	104.5	104.6	6.7	3.3	43.2	53.9	2.9	36.4	59.8	3.8
Myanmar (Burma)	37.5	20.6	51.2	54.9	106.4	105.0	5.3	3.3	39.6	56.4	4.0	34.0	61.4	4.6
Nepal	43.4	33.8	46.2	57.8	96.6	98.2	6.2	5.0	42.9	54.1	3.0	42.0	54.5	3.5
Oman	46.1	38.1	54.9	71.8	104.3	105.8	7.2	7.2	44.6	52.8	2.6	47.7	49.9	2.3
Pakistan	47.3	32.1	53.4	61.1	101.3	103.1	7.0	5.0	44.4	52.7	2.9	41.8	55.0	3.2
Philippines	35.9	27.9	59.9	67.5	105.5	104.4	5.0	3.6	41.9	55.3	2.8	36.7	59.7	3.6
Saudi Arabia	45.9	37.5	58.8	67.8	104.0	104.2	7.3	5.9	44.3	52.9	2.8	40.7	56.4	2.9
Singapore	17.2	12.8	70.8	80.0	106.6	105.3	1.9	1.8	27.0	68.2	4.7	22.6	70.3	7.1
Sri Lanka	28.5	16.8	66.8	71.8	105.4	105.6	3.8	2.1	35.3	60.4	4.3	26.2	67.2	6.6
Syria	46.0	31.1	60.1	68.5	106.2	105.9	7.4	4.0	48.5	48.3	3.2	40.8	56.1	3.1
Tajikistan	37.2	33.6	64.5	64.1	108.3	109.3	5.9	3.9	42.9	52.5	4.6	36.5	55.9	4.6
Thailand	31.6	16.9	61.2	68.5	106.6	109.0	4.3	1.7	40.0	56.5	3.5	25.2	69.1	5.8
Turkey	32.0	18.6	60.3	71.0	107.8	107.4	4.5	2.5	39.2	56.0	4.7	28.3	65.7	5.9
Turkmenistan	35.3	28.9	61.6	60.9	11.2	111.2	5.3	3.6	41.3	54.4	4.3	37.4	58.3	4.2
United Arab Emirates	30.5	18.0	66.8	74.1	106.5	102.7	5.7	3.5	28.6	70.1	1.3	28.1	69.4	2.5
Uzbekistan	34.4	26.2	65.1	63.7	111.0	110.9	5.1	3.5	40.9	54.0	5.1	37.5	57.9	4.6
Vietnam	38.3	21.6	55.8	69.3	108.2	107.7	5.6	3.0	42.5	52.7	4.8	34.3	60.5	5.2
Yemen	53.7	43.4	44.1	59.8	101.1	101.7	7.6	7.6	50.2	47.2	2.6	48.3	49.3	2.3
EUROPE	14.8	11.0	71.3	74.3	111.4	110.6	2.0	1.5	22.2	65.5	12.3	17.5	67.9	14.6
Albania	30.3	19.5	68.9	71.6	106.6	108.6	4.2	2.6	35.9	58.9	5.2	29.7	64.4	6.0
Austria	11.5	9.9	72.0	77.7	110.4	108.1	1.7	1.4	20.4	64.2	15.4	17.1	68.5	14.4
Belarus	16.1	9.3	71.1	68.0	114.7	119.3	2.1	1.4	22.9	66.4	10.7	18.8	67.3	13.8
Belgium	12.4	10.9	72.3	77.8	109.6	109.4	1.7	1.6	20.2	65.5	14.3	17.4	66.2	16.4
Bosnia-Herzegovina	19.6	12.9	69.9	71.5	107.0	107.0	2.2	1.4	27.3	66.7	6.1	18.9	71.2	9.8
Bulgaria	15.8	8.1	71.3	70.9	107.9	110.2	2.2	1.5	22.1	66.0	11.9	16.9	67.2	15.8
Croatia	15.6	12.8	70.6	73.7	110.4	111.6	2.0	1.6	21.2	67.2	11.7	17.3	68.0	14.6
Czech Republic	17.4	9.1	70.6	74.5	110.4	111.0	2.3	1.4	23.5	63.2	13.4	17.6	69.8	12.6
Denmark	12.3	12.2	74.2	76.5	108.4	106.8	1.7	1.8	20.8	64.7	14.4	18.6	66.7	14.7
Estonia	15.0	8.4	69.7	69.5	115.3	119.0	2.1	1.3	21.7	65.8	12.5	17.6	68.5	13.9
Finland	13.6	10.8	72.7	77.4	112.6	110.9	1.6	1.8	20.3	67.7	12.0	18.4	67.1	14.6
France	14.0	12.3	73.7	78.8	111.6	110.8	1.9	1.6	22.3	63.8	14.0	18.3	65.4	16.2
Germany	10.4	9.3	72.5	77.4	109.4	108.1	1.5	1.3	18.5	65.9	15.6	15.4	68.8	15.9
Greece	15.6	9.8	73.7	78.4	105.7	106.5	2.3	1.4	22.8	64.0	13.1	15.3	66.9	17.8
Hungary	16.2	9.3	69.4	71.4	109.8	111.9	2.1	14.0	21.9	64.6	13.4	17.0	68.5	14.5
Iceland	19.2	14.9	76.3	79.4	108.0	105.1	2.3	2.2	27.6	62.7	10.1	23.8	64.9	11.3

COUNTRY	CRUDE BIRTHRATE (births per 1,000 population)		LIFE EXPECTANCY AT BIRTH (years)		LIFE EXPECTANCY OF FEMALES AS A PERCENTAGE OF MALES (years)		TOTAL FERTILITY RATE		PERCENTAGE OF POPULATION IN SPECIFIC AGE GROUPS					
									1980			2000		
	1975–80	1995-00	1975-80	1995-00	1975-80	1995-00	1975-80	1995-00	<15	15-65	65	<15	15-65	>65
Ireland	21.2	14.5	72.0	76.8	107.2	106.7	3.5	1.8	30.6	58.7	10.7	21.2	67.5	11.4
Italy	13.0	9.1	73.6	79.0	109.2	108.0	1.9	1.2	22.3	64.6	13.1	14.2	68.1	17.7
Latvia	14.0	7.8	69.2	68.4	115.6	119.3	2.0	1.4	20.4	66.5	13.0	18.2	67.5	14.4
Lithuania	15.4	9.8	70.8	69.1	114.2	118.7	2.1	1.5	23.6	65.1	11.3	19.5	67.0	13.5
Macedonia	22.6	13.7	69.6	73.8	105.2	105.6	2.7	1.9	28.6	64.5	6.9	22.3	68.3	9.4
Moldova	19.6	12.9	64.8	64.5	111.2	112.5	2.4	1.8	26.7	65.5	7.8	23.4	66.8	9.8
Netherlands	12.7	12.1	75.3	78.3	109.0	108.0	1.6	1.6	22.3	66.2	11.5	18.2	68.2	13.6
Norway	12.9	12.8	75.3	78.7	108.9	108.0	1.8	1.9	22.2	63.1	14.8	19.8	65.1	15.0
Poland	19.2	10.1	70.9	73.2	111.9	113.2	2.3	1.7	24.3	65.6	10.1	19.8	68.4	11.8
Portugal	18.2	11.5	70.2	75.8	110.6	109.7	2.4	1.5	25.9	63.6	10.5	16.7	67.5	15.7
Romania	19.1	10.8	69.6	69.9	107.0	112.1	2.6	1.4	26.7	63.1	10.3	18.5	68.4	13.2
Russia	15.8	9.0	67.4	67.2	118.1	119.6	1.9	1.4	21.6	68.1	10.2	18.0	69.3	12.7
Slovakia	20.6	10.0	70.4	73.7	110.9	111.5	2.5	1.5	26.1	63.5	10.4	20.0	68.8	11.1
Slovenia	16.6	9.3	71.0	74.9	111.6	109.8	2.2	1.3	23.4	65.3	11.4	15.7	70.2	14.2
Spain	17.4	9.2	74.3	78.8	108.4	109.3	2.6	1.2	26.6	62.7	10.7	15.0	68.4	16.5
Sweden	11.7	10.0	75.2	79.6	109.3	106.6	1.7	1.8	19.6	64.1	16.3	19.2	64.3	16.7
Switzerland	11.6	10.4	75.2	79.6	109.2	109.3	1.5	1.5	19.7	66.4	13.8	17.2	68.1	14.7
Ukraine	14.9	9.0	69.3	66.0	114.8	115.6	2.0	1.4	21.4	66.7	11.9	17.8	67.9	14.3
United Kingdom	12.4	11.7	72.8	77.7	109.0	106.6	1.7	1.7	20.9	64.0	15.1	18.9	65.5	15.8
Yugoslavia (Serbia-Montenegro)	18.4	13.5	70.3	73.9	106.5	107.1	2.4	1.8	24.1	66.1	9.8	19.8	66.9	13.3
OCEANIA	20.9	23.7	68.2	72.0	108.7	106.7	2.8	2.5	29.3	62.7	8.0	25.5	64.9	9.7
Australia	16.0	13.0	73.4	79.8	109.8	108.0	2.1	1.9	25.3	65.1	9.6	21.0	67.1	11.9
Fiji	33.2	23.5	67.1	67.9	105.3	105.6	4.0	2.8	39.1	58.0	2.8	31.3	64.3	4.5
New Zealand	17.2	14.3	72.4	77.8	109.2	108.1	2.2	2.0	26.7	63.3	10.0	23.0	65.6	11.3
Papua New Guinea	39.6	32.7	49.7	63.1	101.0	103.5	5.9	4.7	43.0	55.5	1.6	38.7	58.3	3.0
Solomon Islands	45.0	34.8	65.3	71.3	106.2	105.7	7.1	5.0	47.6	49.3	3.1	43.0	54.1	2.9
DEVELOPING COUNTRIES	32.8	24.1	56.7	62.3	103.8	104.8	4.7	3.1	39.3	56.6	4.1	32.8	62.2	5.0
DEVELOPED COUNTRIES	14.9	11.2	72.2	75.9	110.8	111.2	1.9	1.6	22.5	65.9	11.6	18.3	67.5	14.2

Sources: United Nations Population Division World Resources 2000–2001; U.S. Bureau of the Census International Database (2000).

Table H
World Countries: Mortality, Health, and Nutrition, 1980–1999

COUNTRY	MORTALITY						HEALTH			NUTRITION	
	Infant Mortality		Adult Mortality								
	Infant Mortality (per 1,000 live births)	Under-five Mortality (per 1,000)	Male (per 1,000)		Female (per 1,000)		Health Expenditure Per Capita ($US) 1990-1998[a]	Physicians Per 1,000 People 1990-1998[a]	Hospital Beds Per 1,000 People 1990-1998[a]	Average daily per capita supply of calories (kilocalories)[c] 1987	Average daily per capita supply of calories (kilocalories)[c] 1997
	1999	1999	1980	1999	1980	1999					
Albania	24	–	140	175	82	84	36	1.4	3.2	2,556	2,961
Algeria	34	39	226	153	197	117	68	1.0	2.1	2,757	2,853
Angola	127	208	569	427	458	375	–	0.0[b]	1.3	2,063	2,183
Argentina	18	22	205	160	102	78	852	2.7	3.3	3,096	3,093
Armenia	14	18	158	159	85	77	27	3.0	0.7	–	2,371
Australia	5	5	178	108	85	55	1,692	2.5	8.5	3,159	3,224
Austria	4	5	197	121	92	59	2,162	3.0	8.9	3,419	3,536
Azerbaijan	16	21	262	205	127	98	9	3.8	9.7	–	2,236
Bangladesh	61	89	383	276	388	290	12	0.2	0.3	2,062	2,086
Belarus	11	14	255	335	95	115	83	4.3	12.2	–	3,226
Belgium	5	6	173	129	90	61	2,184	3.4	7.2	3,454	3,619
Benin	87	145	486	371	397	312	12	0.1	0.2	1,961	2,487
Bolivia	59	83	357	261	273	210	69	1.3	1.7	2,153	2,174
Bosnia-Herzegovina	13	18	181	166	108	90	–	0.5	1.8	–	2,266
Botswana	58	95	341	786	278	740	127	0.2	1.6	2,337	2,183
Brazil	32	40	221	256	161	139	309	1.3	3.1	2,745	2,974
Bulgaria	14	17	190	221	106	109	69	3.5	10.6	3,699	2,686
Burkina Faso	105	210	467	551	362	522	10	0.0[b]	1.4	2,181	2,121
Burundi	105	176	489	582	400	546	5	0.1	0.7	2,023	1,685
Cambodia	100	143	473	364	355	315	17	0.1	2.1	1,868	2,048
Cameroon	77	154	489	477	415	419	31	0.1	2.6	2,178	2,111
Canada	5	6	161	106	85	53	1,824	2.1	4.2	3,105	3,119
Central African Republic	96	151	540	608	424	555	9	0.1	0.9	1,914	2,016
Chad	101	189	556	438	449	383	7	0.0[b]	0.7	1,596	2,032
Chile	10	12	218	140	120	72	289	1.1	2.7	2,518	2,796
China	30	37	185	164	148	129	33	2.0	2.9	2,608[d]	2,897[d]
Colombia	23	28	237	210	162	115	227	1.1	1.5	2,341	2,597
Congo Republic	89	144	408	487	298	414	41	0.3	3.4	2,326	2,144
Costa Rica	12	14	159	116	100	68	267	0.9	1.7	2,717	2,649
Côte d'Ivoire	111	180	421	524	346	497	29	0.1	0.8	2,677	2,610
Croatia	8	9	233	194	106	76	428	2.0	5.9	–	2,445
Cuba	7	8	135	123	94	78	83	5.3	5.1	3,125	2,480
Czech Republic	5	5	225	173	102	81	392	3.0	8.7	–	3,244
Democratic Republic of the Congo (formerly Zaire)	85	161	–	515	–	482	–	0.1	1.4	2,132	1,755
Denmark	5	6	163	140	102	79	2,732	2.9	4.6	3,211	3,407
Dominican Republic	39	47	183	156	138	104	93	2.2	1.5	2,330	2,288
Ecuador	28	35	229	176	176	138	59	1.7	1.6	2,430	2,679
Egypt	47	61	257	193	204	168	48	1.6	2.1	3,120	3,287
El Salvador	30	36	410	207	178	125	143	1.0	1.6	2,312	2,562
Eritrea	60	105	–	484	–	431	–	0.0[b]	–	–	1,622
Estonia	10	12	291	288	110	94	219	3.1	7.4	–	2,849
Ethiopia	104	180	491	567	401	523	4	0.0[b]	0.2	1,677	1,858
Finland	4	5	206	136	74	59	1,722	3.0	7.8	2,941	3,100

-133-

COUNTRY	MORTALITY						HEALTH			NUTRITION	
	Infant Mortality		Adult Mortality								
	Infant Mortality (per 1,000 live births)	Under-five Mortality (per 1,000)	Male (per 1,000)		Female (per 1,000)		Health Expenditure Per Capita ($US) 1990-1998[a]	Physicians Per 1,000 People 1990-1998[a]	Hospital Beds Per 1,000 People 1990-1998[a]	Average daily per capita supply of calories (kilocalories)[c] 1987	Average daily per capita supply of calories (kilocalories)[c] 1997
	1999	1999	1980	1999	1980	1999					
France	5	5	190	124	85	50	2,377	3.0	8.5	3,543	3,518
Gabon	84	133	474	386	387	344	121	0.2	3.2	2,460	2,556
The Gambia	75	110	584	411	466	349	13	0.0[b]	0.6	2,498	2,350
Georgia	15	20	210	192	94	81	14	3.8	4.8	–	2,614
Germany	5	5	177	131	90	66	2,769	3.5	9.3	3,478	3,382
Ghana	57	109	400	316	334	272	19	–	1.5	1,979	2,611
Greece	6	7	134	114	86	61	957	4.0	5.0	3,481	3,649
Guatemala	40	52	336	288	266	186	78	0.9	1.0	2,384	2,339
Guinea	96	167	589	442	507	438	19	0.2	0.6	2,060	2,232
Guinea-Bissau	127	214	535	474	517	421	–	0.2	1.5	2,378	2,430
Haiti	70	118	348	438	275	344	21	0.2	0.7	1,848	1,869
Honduras	34	46	306	184	237	113	74	0.8	1.1	2,206	2,403
Hong Kong, China	3	5	150	106	87	54	1,134	1.3	–	–	–
Hungary	8	10	270	–	130	–	290	3.5	8.3	3,768	3,313
India	71	90	261	218	279	206	20	0.4	0.8	2,228	2,496
Indonesia	42	52	368	235	308	183	8	0.2	0.7	2,458	2,886
Iran	26	33	221	156	190	139	128	0.8	1.6	2,659	2,836
Iraq	101	128	207	196	191	169	–	0.6	1.5	3,418	2,619
Ireland	6	7	175	124	103	71	1,428	2.2	3.7	3,623	3,565
Israel	6	8	138	110	85	67	1,607	4.6	6.0	3,075	3,278
Italy	5	6	163	116	80	54	1,701	5.9	6.5	3,512	3,507
Jamaica	20	24	186	137	121	84	157	1.3	2.1	2,630	2,553
Japan	4	4	129	97	70	45	2,284	1.9	16.5	2,870	2,932
Jordan	26	31	–	156	–	118	123	1.7	1.8	2,780	3,014
Kazakhstan	22	28	312	380	140	166	86	3.5	8.5	–	3,085
Kenya	76	118	417	591	339	546	31	0.1	1.6	2,025	1,977
Korea, North	58	93	270	311	156	208	–	–	–	2,509	1,837
Korea, South	8	9	270	198	156	93	349	1.3	5.1	3,110	3,155
Kuwait	11	13	172	122	116	64	551	1.9	2.8	3,021	3,096
Kyrgyzstan	26	38	296	300	131	138	15	3.1	9.5	–	2,447
Laos	93	143	531	376	439	317	7	0.2	2.6	2,102	2,108
Latvia	14	18	281	297	106	98	167	3.4	10.3	–	2,864
Lebanon	26	32	241	175	181	132	361	2.3	2.7	3,040	3,277
Lesotho	92	141	371	518	279	486	–	0.1	–	2,216	2,244
Libya	22	28	276	183	218	125	–	1.3	4.3	3,308	3,289
Lithuania	9	12	243	261	92	86	183	3.9	9.6	–	3,261
Macedonia	16	17	–	160	–	102	113	2.3	5.2	–	2,664
Madagascar	90	149	353	327	278	287	5	0.3	0.9	2,292	2,022
Malawi	132	227	429	548	349	541	10	0.0[b]	1.3	2,027	2,043
Malaysia	8	10	230	183	149	111	81	0.5	2.0	2,616	2,977
Mali	120	223	454	470	362	406	11	0.1	0.2	1,967	2,030
Mauritania	88	142	505	346	416	294	19	0.1	0.7	2,509	2,622
Mauritius	19	23	277	207	181	113	120	0.9	3.1	–	–
Mexico	29	36	205	166	121	104	202	1.6	1.1	3,022	3,097
Moldova	17	22	289	310	173	173	33	3.6	12.1	–	2,567

COUNTRY	MORTALITY						HEALTH			NUTRITION	
	Infant Mortality		Adult Mortality								
	Infant Mortality (per 1,000 live births)	Under-five Mortality (per 1,000)	Male (per 1,000)		Female (per 1,000)		Health Expenditure Per Capita ($US)	Physicians Per 1,000 People	Hospital Beds Per 1,000 People	Average daily per capita supply of calories (kilocalories)[c]	Average daily per capita supply of calories (kilocalories)[c]
	1999	1999	1980	1999	1980	1999	1990-1998[a]	1990-1998[a]	1990-1998[a]	1987	1997
Mongolia	58	73	320	199	273	168	24	2.6	11.5	2,034	1,917
Morocco	48	62	264	199	207	145	49	0.4	1.0	3,047	3,078
Mozambique	131	203	468	580	361	514	8	–	0.9	1,785	1,832
Myanmar (Burma)	77	120	284	278	313	228	102	0.3	0.6	2,697	2,862
Namibia	63	108	427	524	366	475	143	0.2	–	2,199	2,183
Nepal	75	109	376	264	395	275	11	0.0[b]	0.2	2,144	2,366
Netherlands	5	5	133	112	74	62	2,140	2.6	11.3	3,076	3,284
New Zealand	5	6	177	126	91	66	1,128	2.3	6.2	3,201	3,395
Nicaragua	34	43	277	200	189	137	54	0.8	1.5	2,330	2,186
Niger	116	252	562	468	453	374	5	0.0[b]	0.1	2,033	2,097
Nigeria	83	151	535	444	453	390	30	0.2	1.7	2,103	2,735
Norway	4	4	144	111	71	58	2,953	2.5	14.7	3,304	3,357
Oman	17	24	389	139	326	103	–	1.3	2.2	–	–
Pakistan	90	126	283	186	291	153	18	0.6	0.7	2,224	2,476
Panama	20	25	–	140	–	83	246	1.7	2.2	2,302	2,430
Papua New Guinea	58	77	514	369	478	330	27	0.1	4.0	2,137	2,224
Paraguay	24	27	198	185	144	130	86	1.1	1.3	2,564	2,566
Peru	39	48	287	199	229	140	141	0.9	1.5	2,276	2,302
Philippines	31	41	323	193	259	146	33	0.1	1.1	2,244	2,366
Poland	9	10	254	227	105	88	264	2.3	5.3	3,441	3,366
Portugal	6	6	199	152	95	70	803	3.1	4.0	3,400	3,667
Puerto Rico	10	–	159	152	78	58	–	1.8	3.3	–	–
Romania	20	24	216	262	119	119	63	1.8	7.6	2,944	3,253
Russia	16	20	341	382	120	138	133	4.6	12.1	–	2,904
Rwanda	123	203	503	604	409	566	10	0.0[b]	1.7	2,042	2,057
Saudi Arabia	19	25	283	160	241	129	611	1.7	2.3	2,488	2,783
Senegal	67	124	586	459	516	389	23	0.1	0.4	2,104	2,418
Sierra Leone	168	283	540	544	527	483	8	–	–	2,126	2,035
Singapore	3	4	199	130	115	72	841	1.4	3.6	–	–
Slovakia	8	10	226	206	105	87	285	3.0	7.5	–	2,984
Slovenia	5	6	250	165	105	72	746	2.1	5.7	–	3,101
South Africa	62	76	–	601	–	533	230	0.6	–	2,976	2,990
Spain	5	6	144	127	69	55	1,043	4.2	3.9	3,150	3,310
Sri Lanka	15	19	210	150	152	96	26	0.2	2.7	2,253	2,302
Sudan	67	109	537	384	462	338	126	0.1	1.1	2,208	2,395
Sweden	4	4	142	1,010	76	57	2,146	3.1	3.8	2,898	3,194
Switzerland	5	5	145	104	70	49	3,835	1.9	18.1	3,358	3,223
Syria	26	30	–	202	–	135	116	1.3	1.4	3,166	3,352
Tajikistan	20	34	190	232	129	140	13	2.1	8.8	–	2,001
Tanzania	95	152	451	542	370	500	8	0.0[b]	0.9	2,288	1,995
Thailand	28	33	280	240	210	147	112	0.4	2.0	2,133	2,360
Togo	77	143	457	478	375	435	8	0.1	1.5	1,946	2,469
Trinidad and Tobago	16	20	234	180	166	132	204	0.8	5.1	2,975	2,661
Tunisia	24	30	227	159	224	133	108	0.7	1.7	3,067	3,283
Turkey	36	45	–	177	–	145	177	1.2	2.5	3,496	3,525

Table H (Continued)
World Countries: Mortality, Health, and Nutrition, 1980–1999

COUNTRY	MORTALITY						HEALTH			NUTRITION	
	Infant Mortality		Adult Mortality								
	Infant Mortality (per 1,000 live births)	Under-five Mortality (per 1,000)	Male (per 1,000)		Female (per 1,000)		Health Expenditure Per Capita ($US)	Physicians Per 1,000 People	Hospital Beds Per 1,000 People	Average daily per capita supply of calories (kilocalories)[c]	Average daily per capita supply of calories (kilocalories)[c]
	1999	1999	1980	1999	1980	1999	1990-1998[a]	1990-1998[a]	1990-1998[a]	1987	1997
Turkmenistan	33	45	263	281	154	158	31	0.2	11.5	–	2,306
Uganda	88	162	463	597	395	590	18	0.0[b]	0.9	2,113	2,085
Ukraine	14	17	282	346	112	134	42	4.5	11.8	–	2,795
United Arab Emirates	8	9	153	125	106	92	1,428	1.8	2.6	3,038	3,390
United Kingdom	6	6	160	119	96	66	1,597	1.7	4.2	3,215	3,276
United States	7	8	194	143	102	78	4,108	2.7	3.7	3,430	3,699
Uruguay	15	17	176	168	91	74	621	3.7	4.4	2,613	2,816
Uzbekistan	22	29	219	227	116	125	–	3.3	8.3	–	2,433
Venezuela	20	23	219	155	123	88	171	2.4	1.5	2,602	2,321
Vietnam	37	42	262	205	204	144	18	0.6	1.7	2,193	2,484
West Bank and Gaza	23	26	–	164	–	106	81	0.5	1.2	–	–
Yemen	79	97	382	307	304	283	18	0.2	0.6	2,126	2,051
Yugoslavia (Serbia-Montenegro)	12	16	164	176	106	106	–	2.0	5.3	–	3,031
Zambia	114	187	482	607	413	597	23	0.1	–	2,017	1,970
Zimbabwe	70	118	389	569	321	526	49	0.1	0.5	2,112	2,145

Sources: *World Development Indicators* (World Bank, Washington, DC, 2001); *World Resources 2000–2001* (World Resources Institute, Washington, DC)

a. Data are for the most recent year available
b. Less than 0.05
c. Has replaced calories available as a percentage of need as a benchmark for nutrition.
d. Data for China include Taiwan

Table I
World Countries: Education and Literacy, 1990–1999

COUNTRY	EDUCATIONAL INPUTS					OUTCOMES							
	Public Expenditure on Education 1994–1997[b] (% of GNI[c])	Primary Pupil-Teacher Ratio 1997 (pupils per teacher)	Primary School Enrollment 1997 (% of age group)[1]	Secondary School Enrollment 1997 (% of age group)[1]	Tertiary School Enrollment 1997 (% of age group)[1]	ADULT ILLITERACY (% above age 15)				YOUTH ILLITERACY (% aged 15–24)			
						Male		Female		Male		Female	
						1990	1999	1990	1999	1990	1999	1990	1999
Albania	3.1	18	107	38	12	14	9	32	23	3	1	7	3
Algeria	5.1	27	108	63	12	32	23	59	44	13	8	32	16
Angola	–	29	–	–	–	–	–	–	–	–	–	–	–
Argentina	3.5	17	111	73	36	4	3	4	3	2	2	2	1
Armenia	2.0	19	87	90	12	1	1	4	3	0[a]	0[a]	1	0[a]
Australia	5.4	18	101	153[d]	80	–	–	–	–	–	–	–	–
Austria	5.4	12	100	103	48	–	–	–	–	–	–	–	–
Azerbaijan	3.0	20	106	77	17	–	–	–	–	–	–	–	–
Bangladesh	2.2	–	–	–	–	54	48	77	71	45	40	68	61
Belarus	5.9	19	98	93	44	0[a]	0[a]	1	1	0[a]	0[a]	0[a]	0[a]
Belgium	3.1	12	103	146[d]	56	–	–	–	–	–	–	–	–
Benin	3.2	50	78	18	3	59	45	84	76	37	23	74	63
Bolivia	4.9	–	–	–	–	13	8	30	21	4	2	11	7
Bosnia-Herzegovina	–	–	–	–	–	–	–	–	–	–	–	–	–
Botswana	8.6	28	108	65	6	34	26	30	21	21	16	13	8
Brazil	5.1	24	125	62	15	18	15	20	15	12	10	9	6
Bulgaria	3.2	17	99	77	41	2	1	4	2	1	0[a]	1	1
Burkina Faso	1.5	47	40	–	1	75	67	92	87	64	55	86	78
Burundi	4.0	42	51	7	–	50	44	73	61	42	36	55	40
Cambodia	2.9	44	113	24	1	49	41	86	79	34	25	73	59
Cameroon	–	49	85	27	–	28	19	46	31	10	6	15	7
Canada	6.9	16	102	105	88	–	–	–	–	–	–	–	–
Central African Republic	–	–	–	–	–	53	41	79	67	34	25	61	43
Chad	1.7	67	58	10	1	63	50	81	68	42	28	62	42
Chile	3.6	30	101	75	32	6	4	6	5	2	2	2	1
China	2.3	24	123	70	6	14	9	33	25	3	1	8	4
Colombia	4.1	25	113	67	17	11	9	12	9	6	4	4	3
Congo Republic	6.1	70	114	53	–	23	13	42	27	5	2	10	4
Costa Rica	5.4	29	104	48	30	6	5	6	5	3	2	2	1
Côte d'Ivoire	5.0	41	71	25	6	56	46	77	63	40	31	59	42
Croatia	5.3	19	87	82	28	1	1	5	3	0[a]	0[a]	0[a]	0[a]
Cuba	6.7	12	106	81	12	5	3	5	4	1	0[a]	1	0[a]
Czech Republic	5.1	18	104	99	24	–	–	–	–	–	–	–	–
Democratic Republic of the Congo (formerly Zaire)	–	45	72	26	2	38	28	66	51	19	12	42	27
Denmark	8.1	10	102	121	48	–	–	–	–	–	–	–	–
Dominican Republic	2.3	28	94	54	23	20	17	21	17	13	10	12	9
Ecuador	3.5	25	127	50	–	10	7	15	11	4	3	5	4
Egypt	4.8	23	101	78	20	40	34	66	57	29	24	49	38
El Salvador	2.5	33	97	37	18	24	19	31	24	15	11	17	13
Eritrea	1.8	44	53	20	1	42	33	72	61	27	20	54	39
Estonia	7.2	17	94	104	42	–	–	–	–	–	–	–	–
Ethiopia	4.0	43	43	12	1	64	57	80	68	52	46	64	48
Finland	7.5	18	99	118	74	0[a]	–	–	–	–	–	–	–
France	6.0	19	105	111	51	–	–	–	–	–	–	–	–
Gabon	2.9	56	162	56	8	–	–	–	–	–	–	–	–
The Gambia	4.9	30	77	25	2	68	57	80	72	49	36	66	52

-137-

Table I *(Continued)*
World Countries: Education and Literacy, 1990–1999

COUNTRY	EDUCATIONAL INPUTS					OUTCOMES							
	Public Expenditure on Education 1994–1997[b] (% of GNI[c])	Primary Pupil-Teacher Ratio 1997 (pupils per teacher)	Primary School Enrollment 1997 (% of age roup)[1]	Secondary School Enrollment 1997 (% of age group)[1]	Tertiary School Enrollment 1997 (% of age group)[1]	ADULT ILLITERACY (% above age 15)				YOUTH ILLITERACY (% aged 15–24)			
						Male		Female		Male		Female	
						1990	1999	1990	1999	1990	1999	1990	1999
Georgia	5.2	18	88	77	42	–	–	–	–	–	–	–	–
Germany	4.8	17	104	104	47	–	–	–	–	–	–	–	–
Ghana	4.2	33	79	–	–	30	21	53	39	12	7	25	13
Greece	3.1	14	93	95	47	2	2	8	4	1	0[a]	0[a]	0[a]
Guatemala	1.7	35	88	26	9	31	24	47	40	20	15	34	28
Guinea	1.9	49	54	14	1	–	–	–	–	–	–	–	–
Guinea-Bissau	–	–	62	–	–	54	42	89	82	30	19	79	68
Haiti	–	35	–	–	–	57	49	63	53	44	37	46	36
Honduras	3.6	35	111	–	10	31	26	32	26	23	19	20	16
Hong Kong, China	2.9	–	94	73	–	5	4	16	10.0	2	1	1	0[a]
Hungary	4.6	12	103	98	24	1	1	1	1	0[a]	0[a]	0[a]	0[a]
India	3.2	62	100	49	7	38	32	64	56	27	21	46	36
Indonesia	1.4	22	113	56	11	13	9	27	19	3	2	7	3
Iran	4.0	30	98	77	18	27	17	45	31	8	4	18	9
Iraq	–	20	85	42	–	43	35	67	55	29	23	48	34
Ireland	6.0	22	105	118	41	–	–	–	–	–	–	–	–
Israel	7.6	14	98	88	41	3	2	9	6	1	0a	2	0a
Italy	4.9	11	101	95	47	2	1	3	2	0[a]	0[a]	0[a]	0[a]
Jamaica	7.4	31	100	–	8	22	18	14	10	13	10	5	3
Japan	3.6	19	101	103	41	–	–	–	–	–	–	–	–
Jordan	6.8	21	71	57	18	10	6	28	17	2	1	4	0a
Kazakhstan	4.4	18	98	87	33	–	–	–	–	–	–	–	–
Kenya	6.5	31	85	24	–	19	12	39	25	7	4	13	6
Korea, North	–	–	–	–	–	–	–	–	–	–	–	–	–
Korea, South	3.7	31	94	102	68	2	1	7	4.0	0[a]	0[a]	0[a]	0[a]
Kuwait	5.0	14	77	65	19	20	16	27	21	12	9	13	7
Kyrgyzstan	5.3	20	104	79	12	–	–	–	–	–	–	–	–
Laos	2.1	30	112	29	3	47	37	80	68	28	18	62	44
Latvia	6.3	13	96	84	33	0[a]	0[a]	0[a]	0[a]	0[a]	0[a]	0[a]	0[a]
Lebanon	2.5	–	111	81	27	12	8	27	20	5	3	11	7
Lesotho	8.4	46	108	31	2	35	28	11	7	23	18	3	2
Libya	–	–	–	–	–	17	10	49	33	1	0a	17	7
Lithuania	5.4	16	98	86	31	1	0[a]	1	1	0[a]	0[a]	0[a]	0[a]
Macedonia	5.1	–	99	63	20	–	–	–	–	–	–	–	–
Madagascar	1.9	47	92	16	2	34	27	50	41	22	17	33	24
Malawi	5.4	59	134	17	1	31	26	64	55	24	20	49	40
Malaysia	4.9	19	101	64	12	13	9	25	17	5	3	6	3
Mali	2.2	80	49	13	1	67	53	81	67	46	29	63	42
Mauritania	5.1	50	79	16	4	53	48	74	69	44	39	65	60
Mauritius	4.6	24	106	65	6	15	12	25	19	9	7	9	6
Mexico	4.9	28	114	64	16	10	7	15	11	4	3	6	4
Moldova	10.6	23	97	81	27	1	1	4	2	0[a]	0[a]	0[a]	0[a]
Mongolia	5.7	31	88	56	17	35	27	59	48	21	16	39	27
Morocco	5.0	28	86	39	11	47	39	75	65	32	24	58	43
Mozambique	–	58	60	7	1	51	41	82	72	34	26	68	55
Myanmar (Burma)	1.2	46	121	30	5	13	11	26	20	10	9	14	10
Namibia	9.1	–	131	62	8	23	18	28	20	14	10	11	7
Nepal	3.2	39	113	42	5	53	42	86	77	34	25	73	59

Table I *(Continued)*
World Countries: Education and Literacy, 1990–1999

COUNTRY	EDUCATIONAL INPUTS					OUTCOMES							
	Public Expenditure on Education 1994–1997[b] (% of GNI[c])	Primary Pupil-Teacher Ratio 1997 (pupils per teacher)	Primary School Enrollment 1997 (% of age roup)[†]	Secondary School Enrollment 1997 (% of age group)[†]	Tertiary School Enrollment 1997 (% of age group)[†]	ADULT ILLITERACY (% above age 15)				YOUTH ILLITERACY (% aged 15–24)			
						Male		Female		Male		Female	
						1990	1999	1990	1999	1990	1999	1990	1999
Netherlands	5.1	14	108	132[d]	47	–	–	–	–	–	–	–	–
New Zealand	7.3	18	101	113	63	–	–	–	–	–	–	–	–
Nicaragua	3.9	36	102	55	12	36	33	34	30	32	29	28	24
Niger	2.3	41	29	7	–	82	77	95	92	75	68	91	87
Nigeria	0.7	34	98	33	–	41	29	62	46	19	11	34	18
Norway	7.4	7	100	119	62	–	–	–	–	–	–	–	–
Oman	4.5	26	76	67	8	33	21	62	40	5	1	25	5
Pakistan	2.7	40	–	–	–	50	41	79	70	36	24	67	52
Panama	5.1	–	106	69	32	10	8	12	9	4	3	5	4
Papua New Guinea	–	38	80	14	3	34	29	52	44	25	20	38	30
Paraguay	4.0	21	111	47	10	8	6	12	8	4	3	5	3
Peru	2.9	27	123	73	26	8	6	21	15	3	2	8	5
Philippines	3.4	35	117	78	29	7	5	8	5	3	2	3	1
Poland	7.5	15	96	98	25	0[a]	0[a]	1	0[a]	0[a]	0[a]	0[a]	0[a]
Portugal	5.8	12	128	111[d]	39	9	6	16	11	1	0[a]	0[a]	0[a]
Puerto Rico	–	–	–	–	–	9	7	9	6	5	3	3	2
Romania	3.6	20	104	78	23	1	1	5	3	1	1	1	0[a]
Russia	3.5	20	107	–	43	0[a]	0[a]	1	1	0[a]	0[a]	0[a]	0[a]
Rwanda	–	–	–	–	–	37	27	56	41	22	15	33	20
Saudi Arabia	7.5	13	76	61	16	22	17	49	34	9	5	21	10
Senegal	3.7	58	71	16	3	62	54	81	73	50	41	70	59
Sierra Leone	–	–	–	–	–	–	–	–	–	–	–	–	–
Singapore	3.0	25	94	74	39	6	4	17	12	1	0[a]	1	0[a]
Slovakia	5.0	20	102	94	22	–	–	–	–	–	–	–	–
Slovenia	5.7	14	98	92	36	0[a]	0[a]	1	0[a]	0[a]	0[a]	0[a]	0[a]
South Africa	7.9	45	133	95	19	18	14	20	16	11	9	12	9
Spain	5.0	15	107	120	51	2	2	5	3	0[a]	0[a]	0[a]	0[a]
Sri Lanka	3.4	28	109	75	5	7	6	15	11	4	3	6	4
Sudan	0.9	29	51	21	–	39	31	68	55	24	18	46	30
Sweden	8.3	12	107	140[d]	50	–	–	–	–	–	–	–	–
Switzerland	5.4	12	97	100	33	–	–	–	–	–	–	–	–
Syria	3.1	23	101	43	16	18	12	53	41	8	5	33	22
Tajikistan	2.2	24	95	78	20	1	1	3	1	0[a]	0[a]	0[a]	0[a]
Tanzania	–	37	67	6	1	23	16	49	34	10	7	22	12
Thailand	4.8	–	89	59	22	5	3	11	7	1	1	2	2
Togo	4.5	46	120	27	4	36	26	71	60	19	13	55	42
Trinidad and Tobago	3.6	25	99	74	8	6	5	11	8	3	2	4	3
Tunisia	7.7	24	118	64	14	28	20	54	41	7	3	25	12
Turkey	2.2	24	107	58	21	11	7	33	24	3	1	12	6
Turkmenistan	–	–	–	–	–	–	–	–	–	–	–	–	–
Uganda	2.6	35	74	12	2	31	23	57	45	20	15	39	29
Ukraine	7.3	21	–	–	42	0[a]	0[a]	1	1	0[a]	0[a]	0[a]	0[a]
United Arab Emirates	1.8	16	89	80	12	29	26	30	22	19	15	11	6
United Kingdom	5.3	19	116	129[d]	52	–	–	–	–	–	–	–	–
United States	5.4	16	102	97	81	–	–	–	–	–	–	–	–
Uruguay	3.3	20	109	85	30	4	3	3	2	1	1	1	0[a]
Uzbekistan	7.7	21	78	94	–	10	7	23	16	3	2	8	5

Table I *(Continued)*
World Countries: Education and Literacy, 1990–1999

COUNTRY	EDUCATIONAL INPUTS					OUTCOMES							
	Public Expenditure on Education 1994–1997[b] (% of GNI[c])	Primary Pupil-Teacher Ratio 1997 (pupils per teacher)	Primary School Enrollment 1997 (% of age roup)[1]	Secondary School Enrollment 1997 (% of age group)[1]	Tertiary School Enrollment 1997 (% of age group)[1]	ADULT ILLITERACY (% above age 15)				YOUTH ILLITERACY (% aged 15–24)			
						Male		Female		Male		Female	
						1990	1999	1990	1999	1990	1999	1990	1999
Venezuela	5.2	21	91	40	–	10	7	12	8	5	3	3	2
Vietnam	3.0	33	114	57	7	6	5	13	9	5	3	5	3
West Bank and Gaza	–	–	–	–	–	–	–	–	–	–	–	–	–
Yemen	7.0	30	70	34	4	45	33	87	76	26	18	75	56
Yugoslavia (Serbia-Montenegro)	–	–	69	62	22	–	–	–	–	–	–	–	–
Zambia	2.2	39	89	27	3	22	15	41	30	14	10	24	15
Zimbabwe	–	39	112	50	7	13	8	25	16	3	2	9	5

1. Large numbers of nontraditional students outside of age group may increase percentages enrolled to above 100 percent in certain countries.
a. Less than 0.5
b. Data are for the most recent year available
c. Gross National Income (GNI) has replaced GNP in the World Bank Atlas Method's estimate of national income
d. Includes training for the unemployed.

Source: World Development Indicators (World Bank, Washington, DC, 1998–1999).

Table J
World Countries: Agricultural Operations, 1996-2000

COUNTRY			AGRICULTURAL INPUTS				AGRICULTURAL OUTPUT AND PRODUCTIVITY			
			Agricultural Machinery							
	Arable Land (hectares per capita)	Irrigated Land (% of cropland)	Land Under Cereal Production (thousand hectares)	Fertilizer Consumption (hundreds of grams per hectare of arable land)	Tractors per Thousand Agricultural Workers	Tractors per Hundred Hectares of Agricultural Land	Crop Production Index (1989-91=100)	Food Production Index (1989-91=100)	Livestock Production Index (1989-91=100)	Agricultural Productivity (agricultural value added per worker in 1995$)
	1996-1998	1996-1998	1998-2000	1996-1998	1996-1998	1996-1998	1998-2000	1998-2000	1998-2000	1997-1999
Albania	0.17	48.5	214	212	10	141	–	–	–	1,934
Algeria	0.26	6.9	2,478	101	39	121	125.8	131.1	125.3	1,876
Angola	0.26	2.1	888	15	3	34	148.1	144	135.6	126
Argentina	0.70	5.7	10,261	330	190	112	159.5	137.9	105.6	9,983
Armenia	0.13	51.2	183	54	70	354	97.4	78	64.8	5,180
Australia	2.80	4.6	16,197	406	704	61	163.9	137.7	111.4	31,432
Austria	0.17	0.3	817	1,836	1,617	2,527	102.4	106	107.8	28,410
Azerbaijan	0.21	75.1	577	128	34	195	45.8	63.1	74.1	837
Bangladesh	0.06	44.8	11,227	1,460	0	7	110.4	114.5	136.2	292
Belarus	0.61	1.8	2,295	1,371	121	158	86.3	61.7	60.9	3,744
Belgium	0.08	4.2	333	3,834	1,186	1,326	138.6	114.7	114.3	48,529
Benin	0.29	0.6	836	212	0	1	175.6	152.4	123.6	558
Bolivia	0.24	6.2	776	53	4	31	151	137.3	127.1	1,054
Bosnia-Herzegovina	0.14	0.3	370	326	270	580	–	–	–	8,471
Botswana	0.22	0.3	87	110	20	175	70.6	97.6	101.3	681
Brazil	0.33	4.1	16,908	1,020	58	151	121.6	136.8	149.9	4,300
Bulgaria	0.51	17.9	1,938	417	68	58	67.8	72.2	64	6,007
Burkina Faso	0.32	0.7	2,999	115	0	6	146.1	136	136.2	162
Burundi	0.12	6.7	202	25	0	2	89.7	90.3	81.6	140
Cambodia	0.33	7.1	2,010	26	0	3	136	139.2	149.1	406
Cameroon	0.43	0.5	1045	63	0	1	124.6	126.2	119.6	1,072
Canada	1.52	1.6	17,444	591	1,678	156	128.9	128.8	132.8	34,922
Central African Republic	0.56	–	156	2	0	0	128.2	132.8	129.2	460
Chad	0.49	0.6	1,897	35	0	0	177.9	155.2	114	220
Chile	0.14	78.4	574	2,225	52	256	126.3	133.1	143.7	4,997
China	0.10	38.3	90,212	2,860	1	56	141.5	168.5	209.9	316
Colombia	0.05	20.7	1,041	2,826	6	105	100	118.5	125.8	3,454
Congo Republic	0.06	0.5	3	255	1	41	114.5	118	129	498
Costa Rica	0.06	24.9	91	7,972	22	311	133.6	132.3	120.9	4,973
Côte d'Ivoire	0.21	1.0	1,621	333	1	13	132.4	131.2	127.6	1,104
Croatia	0.30	0.2	608	1,606	13	21	87.2	72.8	54.4	7,123
Cuba	0.33	19.4	209	580	96	214	54.5	58.2	63.6	–
Czech Republic	0.30	0.7	1,614	1,048	167	275	90.3	83.6	76.6	5,091
Democratic Republic of Congo (formerly Zaire)	0.14	0.1	2,118	3	0	4	89	92.1	103.7	283
Denmark	0.44	20.2	1,509	1,827	1,133	597	95.6	107.9	118.5	52,809
Dominican Republic	0.13	17.1	149	937	4	23	89.2	100.7	121.1	2,710
Ecuador	0.13	28.8	854	955	7	57	122.4	134.1	150.1	1,789
Egypt	0.05	99.8	2,631	3,858	11	318	141.4	149.5	156	1,222
El Salvador	0.10	4.4	457	1,619	4	61	108.5	121.2	127.9	1,690
Eritrea	0.11	5.3	412	140	0	11	174.1	133.9	105.7	–
Estonia	0.77	0.4	357	247	519	451	66.8	45.2	39.7	3,646
Ethiopia	0.17	1.8	6,852	159	0	3	121.6	119.9	116.2	144
Finland	0.42	3.0	1,160	1,442	1,196	907	86.4	89.7	93.3	36,384
France	0.31	9.7	9,141	2,708	1,256	698	112.1	107.6	105	50,171
Gabon	0.28	3.0	18	8	7	46	118.2	113.9	118.3	1,889
The Gambia	0.16	1.0	122	59	0	2	114.1	115.9	117.3	222

Table J (Continued)
World Countries: Agricultural Operations, 1996-2000

COUNTRY			AGRICULTURAL INPUTS				AGRICULTURAL OUTPUT AND PRODUCTIVITY			
			Agricultural Machinery							
	Arable Land (hectares per capita)	Irrigated Land (% of cropland)	Land Under Cereal Production (thousand hectares)	Fertilizer Consumption (hundreds of grams per hectare of arable land)	Tractors per Thousand Agricultural Workers	Tractors per Hundred Hectares of Agricultural Land	Crop Production Index (1989-91=100)	Food Production Index (1989-91=100)	Livestock Production Index (1989-91=100)	Agricultural Productivity (agricultural value added per worker in 1995$)
	1996-1998	1996-1998	1998-2000	1996-1998	1996-1998	1996-1998	1998-2000	1998-2000	1998-2000	1997-1999
Georgia	0.14	43.8	372	442	31	212	61.1	78.3	83.5	1,952
Germany	0.14	4.0	6,904	2,423	960	950	114	94.4	86	28,924
Ghana	0.19	0.2	1,317	54	1	11	174.1	163.5	101.8	554
Greece	0.27	35.2	1,286	1,811	289	843	107	100.1	97.8	12,711
Guatemala	0.13	6.6	686	1,604	2	32	120.9	124.5	129	2,099
Guinea	0.13	6.4	743	35	0	6	142.4	143.1	139.6	284
Guinea-Bissau	0.26	4.9	134	13	0	1	119.4	119.9	120.5	306
Haiti	0.07	8.2	448	165	0	2	86.6	95.4	128.8	392
Honduras	0.28	3.7	500	720	7	30	116.5	112.4	130.1	1,008
Hong Kong, China	0.00	31	0	–	0	7	59.3	49.5	44.6	–
Hungary	0.47	4.2	2,598	929	162	191	79.3	74.7	69.2	4,860
India	0.17	33.6	101,190	976	6	91	122.1	124.6	133.5	395
Indonesia	0.09	15.5	15,298	1,434	1	39	117.4	119.1	125.4	742
Iran	0.28	39.8	7,954	691	38	136	151.3	151.4	146.1	3,679
Iraq	0.24	63.6	2,927	702	74	95	82.9	77.7	65	–
Ireland	0.37	–	283	5,135	993	1,239	110	110.3	110.6	–
Israel	0.06	45.5	57	3,423	323	699	105.6	110.7	116	–
Italy	0.14	24.5	4,128	2,169	950	1,774	105.6	104.8	104.2	23,906
Jamaica	0.07	9.1	2	1,353	11	177	122.9	120.8	119.6	1,229
Japan	0.04	54.6	2,054	3,278	681	4,830	88.3	92.4	94.2	30,620
Jordan	0.06	19.4	76	890	30	188	116.7	139.6	198.8	1,434
Kazakhstan	1.98	7.3	11,466	29	70	34	65.6	58.9	45.3	1,414
Kenya	0.14	1.5	1,851	357	1	36	107.1	104.5	104.1	226
Korea, North	0.07	73	1,330	826	19	441	–	–	–	–
Korea, South	0.04	60.5	1,173	5,358	50	779	106.4	112.3	150.3	12,252
Kuwait	0.00	81.0	1	2,944	11	129	163.8	185.7	180.5	–
Kyrgyzstan	0.29	75.4	645	293	36	142	129.1	114.5	78.7	3,430
Laos	0.17	18.9	708	91	0	11	139.5	144.3	161.6	558
Latvia	0.72	1.1	434	191	330	326	70.2	45.8	35.9	2,523
Lebanon	0.04	37.6	39	3,249	111	300	137.6	142.7	161.6	28,243
Lesotho	0.16	–	178	182	6	62	115.9	99.9	88.5	544
Libya	0.35	22.2	319	320	296	187	132.9	161.6	174.4	–
Lithuania	0.79	0.3	1,046	448	294	267	74.4	66.6	58.1	3,192
Macedonia	0.30	8.5	222	747	398	902	108.7	95.8	85.1	2,141
Madagascar	0.18	35.0	1,373	45	1	14	104.2	108.5	105.7	184
Malawi	0.18	1.4	1,547	294	0	8	149.1	153.2	112.4	138
Malaysia	0.08	4.8	702	6,940	23	238	111.2	134.1	149.1	6,578
Mali	0.46	3.0	2,422	92	1	6	145.1	127.2	123.3	279
Mauritania	0.20	9.8	235	60	1	7	152.3	107.3	100.9	469
Mauritius	0.09	17.6	0	3,480	6	37	93.3	103.1	135.3	5,330
Mexico	0.27	23.8	11,061	658	20	68	121.6	128.4	134.6	1,742
Moldova	0.41	14.1	865	668	82	257	54.7	45.2	36.3	1,277
Mongolia	0.57	6.4	261	33	21	53	35.4	87.8	92.3	1,193
Morocco	0.33	12.7	5,166	357	10	47	95.3	100.1	106.7	1,651
Mozambique	0.19	3.2	1,816	21	1	18	143.2	131	103.2	136
Myanmar (Burma)	0.22	15.5	6,302	182	0	9	152.8	148.6	143	–
Namibia	0.50	0.9	298	–	11	39	111.6	97.3	95.5	1,248
Nepal	0.13	38.2	3,283	383	0	16	120.8	121.4	123.5	189

COUNTRY			AGRICULTURAL INPUTS				AGRICULTURAL OUTPUT AND PRODUCTIVITY			
			Agricultural Machinery							
	Arable Land (hectares per capita)	Irrigated Land (% of cropland)	Land Under Cereal Production (thousand hectares)	Fertilizer Consumption (hundreds of grams per hectare of arable land)	Tractors per Thousand Agricultural Workers	Tractors per Hundred Hectares of Agricultural Land	Crop Production Index (1989-91=100)	Food Production Index (1989-91=100)	Livestock Production Index (1989-91=100)	Agricultural Productivity (agricultural value added per worker in 1995$)
	1996-1998	1996-1998	1998-2000	1996-1998	1996-1998	1996-1998	1998-2000	1998-2000	1998-2000	1997-1999
Netherlands	0.06	60.4	203	5,547	603	1,789	107.5	100.3	99.9	51,594
New Zealand	0.41	8.7	130	4,218	437	488	134.1	125.4	116.4	27,083
Nicaragua	0.53	3.2	378	198	7	11	134.2	131.2	116.7	1,919
Niger	0.51	1.3	7,532	7	0	0	151.3	140.1	120.4	205
Nigeria	0.24	0.8	18,440	59	2	10	155.4	152.2	125.6	641
Norway	0.21	–	334	2,203	1,306	1,584	87.8	96.3	100.1	32,848
Oman	0.01	98.4	3	3,779	1	94	113.8	114.9	104	–
Pakistan	0.17	81.2	12,489	1,178	12	150	125.4	143.3	150.4	626
Panama	0.18	4.9	188	753	20	100	97.2	107.2	121.9	2,580
Papua New Guinea	0.01	–	2	2,283	1	193	109.7	113.1	136.6	808
Paraguay	0.43	2.9	554	233	24	75	110.4	132.8	129.4	3,512
Peru	0.15	28.9	1091	498	3	25	162.9	161.7	150.5	1,569
Philippines	0.08	15.6	6,299	1,283	1	21	112.9	128.4	173.5	1,342
Poland	0.36	0.7	8,577	1,148	285	936	85.8	88.7	87.2	1,554
Portugal	0.19	24.0	590	1,288	219	802	85	94.1	117.1	7,621
Puerto Rico	0.01	51.3	0	–	–	–	62.9	81.7	87.5	–
Romania	0.41	30.6	5,496	392	88	176	90.3	93.4	87.9	3,228
Russia	0.86	3.8	46,809	112	101	72	66.8	60.8	51.6	2,282
Rwanda	0.10	0.4	219	4	0	1	88.1	91.5	108.8	234
Saudi Arabia	0.19	42.3	588	865	12	26	94.3	88.5	147.7	10,930
Senegal	0.25	3.1	1,218	108	0	2	102.9	114.2	138	307
Sierra Leone	0.10	5.4	279	62	0	2	81	85.3	109	379
Singapore	0.00	–	–	25,183	20	650	48.2	41.5	39.5	42,903
Slovakia	0.27	11.2	898	751	92	175	–	–	–	3,491
Slovenia	0.12	0.7	95	3,086	3,604	4,311	93.5	104.6	108.7	30,136
South Africa	0.36	8.5	4,742	534	60	68	105.3	103.3	96.5	4,070
Spain	0.36	19.0	6,652	1,474	576	583	107.6	110.7	122.5	21,687
Sri Lanka	0.05	32.1	890	2,517	2	81	113.9	115.7	133.5	734
Sudan	0.60	11.5	7,973	42	2	6	162	155.9	146.3	–
Sweden	0.32	–	1,221	1,068	989	590	93.8	101.1	104.1	34,285
Switzerland	0.06	5.6	188	4,529	635	2,675	99.4	97.1	94.1	–
Syria	0.32	21.3	3,075	737	66	188	158.4	150.5	133	–
Tajikistan	0.13	80.9	405	841	37	395	62.5	58.1	36.9	–
Tanzania	0.12	3.3	3,201	86	1	20	100.3	105.6	118.2	188
Thailand	0.28	23.1	11,425	925	10	123	112.9	113.1	127	939
Togo	0.52	0.3	765	76	0	0	148.1	140.7	128.8	543
Trinidad and Tobago	0.06	2.5	4	1,406	53	358	101.4	105	100.9	2,463
Tunisia	0.31	7.7	1,273	365	38	121	116.6	127	147.2	3,047
Turkey	0.42	14.8	13,655	751	60	330	114.7	113	109.1	1,858
Turkmenistan	0.35	96.2	612	982	81	307	80.3	132.1	134.4	856
Uganda	0.25	0.1	1,382	2	1	9	118.8	116.5	119.8	350
Ukraine	0.65	7.3	12,040	165	87	109	58.2	49.1	45.8	1,383
United Arab Emirates	0.02	88.9	1	7,775	4	69	275.3	250.6	170.8	–
United Kingdom	0.11	1.7	3,290	3,588	898	800	102.8	98.7	97.9	34,730
United States	0.65	12.0	59,953	1,135	1,515	271	121.9	122.9	120	–
Uruguay	0.39	13.5	578	1,102	173	262	149.7	137.8	122.2	8,679
Uzbekistan	0.19	88.3	1,455	1,623	59	380	88.4	116.5	115.8	1,621

Table J (Continued)
World Countries: Agricultural Operations, 1996-2000

COUNTRY		AGRICULTURAL INPUTS					AGRICULTURAL OUTPUT AND PRODUCTIVITY			
		Agricultural Machinery								
	Arable Land (hectares per capita)	Irrigated Land (% of cropland)	Land Under Cereal Production (thousand hectares)	Fertilizer Consumption (hundreds of grams per hectare of arable land)	Tractors per Thousand Agricultural Workers	Tractors per Hundred Hectares of Agricultural Land	Crop Production Index (1989-91=100)	Food Production Index (1989–91=100)	Livestock Production Index (1989–91=100)	Agricultural Productivity (agricultural value added per worker in 1995$)
	1996-1998	1996-1998	1998-2000	1996-1998	1996-1998	1996-1998	1998-2000	1998-2000	1998-2000	1997-1999
Venezuela	0.12	15.4	668	1,058	59	185	105.7	117.3	118.8	5,125
Vietnam	0.07	42.0	8,228	2,933	4	206	158.5	152.2	163.7	236
West Bank and Gaza	–	–	–	–	–	–	–	–	–	–
Yemen	0.09	31.0	694	111	2	40	129.1	130.9	138.6	355
Yugoslavia (Serbia-Montenegro)	–	–	–	–	–	–	–	–	–	–
Zambia	0.56	0.9	693	94	2	11	88.5	99.7	113.2	218
Zimbabwe	0.28	3.5	1,784	537	6	69	121.2	108.2	113.7	369

Source: *World Development Indicators* (World Bank, Washington, DC, 2001).

Table K
Land Use and Deforestation, 1980–2000

COUNTRY	LAND AREA	RURAL POPULATION DENSITY	LAND USE						FOREST AREA	AVERAGE ANNUAL DEFORESTATION
			Arable Land (% of land area)		Permanent Cropland (% of land area)		Other (% of land area)			
	(thousands of sq. km.)	(people per sq. km. of arable land)	Arable Land (% of land area)		Permanent Cropland (% of land area)		Other (% of land area)		(thousands of sq. km.)	Decline in forest area %
	1998	1998	1980	1998	1980	1998	1980	1998	2000	1990-2000
Albania	27	345	21.4	21.1	4.3	4.5	74.4	74.5	10	0.8
Algeria	2,382	159	2.9	3.2	0.3	0.2	96.8	96.6	21	-1.3
Angola	1,247	268	2.3	2.4	0.4	0.4	97.3	97.2	698	0.2
Argentina	2,737	15	9.1	9.1	0.8	0.8	90.1	90.1	346	0.8
Armenia	28	234	–	17.6	–	2.3	–	80.1	4	-1.3
Australia	7,682	5	5.7	7.0	0.0	0.0	94.2	93.0	1,581	0.0
Austria	83	205	18.6	16.9	1.2	1.0	80.2	82.1	39	-0.2
Azerbaijan	87	205	–	19.3	–	3.0	–	77.7	11	-1.3
Bangladesh	130	1,204	68.3	61.4	2.0	2.6	29.6	36.0	13	-1.3
Belarus	207	49	–	29.8	–	0.6	–	69.6	94	-3.2
Belgium[a]	33	35	23.2	24.8	0.4	0.6	76.4	74.6	7	0.2
Benin	111	207	12.2	15.4	4.0	1.4	83.8	83.3	27	2.3
Bolivia	1,084	156	1.7	1.8	0.2	0.2	98.1	98.0	531	0.3
Bosnia-Herzegovina	51	436	–	9.8	–	2.9	–	87.3	23	0.0
Botswana	567	231	0.7	0.6	0.0	0.0	99.3	99.4	124	0.9
Brazil	8,457	62	4.6	6.3	1.2	1.4	94.2	92.3	5,325	0.4
Bulgaria	111	60	34.6	38.8	3.2	2.0	62.2	59.2	37	-0.6
Burkina Faso	274	260	10.0	12.4	0.1	0.2	89.8	87.4	71	0.2
Burundi	26	779	35.8	30.0	10.1	12.9	54.0	57.2	1	9.0
Cambodia	177	263	11.3	21.0	0.4	0.6	88.3	78.4	93	0.6
Cameroon	465	127	12.7	12.8	2.2	2.6	85.1	84.6	239	0.9
Canada	9,221	15	4.9	4.9	0.0	0.0	95.0	95.0	2,446	0.0
Central African Republic	623	108	3.0	3.1	0.1	0.1	96.9	96.8	229	0.1
Chad	1,259	159	2.5	2.8	0.0	0.0	97.5	97.2	127	0.6
Chile	749	111	5.4	2.6	0.3	0.4	94.3	96.9	155	0.1
China[b]	9,327	689	10.4	13.3	0.4	1.2	89.3	85.5	1,635	-1.2
Colombia	1,039	529	3.6	2.0	1.4	2.0	95.0	96.0	496	0.4
Congo Republic	342	630	0.4	0.5	0.1	0.1	99.6	99.4	221	0.1
Costa Rica	51	824	5.5	4.4	4.4	5.5	90.1	90.1	20	0.8
Côte d'Ivoire	318	290	6.1	9.3	7.2	13.8	86.6	76.9	71	3.1
Croatia	56	133	–	26.1	–	2.3	–	71.6	18	-0.1
Cuba	110	77	23.9	33.1	6.4	7.6	69.7	59.3	23	-1.3
Czech Republic	77	84	–	40.1	–	3.0	–	56.9	26	0.0
Democratic Republic of the Congo (formerly Zaire)	2,267	506	3.0	3.0	0.3	0.5	96.6	96.5	1,352	0.4
Denmark	42	33	62.3	55.7	0.3	0.2	37.4	44.0	5	-0.2
Dominican Republic	48	280	22.1	22.1	7.2	9.9	70.6	68.0	14	0.0
Ecuador	277	302	5.6	5.7	3.3	5.2	91.1	89.2	106	1.2
Egypt	995	1,197	2.3	2.8	0.2	0.5	97.5	96.7	1	-3.4
El Salvador	21	582	27.0	27.0	8.0	12.1	65.0	60.9	1	4.6
Eritrea	101	638	–	4.9	–	0.0	–	95.0	16	0.3
Estonia	42	40	–	26.5	–	0.4	–	73.1	21	-0.6
Ethiopia	1,000	513	–	9.9	–	0.6	–	89.4	46	0.8
Finland	305	81	8.4	7.1	–	0.0	–	92.9	219	0.0
France	550	79	31.8	33.4	2.5	2.1	65.7	64.5	153	-0.4
Gabon	258	76	1.1	1.3	0.6	0.7	98.2	98.1	218	0.0

-145-

Table K *(Continued)*
Land Use and Deforestation, 1980–2000

COUNTRY	LAND AREA	RURAL POPULATION DENSITY	LAND USE						FOREST AREA	AVERAGE ANNUAL DEFORESTATION
	(thousands of sq. km.)	(people per sq. km. of arable land)	Arable Land (% of land area)		Permanent Cropland (% of land area)		Other (% of land area)		(thousands of sq. km.)	Decline in forest area %
	1998	1998	1980	1998	1980	1998	1980	1998	2000	1990-2000
The Gambia	10	430	15.9	19.5	–	0.5	–	80.0	5	-1.0
Georgia	70	279	–	11.3	–	4.1	–	84.6	30	0.0
Germany	349	89	34.4	34.0	1.4	0.7	64.1	65.3	107	0.0
Ghana	228	319	8.4	15.8	7.5	7.5	84.2	76.7	63	1.7
Greece	129	149	22.5	22.1	7.9	8.5	69.6	69.4	36	-0.9
Guatemala	108	482	11.7	12.5	4.4	5.0	83.9	82.4	29	1.7
Guinea	246	550	2.0	3.6	0.9	2.4	97.1	94.0	69	0.5
Guinea-Bissau	28	298	9.1	10.7	1.1	1.8	89.9	87.6	22	0.9
Haiti	28	895	19.8	20.3	12.5	12.7	67.7	67.0	1	5.7
Honduras	112	179	13.9	15.1	1.8	3.1	84.3	81.7	54	1.0
Hong Kong, China	1	0	7.0	5.1	1.0	1.0	92.0	93.9	–	–
Hungary	92	76	54.4	52.2	3.3	2.4	42.2	45.4	18	-0.4
India	2,973	438	54.8	54.3	1.8	2.7	43.4	43.0	641	-0.1
Indonesia	1,812	695	9.9	9.9	4.4	7.2	85.6	82.9	1,050	1.2
Iran	1,622	145	8.0	10.4	0.5	1.2	91.5	88.4	73	0.0
Iraq	437	104	12.0	11.9	0.4	0.8	87.6	87.3	8	0.0
Ireland	69	114	16.1	19.7	0.0	0.0	83.9	80.3	7	-3.0
Israel	21	153	15.8	17.0	4.3	4.2	80.0	78.8	1	-4.9
Italy	294	231	32.2	28.2	10.0	9.4	57.7	62.5	100	-0.3
Jamaica	11	664	16.6	16.1	5.5	9.2	77.8	74.7	3	1.5
Japan	377	599	11.4	12.0	1.6	1.0	87.0	87.0	241	0.0
Jordan	89	485	3.4	2.9	0.4	1.5	96.2	95.6	1	0.0
Kazakhstan	2,671	22	–	11.2	–	0.1	–	88.7	121	-2.2
Kenya	569	494	6.7	7.0	0.8	0.9	92.5	92.1	171	0.5
Korea, North	120	548	13.4	14.1	2.4	2.5	84.2	83.4	82	0.0
Korea, South	99	532	20.9	17.3	1.4	2.0	77.8	80.7	63	0.1
Kuwait	18	821	0.1	0.3	–	0.1	–	99.6	0	-5.2
Kyrgyzstan	192	235	–	7.0	–	0.4	–	92.6	10	-2.6
Laos	231	483	2.9	3.5	0.1	0.2	97.0	96.3	126	0.4
Latvia	62	41	–	29.7	–	0.5	–	69.8	29	-0.4
Lebanon	10	262	20.5	17.6	8.9	12.5	70.6	69.9	0	0.3
Lesotho	30	466	9.6	10.7	–	–	–	–	0	0.0
Libya	1,760	39	1.0	1.0	0.2	0.2	98.8	98.8	4	-1.4
Lithuania	65	40	–	45.4	–	0.9	–	53.6	20	-0.2
Macedonia	25	133	–	23.1	–	1.9	–	75.0	9	0.0
Madagascar	582	408	4.3	4.4	0.9	0.9	94.8	94.7	117	0.9
Malawi	94	437	13.3	19.9	0.9	1.3	85.8	78.7	26	2.4
Malaysia	329	537	3.0	5.5	11.6	17.6	85.4	76.9	193	1.2
Mali	1,220	160	1.6	3.8	0.0	0.0	98.3	96.2	132	0.7
Mauritania	1,025	233	0.2	0.5	0.0	0.0	99.8	99.5	3	2.7
Mauritius	2	684	49.3	49.3	3.4	3.0	47.3	47.8	0	0.6
Mexico	1,909	98	12.1	13.2	0.8	1.1	87.1	85.7	552	1.1
Moldova	33	129	–	54.5	–	11.7	–	33.8	3	-0.2
Mongolia	1,567	67	0.8	0.8	0.0	0.0	99.2	99.2	106	0.5
Morocco	446	140	16.6	20.2	1.1	2.1	82.3	77.6	30	0.0
Mozambique	784	339	3.6	4.0	0.3	0.3	96.1	95.7	306	0.2

Table K (Continued)
Land Use and Deforestation, 1980–2000

COUNTRY	LAND AREA	RURAL POPULATION DENSITY	LAND USE						FOREST AREA	AVERAGE ANNUAL DEFORESTATION
	(thousands of sq. km.)	(people per sq. km. of arable land)	Arable Land (% of land area)		Permanent Cropland (% of land area)		Other (% of land area)		(thousands of sq. km.)	Decline in forest area %
	1998	1998	1980	1998	1980	1998	1980	1998	2000	1990-2000
Myanmar (Burma)	658	340	14.6	14.5	0.7	0.9	84.8	84.6	344	1.4
Namibia	823	143	0.8	1.0	0.0	0.0	99.2	99.0	80	0.9
Nepal	143	700	16.0	20.3	0.2	0.5	83.8	79.2	39	1.8
Netherlands	34	186	23.3	26.7	0.9	1.0	75.8	72.3	4	-0.3
New Zealand	268	35	9.3	5.8	3.7	6.4	86.9	87.8	79	-0.5
Nicaragua	121	87	9.5	20.2	1.5	2.4	89.1	77.4	33	3.0
Niger	1,267	163	2.8	3.9	0.0	0.0	97.2	96.1	13	3.7
Nigeria	911	248	30.6	31.0	2.8	2.8	66.6	66.3	135	2.6
Norway	307	123	2.7	3.0	–	–	–	–	89	-0.4
Oman	212	2,785	0.1	0.1	0.1	0.2	99.8	99.7	0	0.0
Pakistan	771	394	25.9	27.8	0.4	0.8	73.7	71.4	25	1.1
Panama	74	244	5.8	6.7	1.6	2.1	92.5	91.2	29	1.6
Papua New Guinea	453	6,379	0.0	0.1	0.9	1.3	99.0	98.5	306	0.4
Paraguay	397	108	4.1	5.5	0.3	0.2	95.6	94.2	234	0.5
Peru	1,280	189	2.5	2.9	0.3	0.4	97.2	96.7	652	0.4
Philippines	298	573	14.5	18.4	14.8	15.1	70.8	66.5	58	1.4
Poland	304	97	48.0	46.0	1.1	1.2	50.9	52.8	93	-0.1
Portugal	92	206	26.5	20.5	7.8	7.7	65.7	71.8	37	-1.7
Puerto Rico	9	2,990	5.6	3.7	5.6	5.1	88.7	91.2	2	0.2
Romania	230	106	42.7	40.5	2.9	2.2	54.4	57.3	64	-0.2
Russia	16,889	27	–	7.5	–	0.1	–	92.4	8,514	0.0
Rwanda	25	929	30.8	33.2	10.3	10.1	58.9	56.6	3	3.9
Saudi Arabia	2,150	82	0.9	1.7	0.0	0.1	99.1	98.2	15	0.0
Senegal	193	219	12.2	11.6	0.0	0.2	87.8	88.2	62	0.7
Sierra Leone	72	649	6.3	6.8	0.7	0.8	93.0	92.5	11	2.9
Singapore	1	0	3.3	1.6	9.8	0.0	86.9	98.4	0	0.0
Slovakia	48	157	–	30.6	–	2.8	–	66.6	20	-0.3
Slovenia	20	427	–	11.5	–	2.7	–	85.8	11	-0.2
South Africa	1,221	140	10.2	12.1	0.7	0.8	89.1	87.1	89	0.1
Spain	499	63	31.1	28.6	9.9	9.6	59.0	61.8	144	-0.6
Sri Lanka	65	1,664	13.2	13.4	15.9	15.8	70.8	70.8	19	1.6
Sudan	2,376	112	5.2	7.0	0.0	0.1	94.8	92.9	616	1.4
Sweden	412	53	7.2	6.8	–	–	–	–	271	0.0
Switzerland	40	553	9.9	10.5	0.5	0.6	89.6	88.9	12	-0.4
Syria	184	151	28.5	25.6	2.5	4.2	69.1	70.2	5	0.0
Tajikistan	141	583	–	5.4	–	0.9	–	93.7	4	-0.5
Tanzania	884	595	2.5	4.2	1.0	1.0	96.5	94.7	388	0.2
Thailand	511	281	32.3	32.9	3.5	7.0	64.2	60.1	148	0.7
Togo	54	137	36.8	40.4	6.6	1.8	56.6	57.7	5	3.4
Trinidad and Tobago	5	460	13.6	14.6	9.0	9.2	77.4	76.2	3	0.8
Tunisia	155	116	20.5	18.7	9.7	12.9	69.7	68.5	5	-0.2
Turkey	770	70	32.9	31.8	4.1	3.3	63.0	65.0	102	-0.2
Turkmenistan	470	160	–	3.5	–	0.1	–	96.4	38	0.0
Uganda	200	357	20.4	25.3	8.0	8.8	71.6	65.9	42	2.0
Ukraine	579	49	–	56.7	–	1.7	–	41.6	96	-0.3
United Arab Emirates	84	1,017	0.2	0.5	0.1	0.5	99.7	99.0	3	-2.8

Table K (Continued)
Land Use and Deforestation, 1980–2000

COUNTRY	LAND AREA	RURAL POPULATION DENSITY	LAND USE						FOREST AREA	AVERAGE ANNUAL DEFORESTATION
	(thousands of sq. km.)	(people per sq. km. of arable land)	Arable Land (% of land area)		Permanent Cropland (% of land area)		Other (% of land area)		(thousands of sq. km.)	Decline in forest area %
	1998	1998	1980	1998	1980	1998	1980	1998	2000	1990-2000
United Kingdom	242	100	28.7	25.9	0.3	0.2	71.1	73.9	26	-0.8
United States	9,159	36	20.6	19.3	0.2	0.2	79.2	80.5	2,260	-0.2
Uruguay	175	24	8.0	7.2	0.3	0.3	91.7	92.5	13	-5.0
Uzbekistan	414	335	–	10.8	–	0.9	–	88.3	20	-0.2
Venezuela	882	117	3.2	3.0	0.9	1.0	95.9	96.0	495	0.4
Vietnam	325	1,080	18.2	17.5	1.9	4.8	79.8	77.7	98	-0.5
West Bank and Gaza	–	–	–	–	–	–	–	–	–	–
Yemen	528	838	2.6	2.8	0.2	0.2	97.2	96.9	4	1.8
Yugoslavia (Serbia-Montenegro)	–	–	–	–	–	–	–	–	29	0.0
Zambia	743	111	6.9	7.1	0.0	0.0	93.1	92.9	312	2.4
Zimbabwe	387	240	6.4	8.3	0.3	0.3	93.4	91.3	190	1.5

a. Includes Luxembourg.
b. Includes Taiwan.

Source: World Development Indicators (World Bank, Washington, DC, 2001).

Table L
World Countries: Energy Production and Use, 1980–1998

COUNTRY	COMMERCIAL ENERGY PRODUCTION		COMMERCIAL ENERGY USE			COMMERCIAL ENERGY USE PER CAPITA			NET ENERGY IMPORTS[a]	
	Thousand Metric Tons of Oil Equivalent		Thousand Metric Tons of Oil Equivalent		Average Annual % Growth	Kg. of Oil Equivalent		Average Annual % Growth	% of Commercial Energy Use	
	1980	1998	1980	1998	1980-98	1980	1998	1980-98	1980	1998
Albania	3,428	864	3,049	947	−7.0	1,142	284	−8.0	−12	9
Algeria	66,741	132,332	12,089	26,506	3.7	648	898	1.0	−452	−399
Angola	11,301	43,035	4,437	7,147	2.9	632	595	−0.2	−155	−502
Argentina	38,813	80,657	41,868	62,349	2.3	1490	1,726	0.9	7	−29
Armenia	1,263	547	1,070	1,939	–	346	511	–	–	72
Australia	86,096	212,012	70,372	105,009	2.4	4,790	5,600	1.0	−22	−102
Austria	7,655	8,999	23,450	28,815	1.5	3,105	3,567	1.1	67	69
Azerbaijan	14,821	16,178	15,001	12,372	–	2,433	1,564	–	–	−31
Bangladesh	9,234	16,725	10,930	19,965	3.6	126	159	1.4	16	16
Belarus	2,566	3,395	2,385	26,470	–	247	2,614	–	–	87
Belgium	7,986	12,810	46,100	58,349	1.8	4,682	5,719	1.5	83	78
Benin	1,212	1,947	1,363	2,240	2.6	394	377	−0.5	11	13
Bolivia	4,241	5,837	2,287	4,621	3.0	427	581	0.7	−85	−26
Bosnia-Herzegovina	–	684	–	1,950	–	–	517	–	–	65
Botswana	–	–	–	–	–	–	–	–	–	–
Brazil	62,083	126,065	111,262	174,964	2.6	914	1,055	0.9	44	28
Bulgaria	7,737	10,116	28,673	19,963	−2.5	3,235	2,418	−2.1	73	49
Burkina Faso	–	–	–	–	–	–	–	–	–	–
Burundi	–	–	–	–	–	–	–	–	–	–
Cambodia	–	–	–	–	–	–	–	–	–	–
Cameroon	6,707	12,965	3,676	6,183	2.6	425	432	−0.3	−82	−110
Canada	207,417	365,674	193,000	234,325	1.6	7,848	7,747	0.4	−7	−56
Central African Republic	–	–	–	–	–	–	–	–	–	–
Chad	–	–	–	–	–	–	–	–	–	–
Chile	5,801	7,905	9,662	23,630	5.8	867	1,594	4.1	40	67
China	608,625	1,020,270	593,118	1,031,410	3.8	604	830	2.4	−3	1
Colombia	18,040	74,422	19,349	30,713	2.8	680	753	0.8	7	−142
Congo Republic	3,970	14,160	845	1,206	2.0	506	433	−0.8	−370	−1074
Costa Rica	767	1102	1,527	2,781	4.0	669	789	1.5	50	60
Côte d'Ivoire	–	–	–	–	–	–	–	–	–	–
Croatia	–	3,956	–	8,136	–	–	1,808	–	–	51
Cuba	4,227	4,448	14,910	11,858	−2.0	1,536	1,066	−2.8	72	62
Czech Republic	41,000	30,555	47,252	41,034	−1.1	4,618	3,986	−1.2	13	26
Democratic Republic of the Congo (formerly Zaire)	8,697	13,546	8,706	13,711	3.0	322	284	−0.3	0	1
Denmark	896	20,177	19,734	20,804	0.9	3,852	3,925	0.7	95	3
Dominican Republic	1,332	1,433	3,464	5,583	2.4	608	676	0.3	62	74
Ecuador	11,755	22,514	5,191	8,973	2.6	652	737	0.3	−126	−151
Egypt	34,168	57,464	15,970	41,798	4.7	391	679	2.4	−114	−37
El Salvador	1,913	1,987	2,537	3,860	2.0	553	640	0.5	25	49
Eritrea	–	–	–	–	–	–	–	–	–	–
Estonia	6951	2,920	6275	4,835	–	4240	3,335	–	–	40
Ethiopia	10,588	16,379	11,157	17,429	2.4	296	284	−0.4	5	6
Finland	6,912	13,591	25,413	33,459	1.7	5,317	6,493	1.3	73	59
France	46,829	125,528	190,111	255,674	2.0	3,528	4,378	1.6	75	51
Gabon	9,441	18,892	1,493	1,668	−0.4	2,160	1,413	−3.4	−532	−1,033
The Gambia	–	–	–	–	–	–	–	–	–	–
Georgia	1,504	729	4,474	2,526	–	882	464	–	–	71
Germany	185,628	131,412	360,441	344,506	−0.1	4,603	4,199	−0.5	48	62

-149-

COUNTRY	COMMERCIAL ENERGY PRODUCTION		COMMERCIAL ENERGY USE			COMMERCIAL ENERGY USE PER CAPITA			NET ENERGY IMPORTS[a]	
	Thousand Metric Tons of Oil Equivalent		Thousand Metric Tons of Oil Equivalent		Average Annual % Growth	Kg. of Oil Equivalent		Average Annual % Growth	% of Commercial Energy Use	
	1980	1998	1980	1998	1980-98	1980	1998	1980-98	1980	1998
Ghana	3,305	5,705	4,027	7,270	3.7	375	396	0.6	18	22
Greece	3,696	9,892	15,960	26,976	3.1	1,655	2,565	2.6	77	63
Guatemala	2,503	4,739	3,754	6,258	3.1	550	579	0.5	33	24
Guinea	–	–	–	–	–	–	–	–	–	–
Guinea-Bissau	–	–	–	–	–	–	–	–	–	–
Haiti	1,877	1,626	2,099	2,072	–0.1	392	271	–2.0	11	22
Honduras	1,315	1,897	1,892	3,333	3.1	530	542	0.0	31	43
Hong Kong, China	39	48	5,439	16,593	5.9	1,079	2,497	4.5	99	100
Hungary	14,957	11,849	28,961	25,255	–1.0	2,705	2,497	–0.7	48	53
India	222,418	413,055	242,592	475,788	3.9	353	486	1.9	8	13
Indonesia	128,403	211,522	59,561	123,074	4.7	402	604	2.9	–116	–72
Iran	84,001	232,481	38,918	102,148	6.1	995	1,649	3.5	–116	–128
Iraq	136,643	110,824	12,030	29,972	4.8	925	1,342	1.7	–1,036	–270
Ireland	1,894	2,465	8,485	13,251	2.5	2,495	3,570	2.2	78	81
Israel	153	619	8,563	18,873	5.2	2,208	3,165	2.6	98	97
Italy	19,644	29,049	138,629	167,933	1.4	2,456	2,916	1.3	86	83
Jamaica	224	655	2,378	4,058	3.8	1,115	1,575	2.8	91	84
Japan	43,247	109,965	346,492	510,106	2.7	2,967	4,035	2.3	88	78
Jordan	1	295	1,714	4,887	5.1	786	1,063	0.6	100	94
Kazakhstan	76,799	64,086	76,799	39,037	–	5,163	2,590	–	–	–64
Kenya	7,891	11,609	9,791	14,527	2.2	589	505	–0.9	19	20
Korea, North	–	–	–	–	–	–	–	–	–	–
Korea, South	9644	27,738	41,238	163,375	9.5	1082	3,519	8.3	77	83
Kuwait	91,636	114,225	12,248	14,598	–0.2	8,908	7,823	–0.7	–648	–682
Kyrgyzstan	2,190	1,227	1,717	2,921	–	473	609	–	–	58
Laos	–	–	–	–	–	–	–	–	–	–
Latvia	261	1774	566	4,275	–	222	1,746	–	–	59
Lebanon	178	200	2,480	5,288	4.6	826	1,256	2.6	93	96
Lesotho	–	–	–	–	–	–	–	–	–	–
Libya	96,550	76,524	7,193	12,420	3.8	2,364	2,343	0.7	–1,242	–516
Lithuania	–	4,510	–	9,347	–	–	2,524	–	–	52
Macedonia	–	–	–	–	–	–	–	–	–	–
Madagascar	–	–	–	–	–	–	–	–	–	–
Malawi	–	–	–	–	–	–	–	–	–	–
Malaysia	18,202	74,912	12,215	43,623	7.9	888	1,967	5.1	–49	–72
Mali	–	–	–	–	–	–	–	–	–	–
Mauritania	–	–	–	–	–	–	–	–	–	–
Mauritius	–	–	–	–	–	–	–	–	–	–
Mexico	149,359	228,187	98,898	147,834	2.1	1,464	1,552	0.2	–51	–54
Moldova	35	63	–	4,053	–	–	943	–	–	98
Mongolia	–	–	–	–	–	–	–	–	–	–
Morocco	877	753	4,778	9,344	4.2	247	336	2.1	82	92
Mozambique	7,413	6,945	8,074	6,863	–1.0	668	405	–2.6	8	–1
Myanmar	9,513	12,405	9,430	13,631	2.0	279	307	0.5	–1	9
Namibia	–	–	–	–	–	–	–	–	–	–
Nepal	4,630	6,886	4,805	7,831	2.7	331	343	0.2	4	12
Netherlands	71,830	62,495	65,000	74,408	1.5	4,594	4,740	0.9	–11	16
New Zealand	5,488	13,837	9,251	17,159	3.8	2,972	4,525	2.7	41	19
Nicaragua	910	1,458	1,566	2,651	2.8	536	553	0.0	42	45
Niger	–	–	–	–	–	–	–	–	–	–

COUNTRY	COMMERCIAL ENERGY PRODUCTION		COMMERCIAL ENERGY USE			COMMERCIAL ENERGY USE PER CAPITA			NET ENERGY IMPORTS[a]	
	Thousand Metric Tons of Oil Equivalent		Thousand Metric Tons of Oil Equivalent		Average Annual % Growth	Kg. of Oil Equivalent		Average Annual % Growth	% of Commercial Energy Use	
	1980	1998	1980	1998	1980-98	1980	1998	1980-98	1980	1998
Nigeria	148,479	184,847	52,846	86,489	2.6	743	716	–0.3	–181	–114
Norway	55,716	206,667	18,792	25,423	1.7	4,593	5,736	1.3	–196	–713
Oman	15,090	52,202	996	7,285	11.5	905	3,165	7.0	–1,415	–617
Pakistan	20,997	42,351	25,472	57,854	4.8	308	440	2.2	18	27
Panama	529	642	1,865	2,383	1.7	957	862	–0.2	72	73
Papua New Guinea	–	–	–	–	–	–	–	–	–	–
Paraguay	1,605	6,868	2,089	4,277	4.5	671	819	1.5	23	–61
Peru	14,655	11,964	11,700	14,400	1.1	675	581	–0.9	–25	17
Philippines	10,670	17,818	21,212	38,313	3.7	439	526	1.4	50	53
Poland	121,848	86,703	123,465	96,440	–1.3	3,470	2,494	–1.8	1	10
Portugal	1,481	2,315	10,291	21,849	4.4	1,054	2,192	4.4	86	89
Puerto Rico	–	–	–	–	–	–	–	–	–	–
Romania	52,587	28,241	65,110	39,611	–3.0	2,933	1,760	–3.0	19	29
Russia	748,647	928,987	763,707	581,774	–	5,494	3,963	–	–	–60
Rwanda	–	–	–	–	–	–	–	–	–	–
Saudi Arabia	533,071	505,121	35,357	103,230	5.2	3,773	5,244	0.9	–1,408	–389
Senegal	1,046	1,653	1,921	2,822	2.2	347	312	–0.5	46	41
Sierra Leone	–	–	–	–	–	–	–	–	–	–
Singapore	–	24	6,062	24,299	9.8	2,656	7,681	7.8	–	100
Slovakia	3,416	4,833	20,810	16,906	–1.4	4,175	3,136	–1.8	84	71
Slovenia	1,623	2,891	4,313	6,649	–	2,269	3,354	–	–	57
South Africa	73,169	144,405	65,417	110,986	2.2	2,372	2,681	–0.1	–12	–30
Spain	15,644	31,920	68,583	112,782	3.1	1,834	2,865	2.8	77	72
Sri Lanka	3,209	4,319	4,536	7,300	2.3	308	389	0.9	29	41
Sudan	7,089	13,527	8,406	14,899	2.8	450	526	0.5	16	9
Sweden	16,133	34,155	40,984	52,472	1.3	4,932	5,928	0.8	61	35
Switzerland	7,030	11,163	20,861	26,605	1.5	3,301	3,742	0.8	66	58
Syria	9,502	35,411	5,348	17,346	5.6	614	1,133	2.3	–78	–104
Tajikistan	1,986	1,268	1,650	3,255	–	416	532	–	–	61
Tanzania	9,502	13,931	10,280	14,660	2.0	553	456	–1.1	8	5
Thailand	11,182	39,347	22,808	68,971	7.9	488	1,153	6.4	51	43
Togo	–	–	–	–	–	–	–	–	–	–
Trinidad and Tobago	13,141	14,651	3,873	8,950	3.9	3,580	6,964	3.0	–239	–64
Tunisia	6,966	7,113	3,907	7,582	3.7	612	812	1.5	–78	6
Turkey	17,190	28,649	31,314	72,512	4.9	704	1,144	2.9	45	60
Turkmenistan	8,034	17,411	7,948	11,122	–	2,778	2,357	–	–	–57
Uganda	–	–	–	–	–	–	–	–	–	–
Ukraine	109,708	80,415	97,893	142,939	–	1,956	2,842	–	–	44
United Arab Emirates	89,716	144,935	6,112	27,336	8.7	5,860	10,035	3.1	–1,368	–430
United Kingdom	197,864	274,230	201,299	232,879	1.1	3,574	3,930	0.8	2	–18
United States	1,553,260	1,695,430	1,811,650	2,181,800	1.4	7,973	7,937	0.4	14	22
Uruguay	763	1,262	2,641	2,992	1.3	906	910	0.6	71	58
Uzbekistan	4,615	50,334	4,821	46,278	–	302	1,930	–	–	–9
Venezuela	139,392	230,563	34,962	56,543	2.5	2,317	2,433	0.0	–299	–308
Vietnam	18,364	42,668	19,573	33,695	3.0	364	440	0.9	6	–27
West Bank and Gaza	–	–	–	–	–	–	–	–	–	–
Yemen	60	19,565	1,424	3,333	4.5	167	201	0.5	96	–487
Yugoslavia (Serbia-Montenegro)	–	–	–	–	–	–	–	–	–	–
Zambia	4,198	5,657	4,551	6,088	1.3	793	630	–1.6	8	7
Zimbabwe	5,793	8,235	6,570	10,065	2.8	937	861	–0.2	12	18

Table L *(Continued)*
World Countries: Energy Production and Use, 1980–1998

COUNTRY	COMMERCIAL ENERGY PRODUCTION		COMMERCIAL ENERGY USE			COMMERCIAL ENERGY USE PER CAPITA			NET ENERGY IMPORTS[a]	
	Thousand Metric Tons of Oil Equivalent		Thousand Metric Tons of Oil Equivalent		Average Annual % Growth	Kg. of Oil Equivalent		Average Annual % Growth	% of Commercial Energy Use	
	1980	1998	1980	1998	1980-98	1980	1998	1980-98	1980	1998
World[1]	6,882,644	9,611,004	6,902,381	9,345,307	2.9	1,627	1,659	0.9	–	–
Low income	797,751	1,290,575	648,676	1,178,897	5.1	442	550	2.5	−23	−10
Middle income	3,302,896	4,605,397	2,481,018	3,409,502	4.4	1,246	1,311	2.3	−33	−35
Lower middle income	1,944,378	2,867,598	1,779,108	2,282,178	5.4	1,126	1,116	3.2	−9	−26
Upper middle income	1,358,518	1,737,798	701,910	1,127,324	2.7	1,713	2,025	1.0	−94	−54
Low & middle income	4,100,647	5,895,972	3,129,694	4,588,399	4.6	905	967	2.3	−31	−29
East Asia & Pacific	814,603	1,446,679	779,155	1,516,091	4.5	571	857	3.0	−5	5
Europe & Central Asia	1,241,543	1,380,292	1,332,941	1,215,898	7.8	3,349	2,637	–	7	−14
Latin America & Carib.	475,245	830,882	379,775	585,082	2.4	1,070	1,183	0.5	−24	−42
Middle East & N. Africa	988,969	1,237,344	145,929	378,338	5.1	838	1,344	2.3	−577	−228
South Asia	260,487	483,335	288,334	568,738	4.0	325	445	1.9	10	−15
Sub-Saharan Africa	319,801	517,440	203,560	324,252	2.3	727	700	−0.5	−57	−60
High income	2,781,997	3,715,032	3,772,688	4,756,908	1.7	4,796	5,366	1.0	27	22
Europe EMU	365,532	420,629	940,146	1,114,343	1.2	3,408	3,834	0.9	61	62

a. A negative value indicates that a country is a net exporter.
1. World Bank estimations; missing data are imputed whenever possible.

Source: World Development Indicators (World Bank, Washington, DC, 2001).

Table M
World Countries: Water Resources

COUNTRY	ANNUAL RENEWABLE WATER RESOURCES[a]		ANNUAL AVERAGE GROUNDWATER RESOURCES[b]		SECTORAL WITHDRAWALS (%)[c]					
	Supply Per Capita (cubic meters) 2000	Withdrawal Per Capita (cubic meters) 2000	Recharge Per Capita (cubic meters) 2000	Withdrawal Per Capita (cubic meters) 2000	Domestic		Industry		Agriculture	
					Surface	Ground	Surface	Ground	Surface	Ground
WORLD	**7,045**	**664**	**–**	**–**	**9**	**65**	**19**	**15**	**67**	**20**
AFRICA	**5,159**	**307**	**–**	**–**	**8**	**–**	**4**	**–**	**63**	**–**
Algeria	442	180	54	117.1	25	46	15	5	60	49
Angola	14,288	57	5,591	–	14	–	10	–	76	–
Benin	1,689	28	295	–	23	–	10	–	67	–
Botswana	1,788	83	1,048	–	30	–	19	–	46[e]	–
Burkina Faso	1,466	39	796	–	19	–	0	–	81	–
Burundi	538	20	314	–	36	–	0	–	64	–
Cameroon	17,766	38	6,629	–	46	–	19	–	35	–
Central African Republic	39,001	26	15,490	–	21	–	6	–	74	–
Chad	1,961	34	1,503	15.7	16	29	2	–	82	71
Congo Republic	75,387	20	67,268	–	62	–	27	–	11	–
Côte d'Ivoire	5,187	66	2,550	–	22	–	11	–	67	–
Democratic Republic of the Congo (formerly Zaire)	18,101	8	8,150	–	61	–	16	–	23	–
Egypt	26	920	19	85.1	6	58	8	0	86	42[k]
Equatorial Guinea	66,275	30	22,092	–	81	–	13	–	6	–
Eritrea	727	–	–	–	–	–	–	–	–	–
Ethiopia	1,758	47	703	–	11	–	3	–	86	–
Gabon	133,754	70	50,566	0.6	72	100	22	0	6	0
The Gambia	2,298	33	383	–	7	–	2	–	91[f]	–
Ghana	1,499	35	1,301	–	35	–	13	–	52	–
Guinea	30,416	141	5,114	–	10	–	3	–	87	–
Guinea-Bissau	13,189	17	11,541	–	60	–	4	–	36	–
Kenya	672	87	100	–	20	–	4	–	76	–
Lesotho	2,430	31	232	–	22	–	22	–	56	–
Liberia	63,412	54	19,023	–	27	–	13	–	60	–
Libya	143	783	116	734.9	9	9	4	4	87	87l
Madagascar	21,139	1,694	3,450	482.9	1	0	0	–	99[g]	–
Malawi	1,605	98	128	–	10	–	3	–	86	–
Mali	5,341	164	1,780	11.6	2	–	1	–	97	–
Mauritania	150	923	112	498.3	6	–	2	–	92	–
Mauritius	–	–	–	–	–	–	–	–	–	–
Morocco	1,058	446	317	97.9	5	16	3	–	92	–
Mozambique	5,081	40	864	–	9	–	2	–	89	–
Namibia	3,592	185	1,217	–	28	–	3	–	68	–
Niger	326	69	233	17.9	16	58	2	4	82	39
Nigeria	1,982	45	780	–	31	–	15	–	54	–
Rwanda	815	134	466	–	5	–	2	–	94	–
Senegal	2,784	202	802	39.2	5	24	3	–	92	72

Table M
World Countries: Water Resources

COUNTRY	ANNUAL RENEWABLE WATER RESOURCES[a]		ANNUAL AVERAGE GROUNDWATER RESOURCES[b]		SECTORAL WITHDRAWALS (%)[c]					
	Supply Per Capita (cubic meters) 2000	Withdrawal Per Capita (cubic meters) 2000	Recharge Per Capita (cubic meters) 2000	Withdrawal Per Capita (cubic meters) 2000	Domestic		Industry		Agriculture	
					Surface	Ground	Surface	Ground	Surface	Ground
Sierra Leone	32,960	98	10,300	–	7	–	4	–	89	–
Somalia	594	115	327	45.8	3	–	0	–	97	–
South Africa	1,110	391	119	64.9	17	11	11	6	72	84
Sudan	1,187	669	237	13	5	–	1	–	94	–
Swaziland	–	–	–	–	–	–	–	–	–	–
Tanzania	2,387	40	895	–	9	–	2	–	89	–
Togo	2,484	28	1,231	–	62	–	13	–	25	–
Tunisia	367	295	433	181.8	14	10	3	4	83	86
Uganda	1,791	20	1,332	–	32	–	8	–	60	–
Zambia	8,747	214	5,137	–	16	–	7	–	77	–
Zimbabwe	1,208	136	428	–	14	–	7	–	79	–
NORTH AMERICA	**21,583**	**1,907**	**–**	**–**	**10**	**–**	**39**	**–**	**46**	**–**
Canada	87,971	1,623	11,879	37.3	11	34	68	11	7	34[m]
United States	8,838	1,844	5,439	432.3	11	20	44	5	40	62[n]
CENTRAL AMERICA	**6,290**	**715**	**–**	**–**	**–**	**–**	**–**	**–**	**–**	**–**
Belize	66,470	469	–	–	12	–	88	–	0	–
Costa Rica	27,936	1540	5,219	–	13	–	7	–	80	–
Cuba	3,393	475	714	408.3	49	–	0	–	51	–
Dominican Republic	2,472	1085	353	–	11	–	0	–	89	–
El Salvador	2,820	137	–	–	34	–	20	–	46	–
Guatemala	11,805	126	2,723	–	9	–	17	–	74	–
Haiti	1,473	139	304	–	5	–	1	–	94	–
Honduras	14,818	293	6,013	–	4	–	5	–	91	–
Jamaica	3,640	371	–	–	15	–	7	–	77	–
Mexico	4,136	812	1,406	275.4	17	13	5	23	78	64[o]
Nicaragua	37,484	267	11,627	–	14	–	2	–	84	–
Panama	51,616	685	14,708	–	28	–	2	–	70	–
Trinidad and Tobago	–	–	–	–	–	–	–	–	–	–
SOUTH AMERICA	**34,791**	**518**	**–**	**–**	**20**	**–**	**11**	**–**	**60**	**–**
Argentina	9,721	822	3,456	180.4	16	11	9	19	75	70
Bolivia	37,941	197	15,609	–	10	–	3	–	87	–
Brazil	31,849	359	11,016	57	21	38	18	25	61	38
Chile	61,007	1,629	9,204	–	5	–	11	–	84	–
Colombia	50,400	228	12,051	–	59	–	4	–	37	–
Ecuador	34,952	1423	10,596	–	12	–	6	–	82	–
Guyana	279,799	1,811	119,582	–	1	–	0	–	98	–
Paraguay	17,102	112	7,459	–	15	–	7	–	78	–
Peru	68,039	849	11,807	139.4	7	25	7	15	86	60

Table M
World Countries: Water Resources

COUNTRY	ANNUAL RENEWABLE WATER RESOURCES[a]		ANNUAL AVERAGE GROUNDWATER RESOURCES[b]		SECTORAL WITHDRAWALS (%)[c]					
	Supply Per Capita (cubic meters) 2000	Withdrawal Per Capita (cubic meters) 2000	Recharge Per Capita (cubic meters) 2000	Withdrawal Per Capita (cubic meters) 2000	Domestic		Industry		Agriculture	
					Surface	Ground	Surface	Ground	Surface	Ground
Suriname	479,467	1,171	191,787	–	6	–	5	–	89	–
Uruguay	17,680	1352	6,892	–	6	–	3	–	91[h]	–
Venezuela	35,002	382	9,393	–	44	–	10	–	46	–
ASIA	**3,668**	**627**	**–**	**–**	**7**	**–**	**9**	**–**	**81**	**–**
Afghanistan	2,421	1,846	1,276	–	1	–	0	–	99	–
Armenia	2,577	817	1,193	–	30	–	4	–	66	–
Azerbaijan	1,049	2,186	842	–	5	–	25	–	70	–
Bangladesh	813	134	163	97.6	12	13	2	1	86	88[p]
Bhutan	44,728	13	–	–	36	–	10	–	54	–
Cambodia	10,795	66	1,576	–	5	–	1	–	94	–
China	2,201	439	649	47.1	5	–	18	–	77	54
Georgia	11,702	635	3,469	549.5	21	–	20	–	59	–
India	1,244	588	413	223.3	5	9	3	2	92	89[q]
Indonesia	13,380	407	2,145	–	6	–	1	–	93	–
Iran	1,898	1,165	620	738.8	6	–	2	–	92	–
Iraq	1,523	2,368	562	13.1	3	50	5	40	92	–
Israel	312	292	80	204.5	29	18	7	2	64[i]	80[r]
Japan	3,393	735	213	108.2	19	29	17	41	64	30[s]
Jordan	102	187	87	100.7	22	30	3	4	75	66[t]
Kazakhstan	4,649	2,019	2,211	143.9	2	21	17	71	81	8[u]
Korea, North	2,787	726	874	–	11	–	16	–	73	–
Korea, South	1,384	531	284	55.1	26	–	11	–	63	17[nn]
Kuwait	–	307	–	142.7	37	0	2	0	60	100[v]
Kyrgyzstan	9,884	2,219	2,894	132	3	50	3	25	94	25
Laos	35,049	260	6,994	–	8	–	10	–	82	–
Lebanon	1,463	444	1,463	153.2	28	13	4	9	68	78
Malaysia	26,074	633	2,877	19	11	62	13	33	76	5
Mongolia	13,073	182	2,291	149.1	20	–	27	–	53	–
Myanmar (Burma)	19,306	102	3,420	–	7	–	3	–	90	–
Nepal	8,282	1397	–	–	1	–	0	–	99	–
Oman	388	658	376	280.7	5	–	2	–	94	–
Pakistan	541	1,269	351	489.5	2	–	2	–	97	90[w]
Philippines	6,305	811	2,369	82.8	8	50	4	50	88	–
Saudi Arabia	111	1,002	44	899.3	9	10	1	–	90	90
Singapore	–	–	–	–	–	–	–	–	–	–
Sri Lanka	2,656	573	414	–	2	–	2	–	96	–
Syria	434	1,069	409	133.5	4	13	2	4	94	83[x]
Tajikistan	10,714	2,095	970	398.7	4	–	4	–	92	–
Thailand	3,420	596	682	15	5	60	4	26	91	14
Turkey	2,943	560	300	124	16	31	11	9	73	60[x]
Turkmenistan	305	5,947	753	100.3	1	53	1	9	98	38

Table M
World Countries: Water Resources

COUNTRY	ANNUAL RENEWABLE WATER RESOURCES[a]		ANNUAL AVERAGE GROUNDWATER RESOURCES[b]		SECTORAL WITHDRAWALS (%)[c]					
	Supply Per Capita (cubic meters) 2000	Withdrawal Per Capita (cubic meters) 2000	Recharge Per Capita (cubic meters) 2000	Withdrawal Per Capita (cubic meters) 2000	Domestic		Industry		Agriculture	
					Surface	Ground	Surface	Ground	Surface	Ground
United Arab Emirates	61	954	49	724.1	24	–	10	19[d]	67	81[y]
Uzbekistan	672	2,626	809	334.3	4	–	2	11	94	57[z]
Vietnam	4,591	814	601	11.9	4	–	10	–	86	–
Yemen	226	253	84	139.2	7	–	1	–	92	–
EUROPE	**3,981**	**704**	**–**	**–**	**14**	**–**	**45**	**–**	**39**	**–**
Albania	8,646	441	2,248	193.6	29	48	0	–	71	52
Austria	6,699	281	2,716	172.5	31	52	60	43	9	5[aa]
Belarus	3,634	266	1,758	115.7	22	52	43	13	35	28[bb]
Belgium	1,181	917	89	79	–	55	–	22	–	4
Bosnia-Herzegovina	8,938	–	–	–	–	–	–	–	–	–
Bulgaria	2,188	1,574	1,629	566.1	3	–	77	–	22	–
Croatia	8,429	170	2459	–	50	–	50	–	0	–
Czech Republic	1,464	244	–	48	39	–	57	–	1	–
Denmark	1,134	170	5,668	169.8	53	40	9	22	16	38[cc]
Estonia	9,105	106	2,865	–	56	–	39	–	5	–
Finland	20,673	477	367	47.8	17	65	82	11	–	24[dd]
France	3,047	704	1,693	103.8	15	56	73	27	12	17
Germany	1,301	583	556	89.4	14	48	86	47	0	4[ee]
Greece	5,073	688	968	195.7	16	37	3	5	81	58
Hungary	598	612	678	96.5	14	35	70	48	5	18[ff]
Iceland	605,049	611	85,419	558.9	50	–	6	–	–	–
Ireland	13,136	326	928	62.3	40	35	21	38	15	29[gg]
Italy	2,804	840	750	243.2	14	39	33	4	53	58
Latvia	7,104	111	934	–	55	–	32	–	13	–
Lithuania	4,239	68	327	55.1	81	–	16	–	3	–
Macedonia	2,965	–	–	–	–	–	–	–	–	–
Moldova	228	677	91	–	9	–	65	–	26	–
Netherlands	697	522	285	70.2	16	32	68	45	–	23[hh]
Norway	85,560	488	21,502	97.5	27	27	68	73	3	–
Poland	1,419	313	929	51.5	20	70	64	30	2	–
Portugal	3,747	739	516	311	8	39	40	23	53	39[ii]
Romania	2,195	851	372	158	–	61	–	38	–	1[jj]
Russia	29,351	520	5,363	85.5	19	–	62	–	20	–
Slovakia	2,413	263	–	113	39	–	50	–	8	–
Slovenia	9,317	250	–	88.9	50	–	50	–	0	–
Spain	2,821	897	729	137.2	13	18	18	2	68	80
Sweden	19,977	310	2,245	72.8	35	92	30	8	4	–
Switzerland	5,416	363	366	126.3	42	72	58	40	0	–
Ukraine	1,052	501	396	77.5	18	30	52	18	30	52[kk]
United Kingdom	2,465	160	167	42.4	65	51	8	47	2	2[ll]

Table M
World Countries: Water Resources

COUNTRY	ANNUAL RENEWABLE WATER RESOURCES[a]		ANNUAL AVERAGE GROUNDWATER RESOURCES[b]		SECTORAL WITHDRAWALS (%)[c]					
	Supply Per Capita (cubic meters) 2000	Withdrawal Per Capita (cubic meters) 2000	Recharge Per Capita (cubic meters) 2000	Withdrawal Per Capita (cubic meters) 2000	Domestic		Industry		Agriculture	
					Surface	Ground	Surface	Ground	Surface	Ground
Yugoslavia (Serbia-Montenegro)	4,135	–	–	–	–	–	–	–	–	–
OCEANIA	**78,886**	**1178**	–	–	–	–	–	–	–	–
Australia	18,638	839	3812	143.2	12	–	6	20[d]	70[j]	67[mm]
Fiji	–	–	–	–	–	–	–	–	–	–
New Zealand	84,673	545	51,270	–	9	–	13	–	55	–
Papua New Guinea	166,644	28	–	–	29	–	22	–	49	–
Solomon Islands	–	–	–	–	–	–	–	–	–	–

a. Annual renewable water resources usually include river flows from other countries.
b. Withdrawal data from most recent year available; varies by country from 1987 to 1995.
c. Total withdrawals may exceed 100% because of groundwater withdrawals or river inflows.
d. Domestic and industrial withdrawals have been combined.
e. An additional 5% is reserved for overflow.
f. Sectoral figures are for 1982.
g. Sectoral figures are for 1984.
h. Sectoral figures are for 1965.
i. Sectoral withdrawals reflect percentages of a total water withdrawal (1.959 cubic km) for 1997, including recycled water.
j. Sectoral figures are for 1985.
k. Sectoral figures are for 1992, Margat Blue Plan.
l. Sectoral percentages are calculated using groundwater withdrawal of 3.81 km^3, which is an estimate provided with sectoral data for 1995 in the Margat Blue Plan.
m. Sectoral data for Canada are calculated using a groundwater withdrawal value of 1.6 km^3 from 1985 as reported by Margat 1990.
n. Sectoral data for the U.S. are calculated using a groundwater withdrawal value of 101.3 km^3 from 1985 as reported by Margat 1990.
o. Sectoral data for Mexico are calculated using a groundwater withdrawal value of 23.5 km^3 from 1985 as reported by Margat 1990.
p. Sectoral data for Bangladesh are calculated using a groundwater withdrawal value of 3.4 km^3 from 1979 as reported by Margat 1990.
q. Sectoral data are from around 1990 as provided by Shiklomonov; total withdrawal data are also from 1990, but are from FAO.
r. Sectoral figures are for 1994, Margat Blue Plan.
s. Sectoral data are from around 1987 as provided by Shiklomonov 1997 based on groundwater withdrawal of 12.88 km^3.
t. Ground water withdrawal and sectoral data are estimated from a bar graph from 1993 from FAO Water Report.
u. Both withdrawal and sectoral data are estimated from a bar graph from FAO Report.
v. Ground water withdrawal and sectoral data are estimated from a bar graph from 1994 from FAO Water Report.
w. Sectoral data for Pakistan are from Shiklomonov who reports approximately 90% for agriculture share; total withdrawal also is approximately 60 km^3 per year for 1990.
x. Sectoral figures are for 1990, Margat Blue Plan.
y. Sectoral percentages for UAE are a combination of data from text and a bar graph for 1995 from FAO Water Report.
z. Sectoral data for Uzbekistan are from 1994 FAO irrigation in the former Soviet Union in figures estimated from a bar graph.
aa. Sectoral data for Austria are calculated using a groundwater withdrawal value of 1.17 km^3 from 1985 as reported by Margat 1990.
bb. Sectoral data for Belarus are calculated using a groundwater withdrawal value of 1.06 km^3 from 1985 as reported by Margat 1990.
cc. Sectoral data calculated using a groundwater withdrawal value of 1.32 km^3 from 1977 as reported by Margat 1990.
dd. Sectoral data calculated using a groundwater withdrawal value of .37 km^3 from 1980 as reported by Margat 1990.
ff. Sectoral data calculated using a groundwater withdrawal value of 1.6 km^3 from 1972 as reported by Margat 1990.
gg. Sectoral data calculated using a groundwater withdrawal value of .17 km^3 from 1980 as reported by Margat 1990.
hh. Sectoral data calculated using a groundwater withdrawal value of 1.28 km^3 from 1981 as reported by Margat 1990.
ii. Sectoral data calculated using a groundwater withdrawal value of 2.0 km^3 from 1980 as reported by Margat 1990.
jj. Sectoral data calculated using a groundwater withdrawal value of 1.18 km^3 from 1975 as reported by Margat 1990.
kk. Sectoral data calculated using a groundwater withdrawal value of 4.22 km^3 from 1985 as reported by Margat 1990.
ll. Sectoral data calculated using a groundwater withdrawal value of 2.38 km^3 from 1975 as reported by Margat 1990.
mm. Sectoral data calculated using a groundwater withdrawal value of 2.46 km^3 from 1983 as reported by Margat 1990.
nn. Sectoral data calculated using a groundwater withdrawal value of 1.2 km^3 from 1985 as reported by Margat 1990.

Source: *World Resources 1998–99* (Washington, DC, World Resources Institute)

Table N
World Countries: Energy Efficiency and Emissions, 1980–1998

COUNTRY	GDP PER UNIT OF ENERGY USE		TRADITIONAL FUEL USE		CARBON DIOXIDE EMISSIONS					
	PPP $ per Kg. of Oil Equivalent		% of Total Energy Use		Total Million Metric Tons		Per Capita Metric Tons		Kg. per PPP $ of GDP	
	1980	1998	1980	1997	1980	1997	1980	1997	1980	1997
Albania	–	10.3	13.1	7.3	5.3	1.7	2.0	0.5	–	0.2
Algeria	5.0	5.4	1.9	1.5	68.2	98.7	3.7	3.4	1.1	0.7
Angola	–	3.8	64.9	69.7	5.4	5.3	0.8	0.5	–	0.2
Argentina	4.7	7.3	5.9	4.0	111.0	140.6	4.0	3.9	0.6	0.3
Armenia	–	4.3	–	0.0	–	2.9	–	0.8	–	0.4
Australia	2.1	4.1	3.8	4.4	205.5	319.6	14.0	17.2	1.4	0.8
Austria	3.5	6.7	1.2	4.7	55.1	62.6	7.3	7.8	0.7	0.3
Azerbaijan	–	1.5	–	0.0	–	32.0	–	4.1	–	1.9
Bangladesh	4.5	8.9	81.3	46.0	7.8	24.6	0.1	0.2	0.2	0.1
Belarus	–	2.5	–	0.8	–	62.3	–	6.1	–	1.0
Belgium	2.4	4.3	0.2	1.6	131.0	106.5	13.3	10.5	1.2	0.4
Benin	1.3	2.4	85.4	89.2	0.7	1.0	0.2	0.2	0.4	0.2
Bolivia	3.4	4.0	19.3	14.0	4.7	11.3	0.9	1.4	0.6	0.6
Bosnia-Herzegovina	–	–	–	10.1	–	4.5	–	1.2	–	–
Botswana	–	–	35.7	–	1.0	3.4	1.1	2.2	0.6	0.3
Brazil	4.4	6.5	35.5	28.7	197.0	307.2	1.6	1.9	0.4	0.3
Bulgaria	0.9	2.0	0.5	1.3	77.9	50.3	8.8	6.1	3.0	1.2
Burkina Faso	–	–	91.3	87.1	0.4	1.0	0.1	0.1	0.1	0.1
Burundi	–	–	97.0	94.2	0.1	0.2	0.0	0.0	0.1	0.1
Cambodia	–	–	100.0	89.3	0.3	0.5	0.0	0.0	–	0.0
Cameroon	2.8	3.5	51.7	69.2	4.1	2.7	0.5	0.2	0.4	0.1
Canada	1.5	3.2	0.4	4.7	426.1	496.6	17.3	16.6	1.5	0.7
Central African Republic	–	–	88.9	87.5	0.1	0.2	0.0	0.1	0.1	0.1
Chad	–	–	95.9	97.6	0.2	0.1	0.0	0.0	0.1	0.0
Chile	3.1	5.4	12.3	11.3	28.3	60.1	2.5	4.1	0.9	0.5
China	0.8	4.0	8.4	5.7	1516.6	3593.5	1.5	2.9	3.3	0.9
Colombia	4.1	7.9	15.9	17.7	42.0	71.9	1.5	1.8	0.5	0.3
Congo Republic	0.8	1.8	77.8	53.0	0.4	0.3	0.2	0.1	0.6	0.1
Costa Rica	5.7	9.5	26.3	54.2	2.7	5.4	1.2	1.6	0.3	0.2
Côte d'Ivoire	–	–	52.8	91.5	5.3	13.3	0.6	0.9	0.5	0.6
Croatia	–	3.9	–	3.2	–	20.1	–	4.4	–	0.6
Cuba	–	–	27.9	30.2	32.4	26.0	3.3	2.3	–	–
Czech Republic	–	3.2	0.6	1.6	–	125.2	–	12.2	–	0.9
Democratic Republic of the Congo (formerly Zaire)	3.5	2.8	73.9	91.7	3.7	2.3	0.1	0.1	0.1	0.1
Denmark	–	6.4	0.4	5.9	63.9	57.7	12.5	10.9	–	0.4
Dominican Republic	3.7	7.5	27.5	14.3	6.9	14.0	1.2	1.7	0.5	0.4
Ecuador	3.0	4.3	26.7	17.5	14.1	21.7	1.8	1.8	0.9	0.6
Egypt	3.5	4.7	4.7	3.2	46.7	118.3	1.1	2.0	0.8	0.6
El Salvador	4.3	6.5	52.9	34.5	2.4	5.9	0.5	1.0	0.2	0.2
Eritrea	–	–	–	96.0	–	–	–	–	–	–
Estonia	–	2.5	–	13.8	–	19.1	–	13.1	–	1.6
Ethiopia	1.4	2.1	89.6	95.9	1.9	3.8	0.0	0.1	0.1	0.1
Finland	1.8	3.4	4.3	6.5	55.8	56.6	11.7	11.0	1.2	0.5
France	2.9	5.0	1.3	5.7	497.2	349.8	9.2	6.0	0.9	0.3
Gabon	1.9	4.5	30.8	32.9	5.0	3.4	7.2	3.0	1.7	0.5

COUNTRY	GDP PER UNIT OF ENERGY USE		TRADITIONAL FUEL USE		CARBON DIOXIDE EMISSIONS					
	PPP $ per Kg. of Oil Equivalent		% of Total Energy Use		Total Million Metric Tons		Per Capita Metric Tons		Kg. per PPP $ of GDP	
	1980	1998	1980	1997	1980	1997	1980	1997	1980	1997
The Gambia	–	–	72.7	78.6	0.2	0.2	0.2	0.2	0.3	0.1
Georgia	–	7.1	–	1.0	–	4.5	–	0.8	–	0.3
Germany	–	5.5	0.3	1.3	–	851.5	–	10.4	–	0.5
Ghana	2.9	4.6	43.7	78.1	2.6	4.8	0.2	0.3	0.2	0.1
Greece	4.2	5.7	3.0	4.5	58.1	87.2	6.0	8.3	0.9	0.6
Guatemala	4.1	6.1	54.6	62.0	4.8	8.3	0.7	0.8	0.3	0.2
Guinea	–	–	71.4	74.2	0.9	1.1	0.2	0.2	–	0.1
Guinea-Bissau	–	–	80.0	57.1	0.1	0.2	0.2	0.2	0.5	0.2
Haiti	3.7	5.3	80.7	74.7	0.9	1.4	0.2	0.2	0.1	0.1
Honduras	2.9	4.5	55.3	54.8	2.3	4.6	0.6	0.8	0.4	0.3
Hong Kong, China	6.4	8.5	0.9	0.7	17.1	23.8	3.4	3.7	0.5	0.2
Hungary	2.0	4.3	2.0	1.6	84.8	59.6	7.9	5.9	1.4	0.6
India	1.9	4.3	31.5	20.7	356.1	1065.4	0.5	1.1	0.8	0.5
Indonesia	2.2	4.6	51.5	29.3	97.5	251.5	0.7	1.3	0.8	0.4
Iran	2.9	3.3	0.4	0.7	120.0	296.9	3.1	4.9	1.1	0.9
Iraq	–	–	0.3	0.1	46.7	92.3	3.6	4.2	–	–
Ireland	2.3	6.4	0.0	0.2	26.1	37.3	7.7	10.2	1.3	0.5
Israel	3.6	5.7	0.0	0.0	22.1	60.4	5.7	10.4	0.7	0.6
Italy	3.9	7.4	0.8	1.0	392.7	424.7	7.0	7.4	0.7	0.3
Jamaica	1.9	2.2	5.0	6.0	8.5	11.0	4.0	4.3	1.9	1.2
Japan	3.3	6.0	0.1	1.6	964.2	1204.2	8.3	9.6	0.8	0.4
Jordan	3.3	3.6	0.0	0.0	5.2	15.7	2.4	3.5	0.9	0.9
Kazakhstan	–	1.8	–	0.2	–	123.0	–	8.0	–	1.7
Kenya	1.1	2.0	76.8	80.3	6.8	7.2	0.4	0.3	0.7	0.2
Korea, North	–	–	3.1	1.4	128.9	260.5	7.3	11.4	–	–
Korea, South	2.8	4.0	4.0	2.4	132.9	457.4	3.5	9.9	1.2	0.6
Kuwait	1.3	2.1	0.0	0.0	25.4	51.0	18.5	28.2	1.6	1.8
Kyrgyzstan	–	4.0	–	0.0	–	6.8	–	1.4	–	0.6
Laos	–	–	72.3	88.7	0.2	0.4	0.1	0.1	–	0.1
Latvia	19.6	3.4	–	26.2	–	8.3	–	3.3	–	0.6
Lebanon	–	3.7	2.4	2.5	6.9	17.7	2.3	4.3	–	1.0
Lesotho	–	–	–	–	–	–	–	–	–	–
Libya	–	–	2.3	0.9	28.5	43.5	9.4	8.4	–	–
Lithuania	–	2.7	–	6.3	–	15.1	–	4.1	–	0.6
Macedonia	–	–	–	6.1	–	10.9	–	5.5	–	1.2
Madagascar	–	–	78.4	84.3	1.6	1.2	0.2	0.1	0.3	0.1
Malawi	–	–	90.6	88.6	0.8	0.8	0.1	0.1	0.3	0.1
Malaysia	2.7	3.9	15.7	5.5	29.1	137.2	2.1	6.3	0.9	0.7
Mali	–	–	86.7	88.9	0.4	0.5	0.1	0.0	0.1	0.1
Mauritania	–	–	0.0	0.0	0.6	3.0	0.4	1.2	0.4	0.8
Mauritius	–	–	59.1	36.1	0.6	1.7	0.6	1.5	0.3	0.2
Mexico	3.1	5.2	5.0	4.5	259.6	379.7	3.8	4.0	0.8	0.5
Moldova	–	2.2	–	0.5	–	10.4	–	2.4	–	1.1
Mongolia	–	–	14.4	4.3	6.9	7.8	4.1	3.3	3.6	2.1
Morocco	6.8	10.2	5.2	4.0	17.7	35.9	0.9	1.3	0.5	0.4
Mozambique	0.6	2.0	43.7	91.4	3.3	1.2	0.3	0.1	0.7	0.1
Myanmar (Burma)	–	–	69.3	60.5	5.0	8.8	0.1	0.2	–	–

COUNTRY	GDP PER UNIT OF ENERGY USE		TRADITIONAL FUEL USE		CARBON DIOXIDE EMISSIONS					
	PPP $ per Kg. of Oil Equivalent		% of Total Energy Use		Total Million Metric Tons		Per Capita Metric Tons		Kg. per PPP $ of GDP	
	1980	1998	1980	1997	1980	1997	1980	1997	1980	1997
Namibia	–	–	–	–	–	–	–	–	–	–
Nepal	1.5	3.5	94.2	89.6	0.6	2.2	0.0	0.1	0.1	0.1
Netherlands	2.2	4.9	0.0	1.1	154.5	163.6	10.9	10.5	1.1	0.5
New Zealand	–	4.0	0.2	0.8	17.9	31.6	5.8	8.4	–	0.5
Nicaragua	3.6	4.0	49.2	42.2	2.1	3.2	0.7	0.7	0.4	0.3
Niger	–	–	79.5	80.6	0.6	1.1	0.1	0.1	0.1	0.2
Nigeria	0.8	1.2	66.8	67.8	69.1	83.7	1.0	0.7	1.6	0.9
Norway	2.4	4.8	0.4	1.1	91.5	68.5	22.4	15.6	2.0	0.6
Oman	–	–	0.0	–	5.9	18.4	5.3	8.2	–	–
Pakistan	2.1	4.0	24.4	29.5	33.3	98.2	0.4	0.8	0.6	0.4
Panama	3.2	6.5	26.6	14.4	3.7	8.0	1.9	2.9	0.6	0.5
Papua New Guinea	–	–	65.4	62.5	1.8	2.5	0.6	0.5	0.5	0.2
Paraguay	4.2	5.4	62.0	49.6	1.6	4.1	0.5	0.8	0.2	0.2
Peru	4.6	7.8	15.2	24.6	24.7	30.1	1.4	1.2	0.5	0.3
Philippines	5.6	7.0	37.0	26.9	38.8	81.7	0.8	1.1	0.3	0.3
Poland	–	3.2	0.4	0.8	465.4	357.0	13.1	9.2	–	1.2
Portugal	5.6	7.0	1.2	0.9	29.9	53.8	3.1	5.4	0.5	0.4
Puerto Rico	–	–	0.0	–	14.7	17.1	4.6	4.5	–	–
Romania	1.6	3.5	1.3	5.7	199.6	111.3	9.0	4.9	1.9	0.8
Russia	–	1.7	–	0.8	–	1444.5	–	9.8	–	1.4
Rwanda	–	–	89.8	88.3	0.3	0.5	0.1	0.1	0.1	0.1
Saudi Arabia	3.0	2.1	0.0	0.0	132.2	273.7	14.1	14.3	1.2	1.3
Senegal	2.3	4.4	50.8	56.2	3.0	3.5	0.5	0.4	0.7	0.3
Sierra Leone	–	–	90.0	86.1	0.6	0.5	0.2	0.1	0.3	0.2
Singapore	2.3	3.1	0.4	0.0	31.1	81.9	12.9	21.9	2.2	1.1
Slovakia	–	3.2	–	0.5	–	38.1	–	7.1	–	0.7
Slovenia	–	4.4	–	1.5	–	15.5	–	7.8	–	0.5
South Africa	2.7	3.3	4.9	43.4	214.9	321.5	7.8	7.9	1.2	0.9
Spain	3.8	5.9	0.4	1.3	214.0	257.7	5.7	6.6	0.8	0.4
Sri Lanka	3.5	8.0	53.5	46.5	3.7	8.1	0.3	0.4	0.2	0.1
Sudan	–	–	86.9	75.1	3.4	3.8	0.2	0.1	–	–
Sweden	2.1	3.6	7.7	17.9	72.6	48.6	8.7	5.5	0.8	0.3
Switzerland	4.4	7.0	0.9	6.0	43.0	42.6	6.8	6.0	0.5	0.2
Syria	2.9	3.3	0.0	0.0	20.3	49.9	2.3	3.3	1.3	1.0
Tajikistan	–	–	–	–	–	5.6	–	0.9	–	–
Tanzania	–	1.1	92.0	91.4	2.0	2.9	0.1	0.1	–	0.2
Thailand	3.0	5.1	40.3	24.6	42.7	226.8	0.9	3.8	0.6	0.6
Togo	–	–	35.7	71.9	0.8	1.0	0.3	0.2	0.2	0.2
Trinidad and Tobago	1.3	1.1	1.4	0.8	16.8	22.3	15.5	17.4	3.4	2.4
Tunisia	4.0	6.9	16.1	12.5	10.3	18.8	1.6	2.0	0.7	0.4
Turkey	3.6	5.8	20.5	3.1	82.8	216.0	1.9	3.5	0.7	0.5
Turkmenistan	–	1.2	–	–	–	31.0	–	6.7	–	2.5
Uganda	–	–	93.6	89.7	0.6	1.2	0.1	0.1	0.1	0.1
Ukraine	–	1.2	–	0.5	–	370.5	–	7.3	–	2.1
United Arab Emirates	4.4	1.8	0.0	–	37.1	82.5	35.6	32.0	1.4	1.6
United Kingdom	–	5.4	0.0	3.3	591.2	527.1	10.5	8.9	–	0.4
United States	1.6	3.8	1.3	3.8	4609.4	5467.1	20.3	20.1	1.6	0.7

COUNTRY	GDP PER UNIT OF ENERGY USE		TRADITIONAL FUEL USE		CARBON DIOXIDE EMISSIONS					
	PPP $ per Kg. of Oil Equivalent		% of Total Energy Use		Total Million Metric Tons		Per Capita Metric Tons		Kg. per PPP $ of GDP	
	1980	1998	1980	1997	1980	1997	1980	1997	1980	1997
Uruguay	5.0	9.9	11.1	21.0	6.2	5.7	2.1	1.8	0.5	0.2
Uzbekistan	–	1.1	–	0.0	–	104.8	–	4.4	–	2.1
Venezuela	1.7	2.4	0.9	0.7	92.0	191.2	6.1	8.4	1.5	1.4
Vietnam	–	4.0	49.1	37.8	17.0	45.5	0.3	0.6	–	0.4
West Bank and Gaza	–	–	–	–	–	–	–	–	–	–
Yemen	–	3.7	0.0	1.4	–	16.7	–	1.0	–	1.3
Yugoslavia (Serbia-Montenegro)	–	–	–	1.5	–	50.2	–	4.7	–	–
Zambia	0.7	1.2	37.4	72.7	3.6	2.6	0.6	0.3	0.9	0.4
Zimbabwe	1.5	3.3	27.6	25.2	9.9	18.8	1.4	1.6	1.0	0.6
WORLD[1]	**2.1**	**4.2**	**7.4**	**8.2**	**14014.6**	**23868.2**	**3.5**	**4.1**	**1.2**	**0.6**
Low income	–	3.4	46.4	29.8	794.9	2527.5	0.5	1.1	0.7	0.6
Middle income	2.2	3.9	10.4	7.3	4304.9	10006.0	2.4	3.8	1.3	0.8
Lower middle income	1.6	3.6	10.7	5.7	2457.8	6957.9	1.7	3.4	1.7	0.9
Upper middle income	3.3	4.3	8.6	10.6	1847.0	3048.1	4.6	5.5	1.0	0.6
Low & middle income	–	3.7	18.5	12.9	5099.8	12533.6	1.5	2.5	1.2	0.7
East Asia & Pacific	–	–	15.1	9.7	2019.6	5075.6	1.4	2.8	2.0	0.8
Europe & Central Asia	–	2.3	3.2	1.3	915.8	3285.6	–	6.9	2.1	1.2
Latin America & Carib.	3.7	5.7	18.4	16.0	884.7	1356.4	2.5	2.8	0.6	0.4
Middle East & N. Africa	3.4	3.5	1.6	1.1	517.8	1113.6	3.1	4.0	1.1	0.9
South Asia	2.0	4.5	34.2	23.8	403.4	1200.5	0.4	0.9	0.7	0.5
Sub-Saharan Africa	–	–	47.2	63.5	358.4	501.8	1.0	0.8	0.9	0.6
High Income	2.2	4.6	1.0	3.4	8914.8	11334.6	12.6	12.8	1.2	0.5
Europe EMU	3.1	5.6	0.7	2.5	1569.7	2378.6	7.9	8.2	0.9	0.4

Source: World Development Indicators (World Bank, Washington, DC, 2001).

1. World Bank estimations. Missing data are inputed wherever possible.

Part IX

Geographic Index

Name/Description	Latitude & Longitude	Page
Abidjan,Cote d'Ivoire (city,nat. cap.)	5N 4W	97
Abu Dhabi, U.A.E. (city, nat. cap.)	24N 54E	95
Accra, Ghana (city, nat. cap.)	64N 0	97
Aconcagua, Mt. 22,881	38S 78W	90
Acre (st., Brazil)	9S 70W	91
Addis Ababa, Ethiopia (city, nat. cap.)	9N 39E	97
Adelaide, S. Australia (city, st. cap.,Aust.)	35S 139E	99
Aden, Gulf of	12N 46E	94
Aden, Yemen (city)	13N 45E	95
Admiralty Islands	1S 146E	98
Adriatic Sea	44N 14E	92
Aegean Sea	39N 25E	92
Afghanistan (country)	35N 65E	95
Aguascalientes (st., Mex.)	22N 110W	90
Aguascalientes, Aguas. (city, st. cap., Mex.)	22N 102W	90
Agulhas, Cape	35S 20E	96
Ahaggar Range	23N 6E	96
Ahmadabad, India (city)	23N 73E	95
Akmola, Kazakhstan (city)	51N 72E	95
Al Fashir, Sudan (city)	14N 25E	97
Al Fayyum, Egypt (city)	29N 31E	97
Al Hijaz Range	30N 40E	94
Al Khufra Oasis	24N 23E	96
Alabama (st., US)	33N 87W	89
Alagoas (st., Brazil)	9S 37W	91
Alaska (st., US)	63N 153W	89 inset
Alaska, Gulf of	58N 150W	89 inset
Alaska Peninsula	57N 155W	88 inset
Alaska Range	60N 150W	88 inset
Albania (country)	41N 20E	93
Albany, Australia (city)	35S 118E	99
Albany, New York (city, st. cap., US)	43N 74W	89
Albert Edward, Mt. 13,090	8S 147E	98
Albert, Lake	2N 30E	96
Alberta (prov., Can.)	55N 117W	89
Albuquerque, NM (city)	35N 107W	89

The geographic index contains approximately 1,500 names of cities, states, countries, rivers, lakes, mountain ranges, oceans, capes, bays, and other geographic features. The name of each geographical feature in the index is accompanied by a geographical coordinate (latitude and longitude) in degrees and by the page number of the primary map on which the geographical feature appears. Where the geographical coordinates are for specific places or points, such as a city or a mountain peak, the latitude and longitude figures give the location of the map symbol denoting that point. Thus, Los Angeles, California, is at 34N and 118W and the location of Mt. Everest is 28N and 87E.

The coordinates for political features (countries or states) or physical features (oceans, deserts) that are areas rather than points are given according to the location of the name of the feature on the map, except in those cases where the name of the feature is separated from the feature (such as a country's name appearing over an adjacent ocean area because of space requirements). In such cases, the feature's coordinates will indicate the location of the center of the feature. The coordinates for the Sahara Desert will lead the reader to the place name "Sahara Desert" on the map; the coordinates for North Carolina will show the center location of the state since the name appears over the adjacent Atlantic Ocean. Finally, the coordinates for geographical features that are lines rather than points or areas will also appear near the center of the text identifying the geographical feature.

Alphabetizing follows general conventions; the names of physical features such as lakes, rivers, mountains are given as: proper name, followed by the generic name. Thus "Mount Everest" is listed as "Everest, Mt." Where an article such as "the," "le," or "al" appears in a geographic name, the name is alphabetized according to the article. Hence, "La Paz" is found under "L" and not under "P."

Geographic Index

Geographic Index

Name/Description	Latitude & Longitude	Page
Ascension (island)	9S 13W	96
Ashburton (riv., Australasia)	23S 115W	94
Ashkhabad, Turkmenistan (city, nat. cap.)	38N 58E	95
Asia Minor	39N 33E	97
Asmera, Eritrea (city, nat. cap.)	15N 39E	97
Astrakhan, Russia (city)	46N 48E	93
Asuncion, Paraguay (city, nat. cap.)	25S 57W	91
Aswan, Egypt (city)	24N 33E	97
Asyuf, Egypt (city)	27N 31E	97
Atacama Desert	23S 70W	90
Athabasca (lake, N.Am.)	60N 109W	88
Athabaska (riv., N.Am.)	58N 114W	88
Athens, Greece (city, nat. cap.)	38N 24E	93
Atlanta, Georgia (city, st. cap., US)	34N 84W	89
Atlantic Ocean	30N 40W	88
Atlas Mountains	31N 6W	96
Auckland, New Zealand (city)	37S 175E	99
Augusta, Maine (city, st. cap., US)	44N 70W	89
Austin, Texas (city, st. cap., US)	30N 98W	89
Australia (country)	20S 135W	99
Austria (country)	47N 14E	93
Ayers Rock 2844	25S 131E	98
Azerbaijan (country)	38N 48E	93
Azov, Sea of	48N 36E	92
Bab el Mandeb (strait)	13N 42E	96
Baffin Bay	74N 65W	88
Baffin Island	70N 72W	88
Baghdad, Iraq (city, nat. cap.)	33N 44E	92
Bahamas (island)	25N 75W	88
Bahia (st., Brazil)	13S 42W	91
Bahia Blanca, Argentina (city)	39S 62W	91
Baikal, Lake	52N 105E	94
Baja California (st., Mex.)	30N 110W	89
Baja California Sur (st., Mex.)	25N 110W	89
Baku, Azerbaijan (city, nat. cap.)	40N 50E	93
Balearic Islands	29N 3E	93
Balkash, Lake	47N 75E	94
Ballarat, Aust. (city)	38S 144E	99
Baltic Sea	56N 18E	92
Baltimore, MD (city)	39N 77W	94
Bamako, Mali (city, nat. cap.)	13N 8W	97
Bandiera Peak 9,843	20S 42W	90
Bangalore, India (city)	13N 75E	95
Bangeta, Mt. 13,520	6S 147E	98
Banghazi, Libya (city)	32N 20E	97
Bangkok, Thailand (city, nat. cap.)	14N 100E	95
Bangladesh (country)	23N 92E	95
Bangui, Cent. African Rep. (city, nat. cap.)	4N 19E	97
Banjul, Gambia (city, nat. cap.)	13N 17W	97

Geographic Index

Name/Description	Latitude & Longitude	Page
Banks Island	73N 125W	88
Barbados (island)	13N 60W	91
Barcelona, Spain (city)	41N 2E	93
Barents Sea	69N 40E	94
Bartle Frere, Mt. 5322	18S 145W	98
Barwon (riv., Australasia)	29S 148E	98
Bass Strait	40S 146E	98
Baton Rouge, Louisiana (city, st. cap., US)	30N 91W	89
Beaufort Sea	72N 135W	88
Beijing, China (city, nat. cap.)	40N 116E	95
Beirut, Lebanon (city, nat. cap.)	34N 35E	93
Belarus (country)	52N 27E	93
Belem, Para (city, st. cap., Braz.)	1S 48W	91
Belfast, Northern Ireland (city)	55N 6W	93
Belgium (country)	51N 4E	93
Belgrade, Yugoslavia (city, nat. cap.)	45N 21E	93
Belhuka, Mt. 14,483	50N 86E	94
Belize (country)	18S 88W	89
Belle Isle, Strait of	52N 57W	88
Belmopan, Belize (city, nat. cap.)	18S 89W	89
Belo Horizonte, M.G. (city, st. cap., Braz.)	20S 43W	91
Belyando (riv., Australasia)	22S 147W	98
Ben, Rio (riv., S.Am.)	14S 67W	90
Bengal, Bay of	15N 90E	94
Benguela, Angola (city)	13S 13E	97
Benin (country)	10N 4E	97
Benin City, Nigeria (city)	6N 6E	97
Benue (riv., Africa)	8N 9E	96
Bergen, Norway (city)	60N 5E	93
Bering Sea	57N 175W	94
Bering Strait	65N 168W	94
Berlin, Germany (city)	52N 13E	93
Bermeo, Rio (riv., S.Am.)	25S 61W	90
Bermuda (island)	30S 66W	89
Bhutan (country)	28N 110E	95
Billings, MT (city)	46N 108W	89
Birmingham, AL (city)	34N 87W	89
Birmingham, UK (city)	52N 2W	93
Biscay, Bay of	45N 5W	92
Bishkek, Kyrgyzstan (city, nat. cap.)	43N 75E	95
Bismarck Archipelago	4S 147E	98
Bismarck, North Dakota (city, st. cap., US)	47N 101W	89
Bismarck Range	6S 145E	98
Bissau, Guinea-Bissau (city, nat. cap.)	12N 16W	97
Black Sea	46N 34E	92
Blanc, Cape	21N 18W	96
Blue Nile (riv., Africa)	10N 36E	96
Blue Mountains	33S 150E	98
Boa Vista do Rio Branco, Roraima (city, st. cap., Braz.)	3N 61W	91

Geographic Index

Name/Description	Latitude & Longitude	Page
Boise, Idaho (city, st. cap., US)	44N 116W	89
Bolivia (country)	17S 65W	91
Boma, Congo Republic (city)	5S 13E	97
Bombay, (Mumbai) India (city)	19N 73E	95
Bonn, Germany (city, nat. cap.)	51N 7E	93
Boothia Peninsula	71N 94W	88
Borneo (island)	0 11E	95
Bosnia-Herzegovina (country)	45N 18E	93
Bosporus, Strait of	41N 29E	92
Boston, Massachusetts (city, st. cap., US)	42N 71W	89
Botany Bay	35S 153E	99
Bothnia, Gulf of	62N 20E	92
Botswana (country)	23S 25E	97
Brahmaputra (riv., Asia)	30N 100E	94
Branco, Rio (riv., S.Am.)	3N 62W	90
Brasilia, Brazil (city, nat. cap.)	16S 48W	91
Bratislava, Slovakia (city, nat. cap.)	48N 17E	93
Brazil (country)	10S 52W	91
Brazilian Highlands	18S 45W	90
Brazzaville, Congo (city, nat. cap.)	4S 15E	97
Brisbane, Queensland (city, st. cap., Aust.)	27S 153E	99
Bristol Bay	58N 159W	88 inset
British Columbia (prov., Can.)	54N 130W	89
Brooks Range	67N 155W	88
Bruce, Mt. 4052	22S 117W	98
Brussels, Belgium (city, nat. cap.)	51N 4E	93
Bucharest, Romania (city, nat. cap.)	44N 26E	93
Budapest, Hungary (city, nat. cap.)	47N 19E	93
Buenos Aires, Argentina (city, nat. cap.)	34S 58W	91
Buenos Aires (st., Argentina)	36S 60W	91
Buffalo, NY (city)	43N 79W	89
Bujumbura, Burundi (city, nat. cap.)	3S 29E	97
Bulgaria (country)	44N 26E	93
Bur Sudan, Sudan (city)	19N 37E	97
Burdekin (riv., Australasia)	19S 146W	98
Burkina Faso (country)	11N 2W	97
Buru (island)	4S 127E	98
Burundi (country)	4S 30E	97
Cairns, Aust. (city)	17S 145E	99
Cairo, Egypt (city, nat. cap.)	30N 31E	97
Calcutta, (Kolkota) India (city)	23N 88E	95
Calgary, Canada (city)	51N 114W	89
Calicut, India (city)	11N 76E	95
California (st., US)	35N 120W	89
California, Gulf of	29N 110W	89
Callao, Peru (city)	13S 77W	91
Cambodia (country)	10N 106E	95
Cameroon (country)	5N 13E	97
Campeche (st., Mex.)	19N 90W	89

Geographic Index

Name/Description	Latitude & Longitude	Page
Campeche Bay	20N 92W	88
Campeche, Campeche (city, st. cap., Mex.)	19N 90W	89
Campo Grande, M.G.S. (city, st. cap., Braz.)	20S 55W	91
Canada (country)	52N 100W	89
Canadian (riv., N.Am.)	30N 100W	88
Canary Islands	29N 18W	96
Canberra, Australia (city, nat. cap.)	35S 149E	99
Cape Breton Island	46N 60W	88
Cape Town, South Africa (city)	34S 18E	97
Caracas, Venezuela (city, nat. cap.)	10N 67W	91
Caribbean Sea	18N 75W	91
Carnarvon, Australia (city)	25S 113E	99
Carpathian Mountains	48N 24E	92
Carpentaria, Gulf of	14S 140E	98
Carson City, Nevada (city, st. cap., US)	39N 120W	89
Cartagena, Colombia (city)	10N 76W	91
Cascade Range	45N 120W	88
Casiquiare, Rio (riv., S.Am.)	4N 67W	90
Caspian Depression	49N 48E	92
Caspian Sea	42N 48E	92
Catamarca (st., Argentina)	25S 70W	91
Catamarca, Catamarca (city, st. cap., Argen.)	28S 66W	91
Cauca, Rio (riv., S.Am.)	8N 75W	90
Caucasus Mountains	42N 40E	92
Cayenne, French Guiana (city, nat. cap.)	5N 52W	91
Ceara (st., Brazil)	4S 40W	91
Celebes (island)	0 120E	94
Celebes Sea	2N 120E	94
Central African Republic (country)	5N 20E	97
Ceram (island)	3S 129E	99
Chaco (st., Argentina)	25S 60W	91
Chad (country)	15N 20E	97
Chad, Lake	12N 12E	97
Changchun, China (city)	44N 125E	95
Chari (riv., Africa)	11N 16E	96
Charleston, SC (city)	33N 80W	89
Charleston, West Virginia (city, st. cap., US)	38N 82W	89
Charlotte, NC (city)	35N 81W	89
Charlotte Waters, Aust. (city)	26S 135E	99
Charlottetown, P.E.I. (city, prov. cap., Can.)	46N 63W	89
Chelyabinsk, Russia (city)	55N 61E	93
Chengdu, China (city)	30N 104E	95
Chesapeake Bay	36N 74W	88
Chetumal, Quintana Roo (city, st. cap., Mex.)	19N 88W	89
Cheyenne, Wyoming (city, st. cap., US)	41N 105W	89
Chiapas (st., Mex.)	17N 92W	89
Chicago, IL (city)	42N 87W	89
Chiclayo, Peru (city)	7S 80W	91
Chidley, Cape	60N 65W	88

Geographic Index

Name/Description	Latitude & Longitude	Page
Chihuahua (st., Mex.)	30N 110W	89
Chihuahua, Chihuahua (city, st. cap., Mex.)	29N 106W	89
Chile (country)	32S 75W	91
Chiloe (island)	43S 74W	90
Chilpancingo, Guerrero (city, st. cap., Mex.)	19N 99W	89
Chimborazo, Mt. 20,702	2S 79W	90
China (country)	38N 105E	95
Chisinau, Moldova (city, nat. cap.)	47N 29E	93
Chongqing, China (city)	30N 107E	95
Christchurch, New Zealand (city)	43S 173E	99
Chubut (st., Argentina)	44S 70W	91
Chubut, Rio (riv., S.Am.)	44S 71W	90
Cincinnati, OH (city)	39N 84W	89
Cleveland (city)	41N 82W	89
Coahuila (st., Mex.)	30N 105W	89
Coast Mountains (Can.)	55N 130W	88
Coast Ranges (US)	40N 120W	88
Coco Island	8N 88W	88
Cod, Cape	42N 70W	88
Colima (st., Mex.)	18N 104W	89
Colima, Colima (city, st. cap., Mex.)	19N 104W	89
Colombia (country)	4N 73W	91
Colombo, Sri Lanka (city, nat. cap.)	7N 80E	95
Colorado (riv., N.Am.)	36N 110W	88
Colorado (st., US)	38N 104W	89
Colorado, Rio (riv., S.Am.)	38S 70W	90
Colorado (Texas) (riv., N.Am.)	30N 100W	88
Columbia (riv., N.Am.)	45N 120W	89
Columbia, South Carolina (city, st. cap., US)	34N 81W	89
Columbus, Ohio (city, st. cap., US)	40N 83W	89
Comodoro Rivadavia, Argentina (city)	68S 70W	91
Comoros (country)	12S 44E	97
Conakry, Guinea (city, nat. cap.)	9N 14W	93
Concord, New Hampshire (city, st. cap., US)	43N 71W	89
Congo (country)	3S 15E	97
Congo (riv., Africa)	3N 22E	96
Congo Basin	4N 22E	96
Congo, Democratic Republic of (country)	5S 15E	97
Connecticut (st., US)	43N 76W	89
Connecticut (riv., N.Am.)	43N 76W	88
Cook, Mt. 12,316	44S 170E	98
Cook Strait	42S 175E	98
Copenhagen, Denmark (city, nat. cap.)	56N 12E	93
Copiapo, Chile (city)	27S 70W	91
Copiapo, Mt. 19,947	26S 70W	90
Coquimbo, Chile (city)	30S 70W	91
Coral Sea	15S 155E	98
Cordilleran Highlands	45N 118W	88
Cordoba (st., Argentina)	32S 67W	91

Geographic Index

Name/Description	Latitude & Longitude	Page
Cordoba, Cordoba (city, st. cap., Argen.)	32S 64W	91
Corrientes (st., Argentina)	27S 60W	91
Corrientes, Corrientes (city, st. cap., Argen.)	27S 59W	91
Corsica (island)	42N 9E	93
Cosmoledo Islands	9S 48E	96
Costa Rica (country)	15N 84W	89
Cote d'Ivoire (country)	7N 86W	97
Cotopaxi, Mt. 19,347	1S 78W	90
Crete (island)	36N 25W	92
Croatia (country)	46N 20W	93
Cuango (riv., Africa)	10S 16E	96
Cuba (country)	22N 78W	89
Cuiaba, Mato Grosso (city, st. cap., Braz.)	16S 56W	91
Cuidad Victoria, Tamaulipas (city, st. cap., Mex.)	24N 99W	89
Culiacan, Sinaloa (city, st. cap., Mex.)	25N 107W	89
Curitiba, Parana (city, st. cap., Braz.)	26S 49W	91
Cusco, Peru (city)	14S 72W	91
Cyprus (island)	36N 34E	92
Czech Republic (country)	50N 16E	93
d'Ambre, Cape	12S 50E	97
Dakar, Senegal (city, nat. cap.)	15N 17W	97
Dakhla, Western Sahara (city)	24N 16W	97
Dallas, TX (city)	33N 97W	89
Dalrymple , Mt. 4190	22S 148E	98
Daly (riv., Australasia)	14S 132E	98
Damascus, Syria (city, nat. cap.)	34N 36E	93
Danube (riv., Europe)	44N 24E	92
Dar es Salaam, Tanzania (city, nat. cap.)	7S 39E	97
Darien, Gulf of	9N 77W	90
Darling (riv., Australasia)	35S 144E	98
Darling Range	33S 116W	98
Darwin, Northern Terr. (city, st. cap., Aust.)	12S 131E	99
Davis Strait	57N 59W	88
Deccan Plateau	20N 80E	94
DeGrey (riv., Australasia)	22S 120E	98
Delaware (st., US)	38N 75W	89
Delaware (riv., N.Am.)	38N 77W	88
Delhi, India (city)	30N 78E	97
Denmark (country)	55N 10E	93
Denmark Strait	67N 27W	92
D'Entrecasteaux Islands	10S 153E	98
Denver, Colorado (city, st. cap., US)	40N 105W	89
Derby, Australia (city)	17S 124E	99
Des Moines (riv., N.Am.)	43N 95W	88
Des Moines, Iowa (city, st. cap., US)	42N 92W	89
Desolacion Island	54S 73W	90
Detroit, MI (city)	42N 83W	89
Dhaka, Bangladesh (city, nat. cap.)	24N 90E	95
Dinaric Alps	44N 20E	92

Geographic Index

Name/Description	Latitude & Longitude	Page
Djibouti (country)	12N 43E	97
Djibouti, Djibouti (city, nat. cap.)	12N 43E	97
Dnepr (riv., Europe)	50N 34E	92
Dnipropetrovsk, Ukraine (city)	48N 35E	93
Dodoma, Tanzania (city)	6S 36E	97
Dominican Republic (country)	20N 70W	89
Don (riv., Europe)	53N 39E	92
Donetsk, Ukraine (city)	48N 38E	93
Dover, Delaware (city, st. cap., US)	39N 75W	89
Dover, Strait of	52N 0	92
Drakensberg	30S 30E	96
Dublin, Ireland (city, nat. cap.)	53N 6W	93
Duluth, MN (city)	47N 92W	89
Dunedin, New Zealand (city)	46S 171E	99
Durango (st., Mex.)	25N 108W	89
Durango, Durango (city, st. cap., Mex.)	24N 105W	89
Durban, South Africa (city)	30S 31E	97
Dushanbe, Tajikistan (city, nat. cap.)	39N 69E	95
Dvina (riv., Europe)	64N 42E	92
Dzhugdzhur Khrebet	58N 138E	94
East Cape (NZ)	37S 180E	98
East China Sea	30N 128E	94
Eastern Ghats	15N 80E	94
Ecuador (country)	3S 78W	91
Edmonton, Alberta (city, prov. cap., Can.)	54N 114W	89
Edward, Lake	0 30E	96
Egypt (country)	23N 30E	97
El Aaiun, Western Sahara (city)	27N 13W	97
El Djouf	25N 15W	96
El Paso, TX (city)	32N 106W	89
El Salvador (country)	15N 90W	89
Elbe (riv., Europe)	54N 10E	92
Elburz Mountains	28N 60E	94
Elbruz, Mt. 18,510	43N 42E	94
Elgon, Mt. 14,178	1N 34E	96
English Channel	50N 0	92
Entre Rios (st., Argentina)	32S 60W	91
Equatorial Guinea (country)	3N 10E	97
Erg Iguidi	26N 6W	96
Erie (lake, N.Am.)	42N 85W	88
Eritrea (country)	16N 38E	97
Erzegebirge Mountains	50N 14E	92
Espinhaco Mountains	15S 42W	90
Espiritu Santo (island)	15S 168E	99
Espiritu Santo (st., Brazil)	20S 42W	91
Essen, Germany (city)	52N 8E	93
Estonia (country)	60N 26E	93
Ethiopia (country)	8N 40E	97
Ethiopian Plateau	8N 40E	96

Geographic Index

Name/Description	Latitude & Longitude	Page
Euphrates (riv., Asia)	28N 50E	94
Everard, Lake	32S 135E	98
Everard Ranges	28S 135E	98
Everest, Mt. 29,028	28N 84E	94
Eyre, Lake	29S 136E	98
Faeroe Islands	62N 11W	92
Fairbanks, AK (city)	63N 146W	89
Falkland Islands (Islas Malvinas)	52S 60W	90
Farewell, Cape (NZ)	40S 170E	98
Fargo, ND (city)	47N 97W	89
Farquhar, Cape	24S 114E	98
Fiji (country)	17S 178E	99
Finisterre, Cape	44N 10W	92
Finland (country)	62N 28E	93
Finland, Gulf of	60N 20E	92
Firth of Forth	56N 3W	92
Fitzroy (riv., Australasia)	17S 125E	98
Flinders Range	31S 139E	98
Flores (island)	8S 121E	98
Florianopolis, Sta. Catarina (city, st. cap., Braz.)	27S 48W	91
Florida (st., US)	28N 83W	89
Florida, Strait of	28N 80W	88
Fly (riv., Australasia)	8S 143E	98
Formosa (st., Argentina)	23S 60W	91
Formosa, Formosa (city, st. cap., Argen.)	27S 58W	91
Fort Worth, TX (city)	33N 97W	89
Fortaleza, Ceara (city, st. cap., Braz.)	4S 39W	91
France (country)	46N 4E	93
Frankfort, Kentucky (city, st. cap., US)	38N 85W	89
Frankfurt, Germany (city)	50N 9E	93
Fraser (riv., N.Am.)	52N 122W	88
Fredericton, N.B. (city, prov. cap., Can.)	46N 67W	89
Fremantle, Australia (city)	33S 116E	99
Freetown, Sierra Leone (city, nat. cap.)	8N 13W	97
French Guiana (country)	4N 52W	91
Fria, Cape	18S 12E	96
Fuzhou, China (city)	26N 119E	95
Gabes, Gulf of	33N 12E	96
Gabes, Tunisia (city)	34N 10E	97
Gabon (country)	2S 12E	97
Gaborone, Botswana (city, nat. cap.)	25S 25E	97
Gairdiner, Lake	32S 136E	98
Galveston, TX (city)	29N 95W	89
Gambia (country)	13N 15W	97
Gambia (riv., Africa)	13N 15W	96
Ganges (riv., Asia)	27N 85E	94
Gascoyne (riv., Australasia)	25S 115E	98
Gaspé Peninsula	50N 70W	88
Gdansk, Poland (city)	54N 19E	93

Geographic Index

Name/Description	Latitude & Longitude	Page
Geelong, Aust. (city)	38S 144E	99
Gees Gwardafuy (island)	15N 50E	96
Genoa, Gulf of	44N 10E	92
Geographe Bay	35S 115E	98
Georgetown, Guyana (city, nat. cap.)	8N 58W	91
Georgia (country)	42N 44E	93
Georgia (st., US)	30N 82W	89
Germany (country)	50N 12E	93
Ghana (country)	8N 3W	97
Gibraltar, Strait of	37N 6W	92
Gibson Desert	24S 124E	98
Gilbert (riv., Australasia)	8S 142E	98
Giluwe, Mt. 14,330	5S 144E	98
Glasgow, Scotland (city)	56N 6W	93
Gobi Desert	48N 105E	94
Godavari (riv., Asia)	18N 82E	94
Godwin-Austen (K2), Mt. 28,250	30N 70E	94
Goiania, Goias (city, st. cap., Braz.)	17S 49W	91
Goias (st., Brazil)	15S 50W	91
Gongga Shan 24,790	26N 102E	94
Good Hope, Cape of	33S 18E	96
Goteborg, Sweden (city)	58N 12E	93
Gotland (island)	57N 20E	92
Grampian Mountains	57N 4W	92
Gran Chaco	23S 70N	90
Grand Erg Occidental	29N 0	96
Grand Teton 13,770	45N 112W	88
Great Artesian Basin	25S 145E	98
Great Australian Bight	33S 130E	98
Great Barrier Reef	15S 145E	98
Great Basin	39N 117W	88
Great Bear Lake (lake, N.Am.)	67N 120W	88
Great Dividing Range	20S 145E	98
Great Indian Desert	25N 72E	94
Great Namaland	25S 16E	96
Great Plains	40N 105W	88
Great Salt Lake (lake, N.Am.)	40N 113W	88
Great Sandy Desert	23S 125E	98
Great Slave Lake (lake, N.Am.)	62N 110W	88
Great Victoria Desert	30S 125E	98
Greater Khingan Range	50N 120E	94
Greece (country)	39N 21E	93
Greenland (Denmark) (country)	78N 40W	89
Gregory Range	18S 145E	98
Grey Range	26S 145E	98
Guadalajara, Jalisco (city, st. cap., Mex.)	21N 103W	89
Guadalcanal (island)	9S 160E	99
Guadeloupe (island)	29N 120W	88
Guanajuato (st., Mex.)	22N 100W	89

Geographic Index

Name/Description	Latitude & Longitude	Page
Guanajuato, Guanajuato (city, st. cap., Mex.)	21N 101W	89
Guangzhou, China (city)	23N 113E	95
Guapore, Rio (riv., S.Am.)	15S 63W	90
Guatemala (country)	14N 90W	89
Guatemala, Guatemala (city, nat. cap.)	15N 91W	89
Guayaquil, Ecuador (city)	2S 80W	91
Guayaquil, Gulf of	3S 83W	90
Guerrero (st., Mex.)	18N 102W	89
Guianas Highlands	5N 60W	90
Guinea (country)	10N 10W	97
Guinea, Gulf of	3N 0	96
Guinea-Bissau (country)	12N 15W	97
Guyana (country)	6N 57W	91
Gydan Range	62N 155E	94
Haiti (country)	18N 72W	89
Hakodate, Japan (city)	42N 140E	95
Halifax Bay	18S 146E	98
Halifax, Nova Scotia (city, prov. cap., Can.)	45N 64W	89
Halmahera (island)	1N 128E	94 inset
Hamburg, Germany (city)	54N 10E	93
Hammersley Range	23S 116W	98
Hann, Mt. 2,800	15S 127E	98
Hanoi, Vietnam (city, nat. cap.)	21N 106E	95
Hanover Island	52S 74W	90
Harare, Zimbabwe (city, nat. cap.)	18S 31E	97
Harbin, China (city)	46N 126E	95
Harer, Ethiopia (city)	10N 42E	97
Hargeysa, Somalia (city)	9N 44E	97
Harrisburg, Pennsylvania (city, st. cap., US)	40N 77W	89
Hartford, Connecticut (city, st. cap., US)	42N 73W	89
Hatteras, Cape	32N 73W	88
Havana, Cuba (city, nat. cap.)	23N 82W	89
Hawaii (st., US)	21N 156W	88 inset
Hebrides (island)	58N 8W	92
Helena, Montana (city, st. cap., US)	47N 112W	89
Helsinki, Finland (city, nat. cap.)	60N 25E	93
Herat, Afghanistan (city)	34N 62E	95
Hermosillo, Sonora (city, st. cap., Mex.)	29N 111W	89
Hidalgo (st., Mex.)	20N 98W	89
Himalayas	26N 80E	94
Hindu Kush	30N 70E	94
Ho Chi Minh City, Vietnam (city)	11N 107E	95
Hobart, Tasmania (city, st. cap., Aust.)	43S 147E	99
Hokkaido (island)	43N 142E	94
Honduras (country)	16N 87W	89
Honduras, Gulf of	15N 88W	88
Honiara, Solomon Islands (city, nat. cap.)	9S 160E	99
Honolulu, Hawaii (city, st. cap., US)	21N 158W	89 inset
Honshu (island)	38N 140E	94

Geographic Index

Name/Description	Latitude & Longitude	Page
Hormuz, Strait of	25N 58E	94
Horn, Cape	55S 70W	90
Houston, TX (city)	30N 95W	89
Howe, Cape	37S 150E	98
Huambo, Angola (city)	13S 16E	97
Huang (riv., Asia)	30N 105E	94
Huascaran, Mt. 22,133	8N 79W	90
Hudson (riv., N.Am.)	42N 76W	89
Hudson Bay	60N 90W	88
Hudson Strait	63N 70W	88
Hue, Vietnam (city)	15N 110E	95
Hughes, Aust. (city)	30S 130E	99
Hungary (country)	48N 20E	93
Huron (lake, N.Am.)	45N 85W	88
Hyderabad, India (city)	17N 79E	95
Ibadan, Nigeria (city)	7N 4E	97
Iceland (country)	64N 20W	93
Idaho (st., US)	43N 113W	89
Iguassu Falls	25S 55W	90
Illimani, Mt. 20,741	16S 67W	90
Illinois (riv., N.Am.)	40N 90W	88
Illinois (st., US)	44N 90W	89
India (country)	23N 80E	95
Indiana (st., US)	46N 88W	89
Indianapolis, Indiana (city, st. cap., US)	40N 86W	89
Indigirka (riv., Asia)	70N 145E	94
Indonesia (country)	2S 120E	95
Indus (riv., Asia)	25N 70E	94
Ionian Sea	38N 19E	92
Iowa (st., US)	43N 95W	89
Iquitos, Peru (city)	4S 74W	91
Iran (country)	30N 55E	95
Iraq (country)	30N 50E	95
Ireland (country)	54N 8W	93
Irish Sea	54N 5W	93
Irkutsk, Russia (city)	52N 104E	95
Irrawaddy (riv., Asia)	25N 95E	94
Irtysh (riv., Asia)	50N 70E	94
Ishim (riv., Asia)	48N 70E	94
Isla de los Estados (island)	55S 60W	90
Islamabad, Pakistan (city, nat. cap.)	34N 73E	95
Isles of Scilly	50N 8W	92
Israel (country)	31N 36E	93
Istanbul, Turkey (city)	41N 29E	93
Italy (country)	42N 12E	93
Jabal Marrah, 10, 131	10N 23E	96
Jackson, Mississippi (city, st. cap., US)	32N 84W	89
Jacksonville, FL (city)	30N 82W	89
Jakarta, Indonesia (city, nat. cap.)	6S 107E	95 inset

Geographic Index

Name/Description	Latitude & Longitude	Page
Jalisco (st., Mex.)	20N 105W	89
Jamaica (country)	18N 78W	89
James Bay	54N 81W	88
Japan (country)	35N 138E	95
Japan, Sea of	40N 135E	94
Japura, Rio (riv., S.Am.)	3S 65W	90
Java (island)	6N 110E	94 inset
Jaya Peak 16,503	4S 136W	98
Jayapura, New Guinea (Indon.) (city)	3S 141E	95 inset
Jebel Toubkal 13,665	31N 8W	96
Jefferson City, Missouri (city, st. cap., US)	39N 92W	89
Jerusalem, Israel (city, nat. cap.)	32N 35E	93
Joao Pessoa, Paraiba (city, st. cap., Braz.)	7S 35W	91
Johannesburg, South Africa (city)	26S 27E	97
Jordan (country)	32N 36E	93
Juan Fernandez (island)	33S 80W	90
Jubba (riv., Africa)	3N 43E	96
Jujuy (st., Argentina)	23S 67W	91
Jujuy, Jujuy (city, st. cap., Argen.)	23S 66W	91
Juneau, Alaska (city, st. cap., US)	58N 134W	89
Jura Mountains	46N 5E	92
Jurua, Rio (riv., S.Am.)	6S 70W	90
Kabul, Afghanistan (city, nat. cap.)	35N 69E	95
Kalahari Desert	25S 20E	96
Kalgourie-Boulder, Australia (city)	31S 121E	99
Kaliningrad, Russia (city)	55N 21E	93
Kamchatka Range	55N 159E	94
Kampala, Uganda (city, nat. cap.)	0 33E	97
Kanchenjunga, Mt. 28,208	30N 83E	94
Kano, Nigeria (city)	12N 9E	97
Kanpur, India (city)	27N 80E	95
Kansas (st., US)	40N 98W	89
Kansas City, MO (city)	39N 95W	89
Kara Sea	69N 65E	94
Karachi, Pakistan (city)	25N 66E	95
Karakorum Range	32N 78E	94
Karakum Desert	42N 52E	92
Kasai (riv., Africa)	5S 18E	96
Kashi, China (city)	39N 76E	95
Katherine, Aust. (city)	14S 132E	99
Kathmandu, Nepal (city, nat. cap.)	28N 85E	95
Katowice, Poland (city)	50N 19E	93
Kattegat, Strait of	57N 11E	92
Kazakhstan (country)	50N 70E	95
Kentucky (st., US)	37N 88W	89
Kenya (country)	0 35E	97
Kenya, Mt. 17, 058	0 37E	96
Khabarovsk, Russia (city)	48N 135E	95
Khambhat, Gulf of	20N 73E	94

Geographic Index

Name/Description	Latitude & Longitude	Page
Kharkiv, Ukraine (city)	50N 36E	93
Khartoum, Sudan (city, nat. cap.)	16N 33E	97
Kiev, Ukraine (city, nat. cap.)	50N 31E	93
Kigali, Rwanda (city, nat. cap.)	2S 30E	97
Kilimanjaro, Mt. 19,340	4N 35E	96
Kimberly, South Africa (city)	29S 25E	97
King Leopold Ranges	16S 125E	98
Kingston, Jamaica (city, nat. cap.)	18N 77W	89
Kinshasa, Congo Republic (city, nat. cap.)	4S 15E	97
Kirghiz Steppe	40N 65E	94
Kisangani, Congo Republic (city)	1N 25E	97
Kitayushu, Japan (city)	34N 130E	95
Klyuchevskaya, Mt. 15,584	56N 160E	94
Kobe, Japan (city)	34N 135E	95
Kodiak Island	58N 152W	88 inset
Kolyma (riv., Asia)	70N 160E	94
Kommunizma, Mt. 24,590	40N 70E	94
Komsomolsk, Russia (city)	51N 137E	95
Korea, North (country)	40N 128E	95
Korea, South (country)	3S 130W	95
Korea Strait	32N 130W	94
Kosciusko, Mt. 7,310	36S 148E	98
Krasnoyarsk, Russia (city)	56N 93E	95
Krishna (riv., Asia)	15N 76E	94
Kuala Lumpur, Malaysia (city, nat. cap.)	3N 107E	95
Kunlun Shan	36N 90E	94
Kunming, China (city)	25N 103E	95
Kuril Islands	46N 147E	94
Kutch, Gulf of	23N 70E	94
Kuwait (country)	29N 48E	93
Kuwait, Kuwait (city, nat. cap.)	29N 48E	93
Kyoto, Japan (city)	35N 136E	95
Kyrgyzstan (country)	40N 75E	95
Kyushu (island)	30N 130W	94
La Pampa (st., Argentina)	36S 70W	91
La Paz, Baja California Sur (city, st. cap., Mex.)	24N 110W	89
La Paz, Bolivia (city, nat. cap.)	17S 68W	91
La Plata, Argentina (city)	35S 58W	91
Laptev Sea	73N 120E	94
La Rioja (st., Argentina)	30S 70W	91
La Rioja, La Rioja (city, st. cap., Argen.)	29S 67W	91
Labrador Peninsula	52N 60W	91
Lachlan (riv., Australasia)	34S 145E	98
Ladoga, Lake	61N 31E	92
Lagos, Nigeria (city, nat. cap.)	7N 3E	97
Lahore, Pakistan (city)	34N 74E	95
Lake of the Woods	50N 92W	88
Lands End	50N 5W	92
Lansing, Michigan (city, st. cap., US)	43N 85W	89

Geographic Index

Name/Description	Latitude & Longitude	Page
Lanzhou, China (city)	36N 104E	95
Laos (country)	20N 105E	95
Las Vegas, NV (city)	36N 115W	89
Latvia (country)	56N 24E	93
Laurentian Highlands	48N 72W	88
Lebanon (country)	34N 35E	93
Leeds, UK (city)	54N 2W	93
Le Havre, France (city)	50N 0	93
Lena (riv., Asia)	70N 125E	94
Lesotho (country)	30S 27E	97
Leveque, Cape	16S 123E	98
Leyte (island)	12N 130E	94
Lhasa, Tibet (China) (city)	30N 91E	95
Liberia (country)	6N 10W	97
Libreville, Gabon (city, nat. cap.)	0 9E	97
Libya (country)	27N 17E	97
Libyan Desert	27N 25E	96
Lille, France (city)	51N 3E	93
Lilongwe, Malawi (city, nat. cap.)	14S 33E	97
Lima, Peru (city, nat. cap.)	12S 77W	91
Limpopo (riv., Africa)	22S 30E	96
Lincoln, Nebraska (city, st. cap., US)	41N 97W	89
Lisbon, Portugal (city, nat. cap.)	39N 9W	93
Lithuania (country)	56N 24E	93
Little Rock, Arkansas (city, st. cap., US)	35N 92W	89
Liverpool, UK (city)	53N 3W	93
Ljubljana, Slovenia (city, nat. cap.)	46N 14E	93
Llanos	33N 103W	90
Logan, Mt. 18,551	62N 139W	88
Logone (riv., Africa)	10N 14E	96
Lome, Togo (city, nat. cap.)	6N 1E	97
London, United Kingdom (city, nat. cap.)	51N 0	93
Londonderry, Cape	14S 125E	98
Lopez, Cape	1S 8E	96
Los Angeles, CA (city)	34N 118W	89
Los Chonos Archipelago	45S 74W	90
Louisiana (st., US)	30N 90W	89
Lower Hutt, New Zealand (city)	45S 175E	99
Luanda, Angola (city, nat. cap.)	9S 13E	97
Lubumbashi, Congo Republic (city)	12S 28E	97
Lusaka, Zambia (city, nat. cap.)	15S 28E	97
Luxembourg (country)	50N 6E	93
Luxembourg, Luxembourg (city, nat. cap.)	50N 6E	93
Luzon (island)	17N 121E	94
Luzon Strait	20N 121E	94
Lyon, France (city)	46N 5E	93
Lyon, Gulf of	42N 4E	92
Maccio, Alagoas (city, st. cap., Braz.)	10S 36W	91
Macdonnell Ranges	23S 135E	98

Geographic Index

Name/Description	Latitude & Longitude	Page
Macedonia (country)	41N 21E	93
Mackenzie (riv., N.Am.)	68N 130W	88
Macquarie (riv., Australasia)	33S 146E	98
Madagascar (country)	20S 46E	97
Madeira, Rio (riv., S.Am.)	5S 60W	90
Madison, Wisconsin (city, st. cap., US)	43N 89W	89
Madras, (Chennai) India (city)	13N 80E	95
Madrid, Spain (city, nat. cap.)	40N 4W	93
Magdalena, Rio (riv., S.Am.)	8N 74W	90
Magellan, Strait of	54S 68W	90
Maine (st., US)	46N 70W	89
Malabo, Equatorial Guinea (city, nat. cap.)	4N 9E	97
Malacca, Strait of	3N 100E	95
Malawi (country)	13S 35E	97
Malaysia (country)	3N 110E	95
Malekula (island)	16S 166E	98
Mali (country)	17N 5W	97
Malpelo Island	8N 84W	88
Malta (island)	36N 16E	92
Mamore, Rio (riv., S.Am.)	15S 65W	90
Managua, Nicaragua (city, nat. cap.)	12N 86W	89
Manaus, Amazonas (city, st. cap., Braz.)	3S 60W	91
Manchester, UK (city)	53N 2W	93
Mandalay, Myamar (city)	22N 96E	95
Manila, Philippines (city, nat. cap.)	115N 121E	95
Manitoba (prov., Can.)	52N 93W	89
Mannar, Gulf of	9N 79E	94
Maoke Mountains	5S 138E	98
Maputo, Mozambique (city, nat. cap.)	26S 33E	97
Maracaibo, Lake	10N 72W	91
Maracaibo, Venezuela (city)	11N 72W	91
Maracapa, Amapa (city, st. cap., Braz.)	0 51W	91
Maranhao (st., Brazil)	4S 45W	91
Maranon, Rio (riv., S.Am.)	5S 75W	90
Marseille, France (city)	43N 5E	93
Maryland (st., US)	37N 76W	89
Masai Steppe	5S 35E	96
Maseru, Lesotho (city, nat. cap.)	29S 27E	97
Mashad, Iran (city)	36N 59E	95
Massachusetts (st., US)	42N 70W	89
Massif Central	45N 3E	92
Mato Grosso	16S 52W	90
Mato Grosso (st., Brazil)	15S 55W	91
Mato Grosso do Sul (st., Brazil)	20S 55W	91
Mauritania (country)	20N 10W	97
Mbandaka, Congo Republic (city)	0 18E	97
McKinley, Mt. 20,320	62N 150W	88 inset
Medellin, Colombia (city)	6N 76W	91
Mediterranean Sea	36N 16E	92

Geographic Index

Name/Description	Latitude & Longitude	Page
Mekong (riv., Asia)	15N 108E	94
Melbourne, Victoria (city, st. cap., Aust.)	38S 145E	99
Melville, Cape	15S 145E	98
Memphis, TN (city)	35N 90W	89
Mendoza (st., Argentina)	35S 70W	91
Mendoza, Mendoza (city, st. cap., Argen.)	33S 69W	91
Merida, Yucatan (city, st. cap. Mex.)	21N 90W	89
Merauke, New Guinea (Indon.) (city)	9S 140E	99
Mexicali, Baja California (city, st. cap., Mex.)	32N 115W	89
Mexico (country)	30N 110W	89
Mexico (st., Mex.)	18N 100W	89
Mexico City, Mexico (city, nat. cap.)	19N 99W	89
Mexico, Gulf of	26N 90W	88
Miami, FL (city)	26N 80W	89
Michigan (st., US)	45N 82W	89
Michigan (lake, N.Am.)	45N 90W	88
Michoacan (st., Mex.)	17N 107W	89
Milan, Italy (city)	45N 9E	93
Milwaukee, WI (city)	43N 88W	89
Minas Gerais (st., Brazil)	17S 45W	91
Mindoro (island)	13N 120E	95
Minneapolis, MN (city)	45N 93W	89
Minnesota (st., US)	45N 90W	89
Minsk, Belarus (city, nat. cap.)	54N 28E	93
Misiones (st., Argentina)	25S 55W	91
Mississippi (riv., N.Am.)	28N 90W	88
Mississippi (st., US)	30N 90W	89
Missouri (riv., N.Am.)	41N 96W	88
Missouri (st., US)	35N 92W	89
Misti, Mt. 19,101	15S 73W	90
Mitchell (riv., Australasia)	16S 143E	98
Mobile, AL (city)	31N 88W	89
Mocambique, Mozambique (city)	15S 40E	97
Mogadishu, Somalia (city, nat. cap.)	2N 45E	97
Moldova (country)	49N 28E	93
Mombasa, Kenya (city)	4S 40E	97
Monaco, Monaco (city)	44N 8E	93
Mongolia (country)	45N 100E	95
Monrovia, Liberia (city, nat. cap.)	6N 11W	97
Montana (st., US)	50N 110W	89
Monterrey, Nuevo Leon (city, st. cap., Mex.)	26N 100W	89
Montevideo, Uruguay (city, nat. cap.)	35S 56W	91
Montgomery, Alabama (city, st. cap., US)	32N 86W	89
Montpelier, Vermont (city, st. cap., US)	44N 73W	89
Montreal, Canada (city)	45N 74W	89
Morelin, Michoacan (city, st. cap., Mex.)	20N 100W	89
Morocco (country)	34N 10W	97
Moroni, Comoros (city, nat. cap.)	12S 42E	97
Moscow, Russia (city, nat. cap.)	56N 38E	93

Geographic Index

Name/Description	Latitude & Longitude	Page
Mountain Nile (riv., Africa)	5N 30E	96
Mozambique (country)	19N 35E	97
Mozambique Channel	19N 42E	96
Munich, Germany (city)	48N 12E	93
Murchison (riv., Australasia)	26S 115E	98
Murmansk, Russia (city)	69N 33E	93
Murray (riv., Australasia)	36S 143E	98
Murrumbidgee (riv., Australasia)	35S 146E	98
Muscat, Oman (city, nat. cap.)	23N 58E	95
Musgrave Ranges	28S 135E	98
Myanmar (Burma) (country)	20N 95E	95
Nairobi, Kenya (city, nat. cap.)	1S 37E	97
Namibe, Angola (city)	16S 13E	97
Namibia (country)	20S 16E	97
Namoi (riv., Australasia)	31S 150E	98
Nan Ling Mountains	25N 110E	94
Nanda Devi, Mt. 25,645	30N 80E	94
Nanjing, China (city)	32N 119E	95
Nansei Shoto (island)	27N 125E	94
Naples, Italy (city)	41N 14E	93
Nashville, Tennessee (city, st. cap., US)	36N 87W	89
Nasser, Lake	22N 32E	96
Natal, Rio Grande do Norte (city, st. cap., Braz.)	6S 5W	91
Naturaliste, Cape	35S 115E	98
Nayarit (st., Mex.)	22N 106W	89
N'Djamena, Chad (city, nat. cap.)	12N 15E	97
Nebraska (st., US)	42N 100W	89
Negro, Rio (Argentina) (riv., S.Am.)	40S 70W	90
Negro, Rio (Brazil) (riv., S.Am.)	0 65W	90
Negros (island)	10N 125E	94
Nelson (riv., N.Am.)	56N 90W	88
Nepal (country)	29N 85E	95
Netherlands (country)	54N 6E	93
Neuquen (st., Argentina)	38S 68W	91
Neuquen, Neuquen (city, st. cap., Argen.)	39S 68W	91
Nevada (st., US)	37N 117W	89
New Britain (island)	5S 152E	98
New Brunswick (prov., Can.)	47N 67W	89
New Caledonia (island)	21S 165E	98
New Delhi, India (city, nat. cap.)	29N 77E	95
New Georgia (island)	8S 157E	98
New Guinea (island)	5S 142E	98
New Hampshire (st., US)	45N 70W	89
New Hanover (island)	3S 153E	98
New Hebrides (island)	15S 165E	98
New Ireland (island)	4S 154E	98
New Jersey (st., US)	40N 75W	89
New Mexico (st., US)	30N 108W	89
New Orleans, LA (city)	30N 90W	89

Geographic Index

Name/Description	Latitude & Longitude	Page
New Siberian Islands	74N 140E	94
New South Wales (st., Aust.)	35S 145E	99
New York (city)	41N 74W	89
New York (st., US)	45N 75W	89
New Zealand (country)	40S 170E	99
Newcastle, Aust. (city)	33S 152E	99
Newcastle, UK (city)	55N 2W	93
Newfoundland (prov., Can.)	53N 60W	89
Nicaragua (country)	10N 90W	89
Niamey, Niger (city, nat. cap.)	14N 2E	97
Nicobar Islands	5N 93E	94
Niger (country)	10N 8E	97
Niger (riv., Africa)	12N 0	96
Nigeria (country)	8N 5E	97
Nile (riv., Africa)	25N 31E	96
Nipigon (lake, N.Am.)	50N 87W	88
Nizhny-Novgorod, Russia (city)	56N 44E	93
Norfolk, VA (city)	37N 76W	89
North Cape (NZ)	36N 174W	98
North Carolina (st., US)	30N 78W	89
North Channel	56N 5W	92
North Dakota (st., US)	49N 100W	89
North Island (NZ)	37S 175W	98
North Saskatchewan (riv., N.Am.)	55N 110W	88
North Sea	56N 3E	92
North West Cape	22S 115W	98
Northern Territory (st., Aust.)	20S 134W	98
Northwest Territories (prov., Can.)	65N 125W	89
Norway (country)	62N 8E	93
Nouakchott, Mauritania (city, nat. cap.)	18N 16W	97
Noumea, New Caledonia (city)	22S 167E	99
Nova Scotia (prov., Can.)	46N 67W	89
Novaya Zemlya (island)	72N 55E	94
Novosibirsk, Russia (city)	55N 83E	95
Nubian Desert	20N 30E	96
Nuevo Leon (st., Mex.)	25N 100W	89
Nullarbor Plain	34S 125W	98
Nyasa, Lake	10S 35E	96
Oakland, CA (city)	38N 122W	89
Oaxaca (st., Mex.)	17N 97W	89
Oaxaca, Oaxaca (city, st. cap., Mex.)	17N 97W	89
Ob (riv., Asia)	60N 78E	94
Ohio (riv., N.Am.)	38N 85W	88
Ohio (st., US)	42N 85W	89
Okavongo (riv., Africa)	18S 18E	96
Okavango Swamp	21S 23E	96
Okeechobee (lake, N.Am.)	28N 82W	88
Okhotsk, Russia (city)	59N 140E	95
Okhotsk, Sea of	57N 150E	94

Geographic Index

Name/Description	Latitude & Longitude	Page
Oklahoma (st., US)	36N 95W	89
Oklahoma City, Oklahoma (city, st. cap., US)	35N 98W	89
Oland (island)	57N 17E	92
Olympia, Washington (city, st. cap., US)	47N 123W	90
Omaha, NE (city)	41N 96W	89
Oman (country)	20N 55E	95
Oman, Gulf of	23N 55E	94
Omdurman, Sudan (city)	16N 32E	97
Omsk, Russia (city)	55N 73E	95
Onega, Lake	62N 35E	92
Ontario (lake, N.Am.)	45N 77W	88
Ontario (prov., Can.)	50N 90W	89
Oodnadatta, Aust. (city)	28S 135E	99
Oran, Algeria (city)	36N 1W	97
Oregon (st., US)	46N 120W	89
Orinoco, Rio (riv., S.Am.)	8N 65W	90
Orizaba Peak 18,406	19N 97W	88
Orkney Islands	60N 0	92
Osaka, Japan (city)	35N 135E	95
Oslo, Norway (city, nat. cap.)	60N 11W	93
Ossa, Mt. 5,305 (Tasm.)	43S 145E	98
Ottawa, Canada (city, nat. cap.)	45N 76W	89
Otway, Cape	40S 142W	98
Ougadougou, Burkina Faso (city, nat. cap.)	12N 2W	97
Owen Stanley Range	9S 148E	98
Pachuca, Hidalgo (city, st. cap. Mex.)	20N 99W	89
Pacific Ocean	20N 115W	88
Pakistan (country)	25N 72E	95
Palawan (island)	10N 119E	94
Palmas, Cape	8N 8W	96
Palmas, Tocantins (city, st. cap., Braz.)	10S 49W	91
Pamirs	32N 70E	94
Pampas	36S 73W	90
Panama (country)	10N 80W	90
Panama, Gulf of	10N 80W	89
Panama, Panama (city, nat. cap.)	9N 80W	89
Papua, Gulf of	8S 144E	98
Papua New Guinea (country)	6S 144E	98
Para (st., Brazil)	4S 54W	91
Paraguay (country)	23S 60W	91
Paraguay, Rio (riv., S.Am.)	17S 60W	90
Paraiba (st., Brazil)	6S 35W	91
Paramaribo, Suriname (city, nat. cap.)	5N 55W	91
Parana (st., Brazil)	25S 55W	91
Parana, Entre Rios (city, st. cap., Argen.)	32S 60W	91
Parana, Rio (riv., S.Am.)	20S 50W	90
Paris, France (city, nat. cap.)	49N 2E	93
Pasadas, Misiones (city, st. cap., Argen.)	27S 56W	91
Patagonia	43S 70W	90

Geographic Index

Name/Description	Latitude & Longitude	Page
Paulo Afonso Falls	10S 40W	90
Peace (riv., N.Am.)	55N 120W	88
Pennsylvania (st., US)	43N 80W	89
Pernambuco (st., Brazil)	7S 36W	91
Persian Gulf	28N 50E	94
Perth, W. Australia (city, st. cap., Aust.)	32S 116E	99
Peru (country)	10S 75W	91
Peshawar, Pakistan (city)	34N 72E	95
Philadelphia, PA (city)	40N 75W	89
Philippine Sea	15N 125E	94
Philippines (country)	15N 120E	95
Phnom Penh, Cambodia (city, nat. cap.)	12N 105E	95
Phoenix, Arizona (city, st. cap., US)	33N 112W	89
Phou Bia 9,249	24N 102E	94
Piaui (st., Brazil)	7S 44W	91
Piaui Range	10S 45W	90
Pic Touside 10,712	20N 12E	96
Pierre, South Dakota (city, st. cap., US)	44N 100W	89
Pietermaritzburg, South Africa (city)	30S 30E	97
Pike's Peak 14,110	36N 110W	88
Pilcomayo, Rio (riv., S.Am.)	23S 60W	90
Pittsburgh, PA (city)	40N 80W	89
Plateau of Iran	26N 60E	94
Plateau of Tibet	26N 85E	94
Platte (riv., N.Am.)	41N 105W	88
Po (riv., Europe)	45N 12E	92
Point Barrow	70N 156W	88 inset
Poland (country)	54N 20E	93
Poopo, Lake	16S 67W	90
Popocatepetl 17,887	17N 100W	88
Port Elizabeth, South Africa (city)	34S 26E	97
Port Lincoln, Aust. (city)	35S 135E	99
Port Moresby, Papua N. G. (city, nat. cap.)	10S 147E	99
Port Vila, Vanatu (city, nat. cap.)	17S 169E	99
Port-au-Prince, Haiti (city, nat. cap.)	19N 72W	89
Portland, OR (city)	46N 123W	89
Porto Alegre, R. Gr. do Sul (city, st. cap., Braz.)	30S 51W	91
Porto Novo, Benin (city, nat. cap.)	7N 3E	97
Porto Velho, Rondonia (city, st. cap., Braz.)	9S 64W	91
Portugal (country)	38N 8W	93
Potomac (riv., N.Am.)	35N 75W	88
Potosi, Bolivia (city)	20S 66W	91
Prague, Czech Republic (city, nat. cap.)	50N 14E	93
Pretoria, South Africa (city, nat. cap.)	26S 28E	97
Pribilof Islands	56N 170W	88 inset
Prince Edward Island (prov., Can.)	50N 67W	89
Pripyat Marshes	54N 24E	92
Providence, Rhode Island (city, st. cap., US)	42N 71W	89
Puebla (st., Mex.)	18N 96W	89

Geographic Index

Name/Description	Latitude & Longitude	Page
Puebla, Puebla (city, st. cap., Mex.)	19N 98W	89
Puerto Monte, Chile (city)	42S 74W	91
Purus, Rio (riv., S.Am.)	5S 68W	90
Putumayo, Rio (riv., S.Am.)	3S 74W	90
Pyongyang, Korea, North (city, nat. cap.)	39N 126E	95
Pyrenees Mountains	43N 2E	92
Qingdao, China (city)	36N 120E	95
Quebec (prov., Can.)	52N 70W	89
Quebec, Quebec (city, prov. cap., Can.)	47N 71W	89
Queen Charlotte Islands	50N 130W	88
Queen Elizabeth Islands	75N 110W	88
Queensland (st., Aust.)	24S 145E	99
Querataro (st., Mex.)	22N 96W	89
Querataro, Querataro (city, st. cap., Mex.)	21N 100W	89
Quintana Roo (st., Mex.)	18N 88W	89
Quito, Ecuador (city, nat. cap.)	0 79W	91
Rabat, Morocco (city, nat. cap.)	34N 7W	97
Race, Cape	46N 52W	88
Rainier, Mt. 14,410	48N 120W	88
Raleigh, North Carolina (city, st. cap., US)	36N 79W	89
Rangoon, Myanmar (Burma) (city, nat. cap.)	17N 96E	95
Rapid City, SD (city)	44N 103W	89
Rawalpindi, India (city)	34N 73E	95
Rawson, Chubuy (city, st. cap., Argen.)	43S 65W	91
Recife, Pernambuco (city, st. cap., Braz.)	8S 35W	91
Red (of the North) (riv., N.Am.)	50N 98W	91
Red (riv., N.Am.)	42N 96W	91
Red Sea	20N 35E	96
Regina, Canada (city)	51N 104W	89
Reindeer (lake, N.Am.)	57N 100W	88
Repulse Bay	22S 147E	98
Resistencia, Chaco (city, st. cap., Argen.)	27S 59W	91
Revillagigedo Island	18N 110W	88
Reykjavik, Iceland (city, nat. cap.)	64N 22W	93
Rhine (riv., Europe)	50N 10E	92
Rhode Island (st., US)	42N 70W	89
Rhone (riv., Europe)	42N 8E	92
Richmond, Virginia (city, st. cap., US)	38N 77W	89
Riga, Gulf of	58N 24E	92
Riga, Latvia (city, nat. cap.)	57N 24E	93
Rio Branco, Acre (city, st. cap., Braz.)	10S 68W	91
Rio de Janeiro (st., Brazil)	22S 45W	91
Rio de Janeiro, R. de Jan. (city, st. cap., Braz.)	23S 43W	91
Rio de la Plata	35S 55W	90
Rio Gallegos, Santa Cruz (city, st. cap., Argen.)	52S 68W	91
Rio Grande (riv., N.Am.)	30N 100W	88
Rio Grande do Norte (st., Brazil)	5S 35W	91
Rio Grande do Sul (st., Brazil)	30S 55W	91
Rio Negro (st., Argentina)	40S 70W	91

Geographic Index

Name/Description	Latitude & Longitude	Page
Riyadh, Saudi Arabia (city, nat. cap.)	25N 47E	93
Roanoke (riv., N.Am.)	34N 75W	88
Roberts, Mt. 4,495	28S 154E	98
Rockhampton, Aust. (city)	23S 150E	99
Rocky Mountains	50N 108W	88
Roebuck Bay	18S 125E	98
Romania (country)	46N 24E	93
Rome, Italy (city, nat. cap.)	42N 13E	93
Rondonia (st., Brazil)	12S 65W	91
Roosevelt, Rio (riv., S.Am.)	10S 60W	90
Roper (riv., Australasia)	15S 135W	98
Roraima (st., Brazil)	2N 62W	91
Ros Dashen Terrara 15,158	12N 40E	96
Rosario, Santa Fe (city, st. cap., Argen.)	33S 61W	91
Rostov, Russia (city)	47N 40E	93
Rotterdam, Netherlands (city)	52N 4E	93
Ruapehu, Mt. 9,177	39S 176W	98
Rub al Khali	20N 50E	94
Rudolph, Lake	3N 34E	96
Russia (country)	58N 56E	93
Ruvuma (riv., Africa)	12S 38E	96
Ruwenzori Mountains	0 30E	96
Rwanda (country)	3S 30E	97
Rybinsk, Lake	58N 38E	92
S. Saskatchewan (riv., N.Am.)	50N 110W	88
Sable, Cape	45N 70W	88
Sacramento (riv., N.Am.)	40N 122W	88
Sacramento, California (city, st. cap., US)	39 121W	89
Sahara	18N 10E	96
Sakhalin Island	50N 143E	94
Salado, Rio (riv., S.Am.)	35S 70W	90
Salem, Oregon (city, st. cap., US)	45N 123W	89
Salt Lake City, Utah (city, st. cap., US)	41N 112W	89
Salta (st., Argentina)	25S 70W	91
Salta, Salta (city, st. cap., Argen.)	25S 65W	91
Saltillo, Coahuila (city, st. cap., Mex.)	26N 101W	89
Salvador, Bahia (city, st. cap., Braz.)	13S 38W	91
Salween (riv., Asia)	18N 98E	94
Samar (island)	12N 124E	94
Samara, Russia (city)	53N 50E	93
Samarkand, Uzbekistan (city)	40N 67E	93
San Antonio, TX (city)	29N 98W	89
San Cristobal (island)	12S 162E	98
San Diego, CA (city)	33N 117W	89
San Francisco, CA (city)	38N 122W	89
San Francisco, Rio (riv., S.Am.)	10S 40W	90
San Joaquin (riv., N.Am.)	37N 121W	88
San Jorge, Gulf of	45S 68W	90
San Jose, Costa Rica (city, nat. cap.)	10N 84W	89

Geographic Index

Name/Description	Latitude & Longitude	Page
San Juan (st., Argentina)	30S 70W	91
San Juan, San Juan (city, st. cap., Argen.)	18N 66W	89
San Lucas, Cape	23N 110W	88
San Luis Potosi (st., Mex.)	22N 101W	89
San Luis Potosi, S. Luis P. (city, st. cap., Mex.)	22N 101W	89
San Matias, Gulf of	43S 65W	90
San Salvador, El Salvador (city, nat. cap.)	14N 89W	89
Sanaa, Yemen (city)	16N 44E	97
Santa Catarina (st., Brazil)	28S 50W	91
Santa Cruz (st., Argentina)	50S 70W	91
Santa Cruz Islands	8S 168E	98
Santa Fe (st., Argentina)	30S 62W	91
Santa Fe de Bogota, Colombia (city, nat. cap.)	5N 74W	91
Santa Fe, New Mexico (city, st. cap., US)	35N 106W	89
Santa Rosa, La Pampa (city, st. cap., Argen.)	37S 64W	91
Santiago, Chile (city, nat. cap.)	33S 71W	91
Santiago del Estero (st., Argentina)	25S 65W	91
Santiago, Sant. del Estero (city, st. cap., Argen.)	28S 64W	91
Santo Domingo, Dominican Rep. (city, nat. cap.)	18N 70W	89
Santos, Brazil (city)	24S 46W	91
Sao Luis, Maranhao (city, st. cap., Braz.)	3S 43W	91
Sao Paulo (st., Brazil)	22S 50W	91
Sao Paulo, Sao Paulo (city, st. cap., Braz.)	24S 47W	91
Sarajevo, Bosnia and Herz. (city, nat. cap.)	43N 18E	93
Sardinia (island)	40N 10E	92
Sarmiento, Mt. 8,100	55S 72W	90
Saskatchewan (riv., N.Am.)	52N 108W	88
Saudi Arabia (country)	25N 50E	95
Savannah (riv., N.Am.)	33N 82W	88
Savannah, GA (city)	32N 81W	89
Sayan Range	45N 90E	94
Seattle, WA (city)	48N 122W	89
Seine (riv., Europe)	49N 3E	92
Senegal (country)	15N 15W	97
Senegal (riv., Africa)	15N 15W	96
Seoul, Korea, South (city, nat. cap.)	38N 127E	95
Sepik (riv., Australasia)	4S 142E	98
Sergipe (st., Brazil)	12S 36W	91
Sev Dvina (riv., Asia)	60N 50E	94
Severnaya Zemlya (island)	80N 88E	94
Shanghai, China (city)	31N 121E	95
Shasta, Mt. 14,162	42N 120W	88
Shenyang, China (city)	42N 123E	95
Shetland Islands	60N 5W	92
Shikoku (island)	34N 130E	94
Shiraz, Iran (city)	30N 52E	95
Sicily (island)	38N 14E	93
Sierra Leone (country)	6N 14W	97
Sierra Madre Occidental	27N 108W	88

Geographic Index

Name/Description	Latitude & Longitude	Page
Sierra Madre Oriental	27N 100W	88
Sierra Nevada	38N 120W	88
Sikhote Alin	45N 135E	94
Simpson Desert	25S 136E	98
Sinai Peninsula	28N 33E	96
Sinaloa (st., Mex.)	25N 110W	89
Singapore (city, nat. cap.)	1N 104E	95
Sitka Island	57N 125W	88
Skagerrak, Strait of	58N 8E	92
Skopje, Macedonia (city, nat. cap.)	42N 21E	93
Slovakia (country)	50N 20E	93
Slovenia (country)	47N 14E	93
Snake (riv., N.Am.)	45N 110W	88
Snowy Mountains	37S 148E	98
Sofia, Bulgaria (city, nat. cap.)	43N 23E	90
Solimoes, Rio (riv., S.Am.)	3S 65W	90
Solomon Islands (country)	7S 160E	98
Somalia (country)	5N 45E	97
Sonora (st., Mex.)	30N 110W	89
South Africa (country)	30S 25E	97
South Australia (st., Aust.)	30S 125E	99
South Cape, New Guinea	8S 150E	98
South Carolina (st., US)	33N 79W	89
South China Sea	15N 115E	98
South Dakota (st., US)	45N 100W	89
South Georgia (island)	55S 40W	90
South Island (NZ)	45S 170E	98
Southampton Island	68N 86W	88
Southern Alps (NZ)	45S 170E	98
Southwest Cape (NZ)	47S 167E	98
Spain (country)	38N 4W	93
Spokane, WA (city)	48N 117W	89
Springfield, Illinois (city, st. cap., US)	40N 90W	89
Sri Lanka (country)	8N 80E	95
Srinagar, India (city)	34N 75E	95
St. Elias, Mt. 18, 008	61N 139W	88
St. George's Channel	53N 5W	92
St. Helena (island)	16S 5W	97
St. John's, Nwfndlnd (city, prov. cap., Can.)	48N 53W	89
St. Louis, MO (city)	39N 90W	89
St. Lawrence (island)	65N 170W	88 inset
St. Lawrence (riv., N.Am.)	50N 65W	88
St. Lawrence, Gulf of	50N 65W	88
St. Marie, Cape	25S 45E	97
St. Paul, Minnesota (city, st. cap., US)	45N 93W	89
St. Petersburg, Russia (city)	60N 30E	93
St. Vincente, Cape of	37N 10W	92
Stanovoy Range	55N 125E	94
Stavanger, Norway (city)	59N 6E	93

Geographic Index

Name/Description	Latitude & Longitude	Page
Steep Point	25S 115E	98
Stockholm, Sweden (city, nat. cap.)	59N 18E	93
Stuart Range	32S 135E	98
Stuttgart, Germany (city)	49N 9E	93
Sucre, Bolivia (city)	19S 65W	91
Sudan (country)	10N 30E	97
Sulaiman Range	28N 70E	94
Sulu Islands	8N 120E	95
Sulu Sea	10N 120E	95
Sumatra (island)	0 100E	94 inset
Sumba (island)	10S 120E	98
Sumbawa (island)	8S 116E	98
Sunda Islands	12S 118E	98
Superior (lake, N.Am.)	50N 90W	88
Surabaya, Java (Indonesia) (city)	7S 113E	95 inset
Suriname (country)	5N 55W	91
Svalbard Islands	75N 20E	94
Swan (riv., Australasia)	34S 115E	98
Sweden (country)	62N 16E	93
Sydney, N.S.Wales (city, st. cap., Aust.)	34S 151E	99
Syr Darya (riv., Asia)	36N 65E	94
Syria (country)	37N 36E	93
Tabasco (st., Mex.)	16N 90W	89
Tabriz, Iran (city)	38N 46E	95
Tahat, Mt. 9,541	23N 8E	96
Taipei, Taiwan (city, nat. cap.)	25N 121E	95
Taiwan (country)	25N 122E	95
Taiwan Strait	25N 120E	94
Tajikistan (country)	35N 75E	95
Takla Makan	37N 90E	94
Tallahassee, Florida (city, st. cap., US)	30N 84W	89
Tallinn, Estonia (city, nat. cap.)	59N 25E	93
Tamaulipas (st., Mex.)	25N 95W	89
Tampico, Mexico (city)	22N 98W	89
Tanganyika, Lake	5S 30E	96
Tanzania (country)	8S 35E	97
Tapajos, Rio (riv., S.Am.)	5S 55W	90
Tarim Basin	37N 85E	94
Tashkent, Uzbekistan (city, nat. cap.)	41N 69E	95
Tasman Sea	38S 160E	98
Tasmania (st., Aust.).	42S 145E	99
Tatar Strait	50N 142E	94
Tbilisi, Georgia (city, nat. cap.)	42N 45E	93
Teguicigalpa, Honduras (city, nat. cap.)	14N 87W	89
Tehran, Iran (city, nat. cap.)	36N 51E	95
Tel Aviv, Israel (city)	32N 35E	93
Tennant Creek, Aust. (city)	19S 134E	99
Tennessee (st., US)	37N 88W	89
Tennessee (riv., N.Am.)	32N 88W	88

Geographic Index

Name/Description	Latitude & Longitude	Page
Tepic, Nayarit (city, st. cap., Mex.)	22N 105W	89
Teresina, Piaui (city, st. cap., Braz.)	5S 43W	91
Texas (st., US)	30N 95W	89
Thailand (country)	15N 105E	95
Thailand, Gulf of	10N 105E	94
Thames (riv., Europe)	52N 4W	92
The Hague, Netherlands (city, nat. cap.)	52N 4E	93
The Round Mountain 5,300	29S 152E	98
Thimphu, Bhutan (city, nat. cap.)	28N 90E	95
Tianjin, China (city)	39N 117E	95
Tibest Massif	20N 20E	96
Tien Shan	40N 80E	94
Tierra del Fuego	54S 68W	90
Tierra del Fuego (st., Argentina)	54S 68W	91
Tigris (riv., Asia)	37N 40E	92
Timor (island)	7S 126E	94
Timor Sea	11S 125E	99
Tirane, Albania (city, nat. cap.)	41N 20E	93
Titicaca, Lake	15S 70W	90
Tlaxcala (st., Mex.)	20N 96W	89
Tlaxcala, Tlaxcala (city, st. cap., Mex.)	19N 98W	89
Toamasino, Madagascar (city)	18S 49E	97
Tocantins (st., Brazil)	12S 50W	91
Tocantins, Rio (riv., S.Am.)	5S 50W	90
Togo (country)	8N 1E	97
Tokyo, Japan (city, nat. cap.)	36N 140E	95
Toliara, Madagascar (city)	23S 44E	97
Tolima, Mt. 17,110	5N 75W	90
Toluca, Mexico (city, st. cap., Mex.)	19N 100W	89
Tombouctou, Mali (city)	24N 3W	97
Tomsk, Russia (city)	56N 85E	95
Tonkin, Gulf of	20N 108E	94
Topeka, Kansas (city, st. cap., US)	39N 96W	89
Toronto, Ontario (city, prov. cap., Can.)	44N 79W	89
Toros Mountains	37N 45E	94
Torrens, Lake	33S 136W	98
Torres Strait	10S 142E	98
Townsville, Aust. (city)	19S 146E	99
Transylvanian Alps	46N 20E	92
Trenton, New Jersey (city, st. cap., US)	40N 75W	89
Tricara Peak 15,584	4S 137E	98
Trinidad and Tobago (island)	9N 60W	90
Tripoli, Libya (city, nat. cap.)	33N 13E	97
Trujillo, Peru (city)	8S 79W	91
Tucson, AZ (city)	32N 111W	89
Tucuman (st., Argentina)	25S 65W	91
Tucuman, Tucuman (city, st. cap., Argen.)	27S 65W	91
Tunis, Tunisia (city, nat. cap.)	37N 10E	97
Tunisia (country)	34N 9E	97

Geographic Index

Name/Description	Latitude & Longitude	Page
Turin, Italy (city)	45N 8E	93
Turkey (country)	39N 32E	93
Turkmenistan (country)	39N 56E	93
Turku, Finland (city)	60N 22E	93
Tuxtla Gutierrez, Chiapas (city, st. cap., Mex.)	17N 93W	89
Tyrrhenian Sea	40N 12E	92
Ubangi (riv., Africa)	0 20E	96
Ucayali, Rio (riv., S.Am.)	7S 75W	90
Uele (riv., Africa)	3N 25E	96
Uganda (country)	3N 30E	97
Ujungpandang, Celebes (Indon.) (city)	5S 119E	95 inset
Ukraine (country)	53N 32E	93
Ulan Bator, Mongolia (city, nat. cap.)	47N 107E	95
Uliastay, Mongolia (city)	48N 97E	95
Ungava Peninsula	60N 72W	88
United Arab Emirates (country)	25N 55E	95
United Kingdom (country)	54N 4W	93
United States (country)	40N 100W	89
Uppsala, Sweden (city)	60N 18E	93
Ural (riv., Asia)	45N 55E	94
Ural Mountains	50N 60E	94
Uruguay (country)	37S 67W	91
Uruguay, Rio (riv., S.Am.)	30S 57W	90
Urumqi, China (city)	44N 88E	95
Utah (st., US)	38N 110W	89
Uzbekistan (country)	42N 58E	93
Vaal (riv., Africa)	27S 27E	96
Valdivia, Chile (city)	40S 73W	91
Valencia, Spain (city)	39N 0	93
Valencia, Venezuela (city)	10N 68W	91
Valparaiso, Chile (city)	33S 72W	91
van Diemen, Cape	11S 130E	98
van Rees Mountains	4S 140E	98
Vanatu (country)	15S 167E	98
Vancouver, Canada (city)	49N 123W	89
Vancouver Island	50N 130W	88
Vanern, Lake	60N 12E	92
Vattern, Lake	56N 12E	92
Venezuela (country)	5N 65W	91
Venezuela, Gulf of	12N 72W	90
Venice, Italy (city)	45N 12E	93
Vera Cruz (st., Mex.)	20N 97W	89
Vera Cruz, Mexico (city)	19N 96W	89
Verkhoyanskiy Range	65N 130E	94
Vermont (st., US)	45N 73W	89
Vert, Cape	15N 17W	96
Vestfjord	68N 14E	92
Viangchan, Laos (city, nat. cap.)	18N 103E	95
Victoria (riv., Australasia)	15S 130E	98

Geographic Index

Name/Description	Latitude & Longitude	Page
Victoria (st., Aust.)	37S 145W	99
Victoria, B.C. (city, prov. cap., Can.)	48N 123W	89
Victoria, Lake	3S 35E	96
Victoria, Mt. 13,238	9S 137E	98
Victoria Riv. Downs, Aust. (city)	17S 131E	99
Viedma, Rio Negro (city, st. cap., Argen.)	41S 63W	91
Vienna, Austria (city)	48N 16E	93
Vietnam (country)	10N 110E	95
Villahermosa, Tabasco (city, st. cap., Mex.)	18N 93W	89
Vilnius, Lithuania (city, nat. cap.)	55N 25E	93
Virginia (st., US)	35N 78W	89
Viscount Melville Sound	72N 110W	88
Vitoria, Espiritu Santo (city, st. cap., Braz.)	20S 40W	91
Vladivostock, Russia (city)	43N 132E	95
Volga (riv., Europe)	46N 46E	92
Volgograd, Russia (city)	54N 44E	93
Volta (riv., Africa)	10N 15E	96
Volta, Lake	8N 2W	96
Vosges Mountains	48N 7E	92
Wabash (riv., N.Am.)	43N 90W	88
Walvis Bay, Namibia (city)	23S 14E	97
Warsaw, Poland (city, nat. cap.)	52N 21E	93
Washington (st., US)	48N 122W	89
Washington, D.C., United St.s (city, nat. cap.)	39N 77W	89
Wellington Island	48S 74W	90
Wellington, New Zealand (city, nat. cap.)	41S 175E	99
Weser (riv., Europe)	54N 8E	92
West Cape Howe	36S 115E	98
West Indies	18N 75W	88
West Siberian Lowland	60N 80E	94
West Virginia (st., US)	38N 80W	89
Western Australia (st., Aust.)	25S 122W	99
Western Ghats	15N 72E	94
Western Sahara (country)	25N 13W	97
White Nile (riv., Africa)	13N 30E	96
White Sea	64N 36E	92
Whitney, Mt. 14,494	33N 118W	88
Wichita, KS (city)	38N 97W	89
Wilhelm, Mt. 14,793	4S 145E	98
Windhoek, Namibia (city, nat. cap.)	22S 17E	97
Winnipeg (lake, N.Am.)	50N 100W	88
Winnipeg, Manitoba (city, prov. cap., Can.)	53N 98W	89
Wisconsin (st., US)	50N 90W	89
Wollongong, Aust. (city)	34S 151E	99
Woodroffe, Mt. 4,724	26S 133W	98
Woomera, Aust. (city)	32S 137E	99
Wrangell (island)	72N 180E	94
Wuhan, China (city)	30N 114E	95
Wyndham, Australia (city)	16S 129E	99

Geographic Index

Name/Description	Latitude & Longitude	Page
Wyoming (st., US)	45N 110W	89
Xalapa, Vera Cruz (city, st. cap., Mex.)	20N 97W	89
Xingu, Rio (riv., S.Am.)	5S 54W	90
Yablonovyy Range	50N 100E	94
Yakutsk, Russia (city)	62N 130E	95
Yamoussoukio, Cote d'Ivoire (city)	7N 4W	97
Yangtze (Chang Jiang) (riv., Asia)	30N 108W	94
Yaounde, Cameroon (city, nat. cap.)	4N 12E	97
Yekaterinburg, Russia (city)	57N 61E	93
Yellowknife, N.W.T. (city, prov. cap., Can.)	62N 115W	89
Yellowstone (riv., N.Am.)	46N 110W	88
Yemen (country)	15N 50E	95
Yenisey (riv., Asia)	68N 85E	94
Yerevan, Armenia (city, nat. cap.)	40N 44E	93
Yokohama, Japan (city)	36N 140E	95
York, Cape	75N 65W	88
Yucatan (st., Mex.)	20N 88W	89
Yucatan Channel	22N 88W	88
Yucatan Peninsula	20N 88W	88
Yugoslavia (country)	44N 20E	93
Yukon (riv., N.Am.)	63N 150W	88 inset
Zacatecas (st., Mex.)	23N 103W	89
Zacatecas, Zacatecas (city, st. cap., Mex.)	23N 103W	89
Zagreb, Croatia (city, nat. cap.)	46N 16E	93
Zagros Mountains	27N 52E	94
Zambezi (riv., Africa)	18S 30E	96
Zambia (country)	15S 25E	97
Zanzibar (island)	5S 39E	96
Zemlya Frantsa Josifa (island)	80N 40E	94
Ziel, Mt. 4,955	23S 134E	98
Zimbabwe (country)	20S 30E	97

Sources

Bercovitch, J. and R. Jackson. (1997). *International conflict: A chronological encyclopedia of conflicts and their management 1945–1995.* Washington, DC: Congressional Quarterly.

BP Statistical Review of World Energy. Online access at: http://www.bp.com/bpstats.

Canadian Forces College, Information Resources Centre. Online access at: http://www.cfcsc.dnd.ca/links/wars/index.html.

Crabb, C. (1993, January). Soiling the planet. *Discover, 14* (1), 74–75. [For information regarding Map 60 on page 83 of this book]

DeBlij, H. J., & Muller, P. (1998). *Geography: Realms, regions and concepts* (8th ed.). New York: John Wiley.

Domke, K. (1988). *War and the changing global system.* New Haven, CT: Yale University Press.

Goode's world atlas. (1995, 19th ed.). New York: Rand McNally.

Gunnemark, Erik V., *Countries, peoples and their languages.* Gothenburg, Sweden: The Geolinguistic Handbook (n.d., early 1990s).

Hammond atlas of the world. (1993). Maplewood, NJ: Hammond.

Information please almanac, atlas, and yearbook 2001. (2000). Boston & New York: Houghton Mifflin.

International Energy Agency. (2001). *Key world energy statistics 2000.* Paris. Online access: http://www.iea.org/statist/keyworld/keystats.htm.

Johnson, D. (1977). *Population, society, and desertification.* New York: United Nations Conference on Desertification, United Nations Environment Programme.

Köppen, W., & Geiger, R. (1954). *Klima der erde* [Climate of the earth]. Darmstadt, Germany: Justus Perthes.

Lindeman, M. (1990). *The United States and the Soviet Union: Choices for the 21st century.* Guilford, CT: Dushkin Publishing Group.

Murphy, R. E. (1968). Landforms of the world [Map supplement No. 9]. *Annals of the Association of American Geographers, 58* (1), 198–200.

National Oceanic and Atmospheric Administration. (1990–1992). Unpublished data. Washington, DC: NOAA.

The New York Times Almanac 2001. (2000). Wright, John W., ed. New York: Penguin Putnam.

NY Times. Online access at: http://archives.nytimes.com/archives/.

Population Reference Bureau (2001). *World population data sheet.* New York: Population Reference Bureau.

Rourke, J. T. (2001). *International politics on the world stage* (8th ed.). Guilford, CT: McGraw-Hill/Dushkin.

Spector, L. S., & Smith, J. R. (1990). *Nuclear ambitions: The spread of nuclear weapons.* Boulder, CO: Westview Press.

Time atlas of world history. (1978). London.

United Nations Development Programme (UNDP, 2001). *Human development indicators, human development report 2001.* New York: Oxford University Press. Online access at: http://www.undp.org/hdr2001/back.pdf.

United Nations Food and Agriculture Organization. *FAOSTAT database.* Online access at: http://apps.fao.org/page/collections?subset=agriculture.

United Nations High Commissioner on Refugees (UNHCR), Population Data Unit, Population and Geographic Data Section. (2000). Online access at: http://www.unhcr.ch/cgibin/texis/vtx/home. *Provisional statistics on refugees and others of concern to UNHCR for the year 2000.* Geneva.

United Nations Population Fund. (2000). *The state of the world's population.* New York: United Nations Population Fund.

United Nations Statistics Division, Department of Economic and Social Affairs, (2001). *Social indicators.* Online access at: http://www.un.org/depts/unsd/social/index.htm.

Uranium Institute. Online access at: http://www.uilondon.org/safetab.htm.

U.S. Arms Control and Disarmament Agency. (1993). *World military expenditures and arms transfers.* Washington, DC: U.S. Government Printing Office.

U.S. Census Bureau. (2000). *International database, United States Census Bureau.* Online access at: http://www.census.gov/ipc/www/idbnew.html.

U.S. Central Intelligence Agency, Office of Public Affairs. 2001. *The World fact book.* Washington, DC. Online access at: http://www.odci.gov/cia/publications/factbook/.

U.S. Department of State, (1999) Undersecretary for Arms Control and International Security. *World military expenditures and arms transfers.* Online access at: http://www.state.gove/www/global/arms/bureau_ac/wmeat98/wmeat98.html.

U.S. Forest Service. (1989). *Ecoregions of the continents.* Washington, DC: U.S. Government Printing Office.

The world almanac and book of facts 2001. (2000). Mahwah, NJ: World Almanac Books.

World Bank. (2001) *World development indicators* 2001. Washington DC. World Bank. Online access at: http://www.worldbank.org/data/.

World Bank. (2001). *World development report 2000/2001: Attacking poverty.* New York: Oxford University Press.

World Health Organization. (1998). *World health statistics annual.* Geneva: World Health Organization.

World Resources Institute. (2000). *World resources 2000-2001. People and ecosystems: The fraying web of life.* Washington, DC: World Resources Institute: Online access at: http://www.wri.org.